THE MEANING OF MALICE

ON THE TRAIL OF THE BLACK WIDOW OF HIGHLAND PARK

JOHN LEAKE

COUNTERPLAY BOOKS
www.counterplaybooks.com

ISBN: 979-8-9862363-2-2

Designed by Daniel Hancock

For Gloria Rehrig. Her undying love of her son and her pursuit of truth and justice inspired me to keep researching this vast story, even when I felt defeated by the wall of silence, obstruction, and folly that surrounds it.

TABLE OF CONTENTS

PART I: The Rise and Fall of a Dallas Socialite

PART II: Wandering Spirit

PART III: Cinderella and the Suicides

PART IV: My Investigation

I will tell you news of your son: give me your blessing:
truth will come to light; murder cannot be hid long;
a man's son may, but at the length truth will out.

–Shakespeare, *The Merchant of Venice*

PART I
THE RISE AND FALL OF
A DALLAS SOCIALITE

CHAPTER 1
A MYSTERY

Many know Love Field airport as the place where President John Kennedy arrived in Dallas on November 22, 1963. Millions have seen the news footage of him and First Lady Jackie stepping off the Air Force Boeing 707 and waving at the crowd on the tarmac. The reel concludes with Kennedy setting forth in his motorcade towards Downtown Dallas for his appointment with death about thirty minutes later. After the larger Dallas Fort Worth Airport opened in 1973, Love Field became a secondary port with regional service. On July 16, 1982, its short-term parking lot was the scene of one of the most perplexing mysteries in Dallas history.

On that day at around 8:00 p.m., an auto mechanic named Lloyd Durrett pulled into the lot and made his way to its west side, near the runway, because he knew its spaces were closest to a pedestrian crosswalk to the terminal entrance. He was giving his sister-in-law and her children a ride to the airport to catch a Southwest flight back to San Antonio, and they had a lot of luggage. He found a space near a powder blue Mercedes 300 TD station wagon, which was parked parallel to the curb adjacent to one of the multilevel structure's load-bearing columns. It was a beautiful car in perfect condition, and Lloyd remarked to his children, who were along for the ride, "Someday I'll save up enough money to buy us one of those." He said this with conviction. He believed the Mercedes 300 TD was the finest family car on the market, a marvel of German engineering.

As he pulled luggage from his trunk, his two kids wandered over to the Mercedes to take a closer look. Peering into the window, his nine-year-old son Jeremy saw a woman inside. Her torso was lying on the passenger seat, and he thought she was taking a nap. His ten-year-old sister thought she looked ill.

"Daddy, there's a lady in this car and she looks sick," his daughter said. Lloyd turned to his kids, standing next to the driver's side window. The first thing he noticed was that the windows were closed, and the engine was off. With the outside air temperature around 95 degrees, he knew he had an emergency on his hands. In such heat, no one could endure sitting in a sealed car for more than a few minutes without the engine and AC running.

He rushed to the car and peered into the window. He saw a woman lying across the gap between the two front seats. It appeared she had initially been sitting in the driver's seat, but then slumped all the way over to her right so that her upper body was lying on the passenger seat. Looking closely at her face, he saw blood coming out of her nose. To Lloyd, who'd served in Vietnam and seen a lot of death, the woman appeared to have been dead for some time. Though the top of her head was next to the passenger side door, her arms were stretched back towards the center console, and her right hand was braced against the driver's side of the gearshift. Her right palm was upturned, and her right fingers were grasping a small revolver.

Lloyd directed his sister-in-law and the kids to the check-in counter, and he then ran around the terminal looking for a police officer or security guard. In those days it wasn't easy to find one, but finally a lady at a ticket counter was able to summon a security guard, who accompanied Lloyd back to the Mercedes. He then spoke with someone on his handheld radio, and about six minutes later a bunch of police cars and an EMT arrived and cordoned off the scene.

Lloyd found the woman's death shocking, but also intriguing, so he remained standing outside the cordoned area, watching. At first glance he'd noticed that she was fit and immaculately groomed. Everything about

2

her, from her perfectly manicured nails and gold wristwatch to her marvelous car, indicated wealth and privilege. She was wearing what appeared to be a tennis outfit. How on earth had this young, upper-class lady wound up shot in her car, parked in the Love Field parking lot? The revolver in her right hand suggested suicide, but that didn't make sense to Lloyd. Why would she choose to spend her last moments in a gloomy, concrete parking garage next to the airport runway, the air infused with jet exhaust? That she'd first shut off the engine and AC before shooting herself also struck him as odd, as it seemed likely that she would've wanted her body to be found quickly, and what difference did it make if the engine ran for a while before she was discovered?

It seemed to Lloyd that the policemen were being lackadaisical with their work. He saw a cop note her license plate number and then go through her wallet, which contained a large sum of cash. A police photographer took some shots, and then they pulled the dead woman from the car and loaded her into the EMT. Her body had stiffened in the position in which he'd first seen her, with her arms stretched back towards the gearshift. Seeing them move her body reminded him of similar scenes he'd witnessed in Vietnam.

"We'll contact her husband," said one of the officers. Lloyd stood there watching as the investigators drove away without remembering to lock the beautiful car and possible crime scene.

The primary investigators at the scene were the DPD homicide detective J.J. Coughlin and Dallas County Medical Examiner field agent E. Gray. They observed that the only injury to the decedent was a single gunshot wound to the right side of her head. Neither her body nor her car displayed any sign of struggle. That, and the fact that she was clutching a pistol in her right hand, indicated she had committed suicide, though no suicide note was found in her purse (found lying on the floor between the bucket seats) or anywhere else in the car.

The pistol found in her right hand was an RG-14 .22 caliber revolver. Its cylinder contained four live cartridges and two spent. One of the discharged cartridges had apparently been fired into the decedent's head.

The investigators could find no trace of a second shot fired in either her car or the surrounding cars or parking structure. This suggested the decedent had previously test fired the pistol somewhere else to make sure it worked. The cheap RG-14 revolver was a proverbial Saturday-Night-Special carried by criminals for shooting their rivals at close range. It had gained national notoriety the year before when John Hinckley used one (purchased from Rocky's Pawn Shop in Dallas) to shoot President Reagan and three other men. The pistol, which in 1981 had a suggested retail price of $47.50, was all that down-and-out Hinckley could afford. The decedent that lay before Detective Coughlin was obviously a lady of wealth and taste, so it seemed odd to him that she would possess such a lowly firearm. No sales receipt was found in her purse or in the car—another indication she hadn't purchased the gun just before she used it to kill herself.

The lady's driver's license identified her as forty-year-old Mary Elizabeth Bagwell. Her car was registered under the name Dr. John Bagwell, whom Coughlin took to be her husband, as the address on both documents was the same. Maplewood Avenue ran through the heart of Highland Park—a wealthy independent township in the middle of Dallas County. Highland Park had its own police force, which meant it wasn't Coughlin's jurisdiction. The thirty-one-year-old detective had acquired most of his experience in South Dallas, investigating gang and drug related homicides. However, because Mrs. Mary Elizabeth Bagwell was found at Love Field, within the City of Dallas, he got the unhappy assignment to notify her next of kin. The Bagwell residence was a stately house with a circular driveway, located near the exclusive Dallas Country Club. Detective Coughlin arrived around 8:30 p.m., just after sunset on July 16. He rang the doorbell and the door opened to reveal a small gathering of people who seemed to be expecting him.

"Did you find her?" one of them asked.

Mary Elizabeth Monroe Bagwell, who went by the name Betsy, was the daughter of Frank and Percye Monroe. She was born in Midland, Texas, where her father was the superintendent of schools. After the birth of her younger brother, Frank Jr., the Highland Park Independent School

District offered Frank Sr. the job of superintendent, a position he held from 1954-74. Throughout Dallas County and in many other parts of Texas, the Town of Highland Park, with its 8,500 inhabitants, is often called "the Bubble" because it is thought to be sheltered from the social and economic ills that afflict the rest of humanity.

The Bubble originated in 1906, when land for a new residential development was purchased. Wilber David Cook—the landscape designer who'd planned Beverly Hills, California—was hired to design the layout. As the 20th century progressed, Highland Park became the preferred neighborhood for many of the wealthiest families in Dallas County. A chief attraction was its independent school district, dedicated to educating the children of the town's residents. For most of its history, its entire student body was white and mostly Anglo-Saxon Protestant.

At Highland Park High School, Betsy Monroe had the studious habits of her parents, and was chosen to be a cheerleader. After graduating from Vanderbilt University, she moved back to Dallas and married John Claude Bagwell whose father, John Spurgeon Bagwell, was one of the city's most prominent medical men. The personification of the Protestant Work Ethic, the elder Bagwell graduated first in his class from the Baptist-affiliated Baylor Medical School and was also the first of his university to receive a post-graduate scholarship to study at the Mayo Clinic. During the sixties he was president of staff of Baylor University Medical Center, where he played a key role in making it one of the nation's premier hospitals. The younger John Bagwell followed in his father's footsteps and became the most renowned cancer doctor in Dallas. By the year 1980, he was the go-to oncologist for Highland Park society.

Betsy gracefully complemented her distinguished husband, tending their splendid home on one of the most beautiful streets in Highland Park and mothering their two attractive and intelligent children. She had many close friends and was a member of the Junior League and Highland Park Presbyterian Church. A docent at the Dallas Museum of Art, she'd also worked on the Dallas Shakespeare festival (her mother was a Shakespeare lover). At forty, she still had her slender, athletic figure and was in glowing physical health. Evaluated by the socially conservative standards of

Highland Park, Betsy Bagwell seemed to have an ideal life—the sort of life that a less fortunate woman might covet. Soon after it ended on July 16, 1982, her friends concluded that the chain of events leading to her violent death had begun when her husband became the treating doctor of the most popular man in Dallas society.

CHAPTER 2
A REMARKABLE PATIENT

Bobby Bridewell was born in Tyler, Texas, which lies in the middle of the legendary East Texas Oil Field. His father was an oilman named William Bridewell, known in petroleum circles by the nickname "Slanthole Billy" for his participation in the Hot Oil Scandal of 1962 in which independent operators were caught horizontal drilling into the leases of majors such as Shell and Texaco. In a couple of ways Bobby was a chip off the old block. Like his father, he was a creative wheeler and dealer, and both father and son were ace golfers who won minor tournaments. But in most other respects, Bobby was the opposite of Billy, perhaps consciously so.

While Billy was widely perceived as a tough old skinflint, Bobby was generous to a fault, constantly entertaining his friends, organizing events, and buying racehorses, his greatest love. At Washington and Lee, where he was called "Tweedy Bob" for his fondness for tweed jackets, he was vice-president of the Dance Board in 1961-1962. When he moved to Dallas after college he became "the one-of-a-kind President of the Dervish Club," as the *Dallas Morning News* referred to him when he held the office in 1968-69. The Dervishes' primary function was (and still is) to escort debutantes to the season's balls and parties. As reported in the *Morning News*'s society page, the '68 Dervish Ball was "the best ever." The evening's highlight had been Bob's toast to the debutantes, addressing them one by one and making comical remarks, eliciting hysterical laughter from the audience. Bobby's dancing ability went beyond traditional ballroom steps. His friend Angus Wynne—also the descendant of a prominent Tyler oil family—was a concert promoter in Dallas, and through him, Bobby became friends with James Brown and other musicians. At one of Brown's concerts in Dallas, Bobby got up on the stage and danced with the Funk Master.

"Bobby could turn even a miserable situation into something fun," Angus reminisced decades later. "I remember one icy evening, as I was on my way to a formal affair, I slid into a phone pole. I didn't break my legs, but I damn sure banged up my knees. Somehow, I managed to make it to the party, which was so dull that I just sat at the bar and got drunk to numb my pain. That's when Bobby walks up and says, 'This isn't much fun, but it's about to get better.' Some friends of his in the Texas Air National Guard were flying into Love Field as we spoke, and Bobby had a plan. So off we went to Love and jumped on this military bird to Vegas. A few hours later we were sitting front row in a lounge listening to Sinatra."

Another friend, Albert Tatum, remembered the time that Bobby organized an outing for a bunch of friends to the Oaklawn Racetrack in Hot Springs, Arkansas. Bobby had just bought a little mare called Go-Go Dash, and he wanted to celebrate her debut in style with a Mint Julep-fueled party. Al couldn't attend, but after the race he spoke with Bobby.

"How did Go-Go Dash do?" he asked.

"I've never been so proud of any animal or human in my entire life," Bobby said. "The little girl ran so hard around the final turn on a wet track with mud kicking in her face, and she beat the favored horse by a nose."

"Congratulations Bobby! How much did you win? Al asked.

"Nothing! The favored horse came in fourth," Bobby said with a laugh.

He began his business career in Dallas working for the real estate investment department of Prudential Life. His experience and contacts from this position helped him to launch his meteoric rise as a hotel developer.

"Bobby was a creative genius at developing and financing projects," explained Walker Harmon, who worked at Bobby's company, Metro Hotels. "In the blink of an eye he could envision a new project and how to get the money for it. And because he was so socially gifted, he could get anybody on the phone and interested in his projects. I remember one day he said to me, 'I'm gonna call Eric Hilton and tell him we want to talk with him about building a new Hilton franchise in Fort Worth.' And just like that, two days later we drove to Austin, sat down with Eric, and got the Fort Worth deal."

Decades later, Walker still got tickled telling the story about their development of the Fort Worth Hilton.

"After construction was completed, Bobby took me on a tour, and as were taking a turn around the covered parking garage, he turns to me with a grin and says, "You know, this garage is a whole floor short of the parking code."

"Oh my God, what are we going to do?" I asked him.

"'Nothing! Bobby said. 'No one will ever notice.' And I'll be damned if he wasn't right," Walker said. "No one at Hilton or in the city ever said a word about the garage being an entire story short."

Sadly, Bobby's high-flying career as president of Metro Hotels was not to last long. In the mid-seventies, exuberance and temptation led him to do some highly leveraged land deals north of Dallas with the intent of flipping them for quick profit. He got caught in a market downturn that left him holding the inventory with massive financing costs. Skilled at accessing capital and moving it around, he was able to manage the situation for a while. However, by mid-1977, his creditors were breathing down his neck. One of them was his father, who'd joined him in managing Metro Hotels, and Billy was characteristically hardnosed. He believed that because Bobby was president, his liabilities imperiled the company.

Growing stress with his father was compounded by another disaster that struck him in 1977. He and his wife owned a horse farm in the little town of Celina, forty miles north of Dallas, where they trained thoroughbred horses. She was a lovely southern belle from Virginia, and he adored her. It was thus a terrible blow to his heart and ego when he caught her *in flagrante delicto* with their horse trainer. In the fall of 1977, his normally buoyant and optimistic spirit was laid low, and his friends grew alarmed at his despondency.

With his thirty-seventh birthday approaching on November 16, his old friend Bo Price hatched a plan for lifting his spirits. Bo had recently learned that a beautiful, thirty-three-year-old widow named Sandra Stegall had set her sights on Bobby. She didn't know about his financial troubles. All she knew was that he was president of Metro Hotels, flew around in a company plane, and was pals with rich guys like Eric Hilton and Richard Pew (a Sun Oil heir). What she *did* understand was that his marriage was troubled, which provided an opportunity for her. Already she'd spent weeks reading everything she could get her hands on about thoroughbred horses, acquiring a small library on the subject. When she finally got to meet Bobby, she would be ready to converse with him about his greatest love.

Word had it that Sandra was not only beautiful, but also a great deal of fun. What better way to cheer Bobby up? And so, Bo set about planning a big birthday bash for his friend with the beguiling woman in attendance. What happened at the party was reminiscent of Plutarch's famous story of Cleopatra smuggling herself into Julius Caesar's headquarters in Alexandria in a rolled rug. A few stout Egyptians hauled it in as though it were a gift from a local merchant. With Caesar watching, they set it on the ground and unrolled it to reveal the ravishing young princess. The great general was delighted by the surprise and instantly smitten.

At the climactic moment of Bobby's thirty-seventh birthday party, a huge cake was rolled into the room, and with everyone singing happy birthday, Sandra popped out of it in a slinky dress. Bobby was surprised and thrilled and soon fell head over heels in love. A whirlwind romance ensued. Two months later, he filed for divorce from his wife, and was legally divorced in May 1978. Shortly thereafter, the invitations went out for his wedding to Sandra on June 26, 1978.

Decades later, some of Bobby's friends remembered how she'd doted on him in their early days. One still vividly recalled the first time he saw them together. They came over to his house for a visit, and while Bobby sat in a lounge chair in the living room, **Sandra** sat on the floor, propping herself against the ottoman on which he was resting his feet, looking up at him with an adoring expression, hanging onto his every word. It seemed that this sort of behavior was a balm for his ego, recently bruised by his wife's infidelity.

Still, some of his friends were surprised at how quickly he planned to remarry, as he'd only just met **Sandra** and the ink on his divorce decree was scarcely dry. Bobby's best friend—a prominent Dallas architect named Phil Shepherd—figured **Sandra** believed she was coming in for a lot of money. Bobby knew she believed this. He didn't trouble himself with the concern that she was a gold-digger, and nor did he disabuse her of her notion that he was rich. He figured it was best to assume that she was marrying him for love, and to avoid speaking about money.

This approach also comported well with the fact that during the same month he was planning to marry **Sandra**, his father asked him to step down as president of Metro Hotels to separate his personal liabilities from the company. In other words, far from marrying a high rolling hotel developer with a company plane, **Sandra** was about to wed a man who would file for bankruptcy just six months later. To be sure, Bobby was resourceful and confident he would work out his financial problems and get back into business. All the same, it was a weirdly ironic situation.

To make matters weirder, **Sandra** had her own liability that emerged just before their wedding when she received notice that a Dallas bank was suing her for her failure to repay a loan. No stranger to dealing with creditors, Bobby asked his lawyer, Roger Marshall, to represent her. However, this lawsuit had a dramatic twist. In the bank's petition to the court, it named a co-defendant, who just happened to be the CEO of a publicly listed company with headquarters in Dallas. He also happened to be married and a churchwarden. To spare his family members from embarrassment, he shall be called Mr. Big.

Somehow **Sandra** had managed to represent Mr. Big as a guarantor of the loan. Believing he'd been tricked, he filed a cross-action suit against her. He and his lawyer seemed confident as they strode into Mr. Marshall's office to take her deposition. **Sandra** then walked in wearing a mink coat, sunglasses, and all the jewelry she could wear. *This guy has no idea what's about* *to hit him*, thought Sandra's attorney as they sat down at the conference table. With a court reporter typing what would soon become public record, Sandra began her deposition. She said the arrangement for the loan had come about after she'd commenced a relationship with the plaintiff.

"Shall I tell you about our sexual encounters?" she asked.

"We would prefer that you not," replied Mr. Big's attorney.

"Why not? I think you'll find them interesting. We had them in the most unusual places. I especially remember the time we—."

"I think that's enough," interjected Mr. Big's attorney. A discussion ensued in which Mr. Big agreed to pay off the debt. His attorney concluded the meeting by saying he would petition the court to dismiss the matter with prejudice.

Mr. Marshall didn't tell Bobby about his new bride's performance. Bobby was in love with her, and as everyone knows, love is blind. But the attorney would never forget Sandra's icy, ruthless cunning, and her total lack of shame as she made the statement. The big-shot CEO was unaccustomed to being pushed around, and he apparently reckoned that Sandra—newly wed to a socially prominent man—would shy from the conflict. Man was he wrong.

Despite these strange and stressful circumstances, the wedding ceremony was a great success with loads of champagne and dancing. *Saturday Night Fever* had just made a splash in cinemas, and Bobby exclaimed, "Behold the great John Travolta!" and proceeded to execute some of the moves showcased in the film. Holding a bottle of champagne in one hand, he danced over to Sandra who was sitting in chair watching him, kneeled, and removed one of her shoes. He then filled it with champagne and drank from it as though it were a chalice.

After their wedding, Bobby sold his house in Tyler and purchased their house on Lorraine Avenue in Highland Park. To many observers, he seemed wonderfully happy with Sandra. She shined as a gracious hostess and gourmet cook, while Bobby held court with his countless friends. At the same time, he strategized about the next phase of his business career.

On January 9, 1979, he filed for bankruptcy. By then it had become tragically clear that he could have worked out a deal with his creditors if he had remained president of Metro Hotels. The latter half of 1978 proved to be the most profitable two quarters in its history. At year's end, Walker Harman—the young man who succeeded him—was wealthy beyond his wildest dreams. But Bobby was never one to be discouraged. Shortly after he filed for bankruptcy, he got to work on a new project that would prove to be the great monument of his career.

CHAPTER 3

THE MANSION

Before oil, cotton was king in Texas, and in the early 20th century a man named Sheppard King made a fortune with the stuff. On the west bank of Turtle Creek, a few miles south of Highland Park, he built a 10,000 square foot mansion in the Italian Renaissance style, using master masons and carpenters and the finest materials brought over from Europe. Upon its completion in 1925, it became a landmark Dallas home. Ten years later, Mr. King fell on hard times, so he sold the mansion to the oilman Freeman Burford.

President Roosevelt and First Lady Eleanor were guests in 1936, and Tennessee Williams lived in the Mansion for a while in the forties, where he wrote the play *Summer and Smoke*. In the late forties, Toddie Lee Wynne bought the property and used it for his American Liberty Oil Company offices. Later it was occupied by insurance and financial services companies. In early 1979, the once grand house had fallen into disrepair and there was talk of demolishing it to build a high-rise office tower.

One day in the early spring of 1979, Walker Harman got a call from Bobby just before lunchtime.

"I'll be there in a few minutes to pick you up," he said. "I wanna show you something." First Bobby drove to a little soul food place in

Downtown to grab some takeout fried chicken, then to a gas station to grab a couple of beers, and then to the old Sheppard King Mansion, where they had a picnic in its front yard.

"This," he said, pointing at the Mansion, "will soon be the most stylish hotel in Dallas. Where the world's rich, famous, and beautiful will stay when they're in town. I've got the whole thing worked out," he continued, pulling a piece of paper from his jacket pocket. On it he'd sketched a plan for renovating the Mansion and converting its grand interior into a fabulous dining room and bar. Old Mr. King's basement silver vault would be a huge wine cellar. As for the modern hotel rooms—they would be added with an adjoining wing with inexpensive modern construction, but with an exterior façade that matched the original building's style. Hilton had done a similar job with the Ortiz Hacienda in Santa Fe.

"I think it's a fabulous vision," Walker said. "But none of our lenders are going to fund something so special with no comps. What you need is a rich guy here in Dallas who'll do it for love and glory." Bobby was already thinking the same, and his friend Phil Shepherd knew just the guy.

Stephen Sands was the son of Caroline Rose Hunt, the second daughter of the legendary oilman H.L. Hunt. Unlike her brothers, Caroline had never been active in business. Before she married her first husband, she held a job as a salesgirl at Neiman-Marcus, and since then she'd worked on several charitable projects. However, in 1979 the idea of working on a creative enterprise appealed to her, and she agreed to invest $21 million in Bobby's vision. The Mansion on Turtle Creek became the first property of her Rosewood Hotels & Resorts, which went on to develop and acquire many of the world's most beautiful hotels.

Bobby was back in business, working as project manager on the most splendid deal of his life. As 1979 ended, his future—and that of his wife Sandra—seemed as bright as they could be. Shortly after New Year's Day, they went to the Highland Park Village Theater with Phil and Frances Shepherd to watch Bob Fosse's new film, *All that Jazz*. With his love of music and dance, Bobby was very excited to see it. About halfway into the film, the strangest thing happened. He broke into the most profuse sweat he could ever remember.

"It's the damnedest thing," he said to Frances. "My clothes are soaking wet." A few days later he found some swollen lymph nodes in one of his armpits. He showed them to his doctor friend Don McKay, who sent him to a specialist. The news was bad. Bobby had lymphoma. An oncologist at Medical City in Dallas initially reckoned his prognosis to be good. The cancer seemed to be limited to the nodes in his armpit and could be eliminated with orally administered chemotherapy. However, a few months later at the Kentucky Derby, an old college friend didn't like Bobby's account of his treatment.

"I implore you to go to M.D. Anderson in Houston," his friend advised. "They've got the best cancer guys." Bobby did as his friend suggested, and the docs in Houston took a sharply different view. In fact, Bobby's lymphoma was advancing and probably had been despite the treatment he'd received from Medical City. He needed to get far more aggressive, and they recommended he see the Baylor University Medical Center oncologist, John C. Bagwell.

Bobby took their advice and was given stronger chemotherapy that robbed him of his energy. Still, he continued his work on the Mansion, whose restaurant opened on August 6, 1980, with much fanfare and a full-page review in the *New York Times*. Initially managed by guys from the 21 Club in New York, the restaurant was a smash success and quickly became the place in Dallas to see and be seen. Nine months later, on May 16, 1981, the Mansion Hotel opened with an opulent gala, attended by the city's crème de la crème. The project also received the Historic Preservation League of Dallas' Keystone Award.

It was an absolute triumph, but the occasion marked the beginning of the end for Bobby. During the latter half of 1981, his condition deteriorated. Still, he soldiered on with his newly formed Bridewell Hotels Corporation, playing a key role in the redevelopment of the Melrose Hotel, a few blocks from the Mansion. And yet, despite his fighting spirit and ever-positive attitude, by December of 1981, his cancer was gaining the upper hand.

CHAPTER 4

BOBBY'S LAST DAYS

In January 1982, it became clear that Bobby was a goner, though there was no telling how long he would hang on. On January 30, a forty-year-old Park Cities resident named John Conklin left a suicide note for his wife in their family home and then drove to his nearby office, where he lay down on a couch and shot himself in the head with a .357 Magnum pistol. A few weeks after his suicide, his wife heard a knock on her door and opened it to see a woman she'd never met. The woman introduced herself as Sandra Bridewell and said that her first husband had committed suicide and that she'd always wanted to talk with someone who'd experienced the same trauma. Mrs. Conklin found this strange, but nevertheless had a conversation with Sandra about her husband's death. Only later did it occur to her that Sandra wasn't so much seeking commiseration as trying to learn about suicide.

It was during the last solemn and agonizing months of Bobby Bridewell's life that Sandra decided to remodel their house on Lorraine Avenue. At the beginning of March, she asked her friend Marion Underwood—a seventy-five-year-old retired schoolteacher—if Bobby could stay in one of her spare bedrooms while a new HVAC was installed in the Bridewell home. Shortly thereafter, Sandra asked three different families if they would look after her three children while she gathered her strength for her husband's imminent death. Britt stayed with Bill and Candy Hill; Kathryn stayed with David and Debbie Thompkins, and Emily stayed with Roger and Sissy Alsabrook. She implied that the arrangements she was making for her dying husband and three children were temporary, perhaps a couple of weeks. But then an entire month elapsed, and then a second.

After Bobby moved in with the Underwood's, Sandra didn't tell him that she also moved the kids into other homes. At his weekly Bible study, he told his friends Bill Hill, Donald McKay, and Boots Nowlin of his concern that Sandra was overwhelmed with the responsibility of looking after three kids on her own. None had the heart to tell him this wasn't true because his wife had lodged the children in other households. In fact, she was frequently observed dining and drinking champagne with friends at the Mansion and signing the bills on Bobby's account. To spare Bobby from receiving the bills, Phil Shepherd and Steve Sands took care of them.

The men in Bobby's Bible study thought there was something very strange about Sandra, and they couldn't fathom why she didn't welcome her dying husband back into his own home. Then Don McKay had an encounter with her that was revealing. One day, while doing some tasks in his workshop (behind his residence), Sandra appeared at his house and asked his wife Janie if she could speak with him. Janie directed her to Don's workshop. A while later, Sandra left, and then Don entered the house.

"Don't ever leave me alone with that woman again!" he exclaimed to his wife. "She just made a pass on me." He didn't go into detail with Janie, but later, at a dinner, she overheard him tell Boots Nowlin, "Sandra told me that Bobby's chemotherapy had made him impotent, so she needed me to satisfy her."

After living a few weeks with Marion Underwood, Bobby checked into a suite in the hotel at 6060 Central Expressway that he'd developed early in his career. His friends frequently visited him, as did their wives, who brought him home-cooked meals. A few of them noticed that Sandra never seemed to be there. On one occasion, a lady made a dish for him. Bobby was taking a nap when she arrived, so she left the casserole and a little note in the anteroom. Later that day she returned home and was shocked to find the dish on her porch with a note that read, "Stay away from my husband!"

In addition to remodeling her house and dining at the Mansion, Sandra said she was busy creating the Bridewell Foundation. The purpose of this tax-exempt, non-profit organization was to fund Camp Esperanza—a summer camp for children afflicted with cancer. The camp was, she claimed, the dream of both Bobby and his oncologist, Dr. John Bagwell. In the name of her dying husband, she solicited donations from his friends. The list of donors was a "Who's Who" of Dallas society. Working together with Children's Medical Center and an existing summer camp in Gainesville, Texas called Camp Sweeney, she set up the annual, one-week program for about 75 young patients in the hospital's Hematology-Oncology Clinic. With the founding of this institution, Sandra followed in the tradition of Dallas society lions such as the Hunt and Wynne families, who'd created the Cattle Baron's Ball and the Six Flags Over Texas Family Night for the benefit of cancer treatment.

While Bobby's wife busied herself with founding a new charity, he was admitted to Baylor University Medical Center for palliative care. One day his old friend Al Tatum visited him. As he entered the room, he saw Bobby sitting up in bed, dreadfully gaunt and bald from the chemotherapy. Sandra was sitting next to him, and they were looking at a notepad on which Bobby was jotting. Bobby looked up at Al, peering over the rim of his glasses with a studious expression.

"We're making a list of guys I approve of Sandra dating after I'm gone," Bobby said. "Tatum, I'm not sure about you, but I think you might make it." This made Sandra and Al laugh.

Tatum had had a soft spot for Sandra since the sixties when they'd briefly dated. After the death of her first husband—purportedly by a self-inflicted gunshot wound to the head—he had reconnected and occasionally escorted her when she needed a date to a charity ball or other formal event. Sandra had always understood that he was a confirmed bachelor and never tried to pressure him into marriage. This had enabled them to have a lot of fun together. Al believed that Sandra's wild, fun-loving spirit perfectly complemented Bobby's, and that the two had been made for each other. This perception caused him to retain his loyalty to her even after most of Bobby's other friends turned against her.

A lady named Barbara Crooks felt the same way. She'd gotten to know Sandra in the seventies, when they were neighbors, and had always found her to be a blast. Barbara also loved Bobby and co-owned a racehorse with him. She often visited Sandra at their house on Lorraine, where they sat on the couch in the living room, drank champagne, talked, and laughed.

During this same period, the wife of one of Bobby's close friends visited him at Baylor hospital. Sandra happened to be there as well, and she offered to run out and get him a milkshake. Bobby handed her a ten-dollar bill and said, "Get yourself one while you're at it." She'd recently been slimming down and looked cute in a little dress. Upon hearing Bobby's suggestion, she put her hands on her hips in a gesture of indignation.

"What! Drink a milkshake and spoil this beautiful figure of mine!"

Shortly before Bobby's end, Sandra visited him in his hospital room and took his credit card from his wallet. Because of his bankruptcy in 1979, he still wasn't qualified for consumer credit. Walker Harman—his successor CEO at Metro Hotels—had provided him with a company card. By a secret arrangement, Bobby paid Walker at the end of each month, and Walker paid the bill. One day Walker received a call at work from the manager of the Marie Leavell dress shop.

"Mrs. Bridewell just walked out of here with several dresses," he said. "My sales staff didn't question if the purchases are authorized, so I'm calling you to ask." Instantly Walker sensed that Bobby hadn't given her the card. She must have taken it while he was in the bathroom or distracted. Walker then went into Billy's office and confessed that he'd provided Bobby with a company credit card, and that Sandra had snatched it and spent five grand on dresses.

"I think we ought to eat it," Walker said. "This is going to be pretty humiliating for Bobby if he finds out what she's done."

"Hell no!" Billy exclaimed. "We're not paying for it, and you're not paying for it out of your pocket either. You call that dress shop and tell them tough shit. And cancel the damned card!"

Walker did as he was told, and the next day he got a call from the manager of an antiques shop. The moron had sold a bunch of valuable pieces to Sandra on a cancelled card and already delivered them to her house.

"Sorry," Walker said. "The card was cancelled, so you'll have to deal with Mrs. Bridewell yourself."

Robert Weeks Bridewell died on Mother's Day, May 9, 1982, at the age of forty-one. His Memorial Service at the Highland Park Presbyterian Church, officiated by Pastor Clayton Bell, was packed with friends who'd loved him and would always remember his ever-cheerful, fun-loving, and optimistic spirit—a spirit still commemorated by a charming equestrian sculpture that stands at the entrance of the Mansion. Sandra looked dynamite in a low-cut red dress that showed off her tuned-up figure. Even during this most solemn of occasions, the men in the audience found their eyes drawn to her, and she basked in the attention. Bobby's pallbearers were his best friends and his oncologist, Dr. John Bagwell.

CHAPTER 5

BETSY BAGWELL

While Bobby was dying, Betsy Bagwell felt sorry for Sandra, and was happy to support her during her time of need. However, after his death, Betsy's sympathy was tested by Sandra's constant calling, asking for favors, and showing up unannounced at the Bagwell home. Betsy was demure and had no experience dealing with such an overbearing person. She also didn't know how to respond to Sandra's ardent declarations of affection for her.

"Betsy is my new best friend," Sandra said to mutual acquaintances, probably with the understanding that it would get back to Betsy.

For the Fourth of July weekend, Betsy travelled to Santa Fe to spend a few days with an old college friend and her husband. Sandra caught wind of this and told Betsy that she too was going to be in the Santa Fe area, just after the Fourth of July, to pick up her daughter Emily from the Brush Ranch Camp.

"I'd love to stay with you for a few days before I pick her up," Sandra said. Betsy replied that she already had a full house with some old friends. Somehow Sandra sensed that Betsy's visitors might not stay for as long as Betsy claimed, so she called the Santa Fe house at the end of the holiday. Betsy's daughter answered the phone and spilled the beans that the visiting couple was about to leave.

"Great," Sandra replied. "See you soon!"

Betsy told her visiting friends that Sandra was driving her nuts. It was terrible that Bobby had died despite John giving him the best treatment known to medical science, and dreadful that Sandra was left alone to raise three kids. But Sandra was just relentless—constantly showing up everywhere, always, and needing things.

"I really don't want to be here with her," Betsy said. And so, she decided to curtail her stay in Santa Fe. Upon Sandra's arrival, Betsy made an excuse for needing to return to Dallas earlier than expected.

"That's okay," Sandra said. "I'll look after the place and lock it up when I leave." Betsy gave her instructions for closing the house, and then returned to Dallas. Later, to her astonishment, Sandra called John and asked for instructions, implying that Betsy hadn't explained it to her. Betsy related this story in a subsequent phone call with her old friend who'd visited her in Santa Fe. This was, she told her friend, the last straw, and it had prompted her to tell John that it was time to get Sandra out of their lives. An opportunity presented itself on Wednesday, July 14. That evening Sandra called the Bagwell house, asked to speak with John, and told him her car had broken down and she needed his help. As John would later claim, when he went to assist with her car, he told her to cease calling him and his wife and coming over to their home.

Sandra was not deterred. On the morning of Friday, July 16—after John had left for work—she called Betsy with devastating news. She'd just found a letter, lodged behind a picture frame, from a married woman and addressed to Bobby. The woman referred to their extramarital affair and indicated that Bobby had fathered her most recent child, conceived the year before. Sandra was beside herself, and said she desperately needed to talk with someone. Would Betsy come over to talk?

Betsy agreed and went to Sandra's house to discuss the letter. Then Sandra had another favor to ask. She was expecting a package from Houston to arrive at Love Field on a Muse Air flight (in 1982 it was possible to check a bulky package into the cargo of commercial flights, even if one wasn't a passenger, and the receiver could pick it up at baggage claim). The trouble was, Sandra's car wouldn't start, so she asked Betsy to give her a ride. Betsy agreed and parked her car in the short-term lot while Sandra went into the terminal to get the package. She returned fifteen minutes later without it and said it was on a later flight. Betsy drove her back to her house, dropped her off, and then went home. Sandra's melodramatic letter story and all her fussing about it seemed dubious. It was yet another act in the Sandra drama, and Betsy called her husband at work to tell him about it.

At 2:00 p.m., Betsy met her two best friends for lunch at the Dallas Country Club and related the morning's events with Sandra—the letter she claimed she'd found behind the picture frame and the fruitless drive to Love Field to pick up a package. Betsy didn't know the alleged author, but the letter struck her as questionable. Both of her friends *did* know the alleged author, and they considered it preposterous. The letter must have been a fabrication. Betsy mentioned that Sandra wanted another ride to the airport to pick up the package scheduled for a later flight.

"What am I to do with this girl?" she asked.

At around 4:00 p.m., Betsy drove from the Dallas Country Club to Sandra's house to pick her up and give her a ride back to Love Field to pick up the package on the later flight and to rent a car. On the way to the airport, they passed by Betsy's house to drop off her daughter Wendy, who'd gone for a swim at the DCC while Betsy lunched with her friends. As the fourteen-year-old girl was getting out of the car, Betsy told her not to spoil her appetite by snacking because she was preparing a pasta feast for dinner. She then drove off with Mrs. Bridewell to Love Field.

At around 5:00 p.m., Dr. Bagwell called home to let Betsy know when he'd be home for dinner. Wendy answered and said that Betsy had left thirty minutes earlier to run an errand with Mrs. Bridewell. He then called Sandra's house and (as he later claimed) spoke with her daughter Kathryn, who said that her mom wasn't home. Dr. Bagwell called his house a second time around 5:30 p.m., and Wendy told him that Betsy still hadn't returned. A while later, sometime after 6:00 p.m., he called Sandra's house again. This time she was at home, and he spoke to her. She told him that, after their trip to Love Field around 4:30 p.m., Betsy had dropped her off at the Highland Park Presbyterian Church around 5:30 p.m.

"I've not seen or heard from her since then," Sandra said.

CHAPTER 6
"SOMETHING HAS HAPPENED TO BETSY."

Sometime around 8:00 p.m., Frank and Percye Monroe got a call from John Bagwell, who said, "Something has happened to Betsy" and that they needed to come over. They went to the Bagwell residence, where John explained that Betsy had left the house that afternoon, not returned home for dinner, and was nowhere to be found. Though he offered no details or theory, Frank got the impression from the way he spoke that Betsy was dead and that he somehow knew it.

Shortly thereafter, the DPD homicide investigator J.J. Coughlin arrived at the Bagwell residence and was confronted with a little group of people who seemed to be expecting him. He found this strange, because no missing person report had been filed for Mrs. Bagwell, and it wasn't a late hour for an adult to be out on a Friday evening. Dr. Bagwell was present, and Coughlin told him that his wife had been found shot to death in her car parked at Love Field. Though everyone was upset by this news, they didn't seem surprised. It was as if they already knew that something terrible had happened to her.

Coughlin explained that, though the incident was being investigated, it appeared to be a case of suicide. Dr. Bagwell and the other family members insisted that Betsy hadn't been suicidal—that she'd had no history of depression, had made no previous suicide threats or attempts, and had been perfectly fine. At the same time, Dr. Bagwell offered no information or theory that could explain how Betsy's shooting death at Love Field had come about. He'd spent the day at the Baylor University Medical Center, where he worked as an oncologist. As he'd learned from his kids, Betsy had been at home that afternoon and had started preparing dinner. Shortly after 4:00 p.m. she ran out to do an errand with a friend and did not return home.

That friend was a thirty-eight-year-old woman named Sandra Bridewell, who was also a resident of Highland Park. Detective Coughlin did not have to ask for her contact information, because at around 9:30 p.m., she showed up at the Bagwell home with a man named Stanley Crooks, who was an attorney. She said that, earlier that evening, while dining at a restaurant with Mr. Crooks and his wife Barbara, she received a call from Dr. Bagwell, who told her that Betsy had never returned home from their errand that afternoon. Sandra was concerned and therefore decided to go to the Bagwell house after dinner concluded.

Detective Coughlin conducted a separate interview with Mrs. Bridewell, apparently outside the Bagwell house. She told him that she and Betsy had driven to Love Field that afternoon to rent a car because hers had stalled. During their time together—which concluded around 5:00 p.m.—they discussed Betsy's husband and his nurse at the hospital. Mrs. Bridewell further stated that Betsy had asked her many questions about suicide. Betsy had seemed particularly curious about the gunshot suicide of Mrs. Bridewell's first husband seven years earlier.

Mrs. Bridewell's statement strengthened Coughlin's perception that Betsy had killed herself. That Dr. Bagwell hadn't seemed surprised by the news of his wife's death suggested he'd known her to be suicidal. Coughlin surmised that he'd found a suicide note and destroyed it because he considered suicide shameful and a poor reflection on his marriage. Coughlin advised medical examiner field investigator Gray of his conversation with Betsy's friend. He didn't mention Sandra's name but referred to her as a "friend of the decedent." Gray noted this conversation in a report for Chief Medical Examiner Charles Petty, who performed an autopsy on Betsy the next (Saturday) morning (July 17, 1982).

Dr. Petty noted that the decedent was clothed with a tennis outfit over a bathing suit. Though her attire offered a clue about her activity during the afternoon before her death, this potential lead wasn't pursued by the Dallas police. Her body and her beautifully manicured hands displayed no injuries, indicating she hadn't struggled prior to receiving the single gunshot to her right temple. The .22 caliber bullet had entered the right temporal region of her brain, travelled right to left, slightly upward and straight, and stopped in the left temporal parietal lobe. Most remarkable was the contact nature of the gunshot wound, indicating the muzzle had been pressed to her skin when the shot was fired. As Dr. Petty knew from large sample studies of gunshots to the head, the great majority of contact wounds are self-inflicted. In addition to analyzing the wound, Dr. Petty swabbed the ventral and dorsal surfaces of her right hand and gave the samples to trace evidence specialist Dr. I.C. Stone. Dr. Stone detected particles of lead and antimony—i.e., gunshot primer residue—in both samples. This result, plus the contact nature of the gunshot wound, led Dr. Petty to conclude that Mary Elizabeth Bagwell had committed suicide.

Frank Monroe Jr., the younger brother of Betsy Bagwell, was a lawyer who lived in Houston. On the morning of Saturday, July 17, he arrived at Camp Longhorn, located on Inks Lake in the central part of Texas, often called the Hill Country. The camp's second term had just concluded, and Frank was there to pick up his son. As he checked into the visitors' center, he was notified to call his parents in Dallas. This was strange and worrisome, and he quickly went to a pay phone and made the call. His mother answered and was extremely distraught.

"Betsy is dead. Someone has killed her," she said. A moment of stunned silence, and then Frank asked how it had happened. His mother said she didn't know. All they knew was that Betsy had been found shot.

"I'll be there as soon as I can," Frank said. He drove his son back to his home in Houston and then caught a flight to Dallas, arriving at Love Field, where his sister had been found the evening before. He first went to his parents' house. They still knew little about the circumstances of Betsy's death and were hoping to learn more from the police. The next day Frank went to the Bagwell residence and spoke briefly with Betsy's kids. He then went upstairs to speak with John Bagwell, who'd just awakened from a nap and was groggy.

"How did this happen?" Frank asked him. John said he didn't know, but before Frank could follow up with questions, another visitor entered and interrupted the conversation.

Frank left the Bagwell house and drove to the Dallas Police Department headquarters. An officer showed him the case file and told him the medical examiner had concluded that Betsy had committed suicide. The weapon found in her right hand had been used to shoot her in the right temple, and the gunshot residue found on her right hand indicated she had fired the shot.

Joy Faye Adam and her husband and two kids lived a block away from the Bagwell residence, and Joy and Betsy had become friends. Their kids were about the same age, and they were both members of the Highland Park Presbyterian Church. Joy had long regarded Betsy as a great lady and dedicated mother, always friendly and helpful. Like everyone else who knew Betsy, Joy was shocked by the news of her shooting death and didn't believe for a second that she'd committed suicide. Above all, there was no way she would abandon her kids. Joy was therefore stunned when, just two days after Betsy was found, she overheard one of her children's friends say that Mrs. Bagwell had killed herself. The boy who said this was the ten-year-old son of Clyde Jackson, who lived across the street from the Bagwell house.

"You shouldn't say that" Joy told the boy. "The police haven't had time to investigate, so it's wrong to say that she committed suicide." For Joy, this was a matter of defending Betsy's honor. To say, without evidence, that she'd taken her life and abandoned her family was terrible. Betsy's body had only just been found a couple of days earlier. Why on earth would anyone jump to that conclusion?

The next day Joy got a call from Clyde Jackson.

"Joy Faye, there's something I want to tell you and I want you to listen carefully," he said. "Betsy Bagwell committed suicide. Do you understand?" Joy was taken aback by his stern tone and imperious manner. Clearly, he was telling her she *had* to accept his assertion that Betsy had committed suicide, and that she should never question it again. In other words, he called to silence her. But why would he do that?

CHAPTER 7

QUESTIONS PERSIST

The next day (Monday, July 19, 1982) a memorial service was held for Betsy at the Highland Park Presbyterian Church with the Reverend Don Riley officiating. Frank Monroe Jr. found the service strangely formal and liturgical, with no eulogy for his sister, and few remembrances of her life and personality. It was yet another feature of Betsy's death that offered no feeling of resolution.

Before the funeral, Betsy's closest friends gathered at the Bagwell residence to accompany the family to the service. An unexpected and unwelcome visitor who appeared was Sandra Bridewell. Right as she entered the house, the husband of one of Betsy's friends asked her to leave. That evening, after the funeral reception, about fifteen of Betsy's closest friends gathered to discuss her death. Soon the conversation focused on the question of how Sandra had murdered her. No one in the room doubted that she had. Different theories were put forth about how she'd planned and executed it, and how she'd gotten away from the crime scene and returned home without being observed. Everyone present assumed their hypotheses were also being considered and analyzed by DPD homicide detectives. In fact, around the same time they were having their discussion, a *Dallas Times Herald* reporter took a statement from

DPD spokesman, Sergeant Tom Sherman.

"Everything is consistent with suicide, and the medical examiner says for all practical purposes, it will be a suicide," he explained. At the time Sergeant Sherman said this, less than three days had elapsed since Betsy's body had been found the previous Friday evening. What kind of investigation had the DPD performed over the weekend?

The *Times Herald* story ("Questions persist in death of woman") appeared the following day. Despite these persistent questions, the report stated that the "police say they consider the death a suicide and have ended their investigation." Law enforcement's perception of the matter contrasted with that of a 'family friend,' who was quoted as saying, "No one can imagine that she would have shot herself."

An attentive reader might have noticed an odd passivity conveyed in the article. It was true that none of Betsy's friends—including those with whom she'd lunched few hours before her death—believed she'd shot herself. And yet it seemed that none of them had spoken to the police or press. The solitary "family friend" who was quoted apparently wished to remain anonymous.

On Thursday, July 22, Detective Coughlin wrote his final Investigative Supplement. It was a succinct (three paragraph) document that he concluded with the statement that the medical examiner had ruled the manner of Betsy's death as suicide. Coughlin therefore reclassified the case from "Unexplained" to "Suicide" and closed it. As far as the DPD was concerned, there was nothing more to examine in the matter of Mary Elizabeth Bagwell.

The residents of Highland Park took a different view of her death. After her funeral, word spread that Betsy's last known contact was Sandra Bridewell. Some remembered Sandra treating Bobby Bridewell with shocking callousness as he lay dying. And come to think of it, hadn't her first husband ended up shot in the head? *Just like Betsy Bagwell.* Women recalled times she'd been an outrageous flirt with married men and wrecked marriages. Surely, they thought, she would be arrested and tried for murdering Betsy.

This didn't happen, and Sandra didn't seem concerned that it would. About a week after Betsy's funeral, Sandra's daughter Emily, an angelic-looking girl, appeared at the Bagwell house. Dr. Bagwell's sister, Judy, happened to be there, and Emily handed her a folded piece of paper. The little girl then turned and went back to the sidewalk in front of the house. Judy glanced at the paper, which displayed a childish drawing of John and Sandra and their five kids, under which was scrawled, "I wish you would marry my mom and take her to Santa Fe, and we would all be so happy." Judy walked out to the sidewalk and looked down the street, where she saw Emily getting into Sandra's car.

Word of this incident spread among Betsy's friends. Obviously, Sandra had put Emily up to it, and they were astonished that the woman could be so brazen to pursue John Bagwell so openly after murdering his wife. Many who'd known Betsy were bewildered that Sandra wasn't arrested. They believed that if she could get away with such a bold crime, she could get away with anything. This gave rise to the perception of Sandra having a demonic aura, perhaps even some sort of dark power that enabled her to evade law enforcement. One woman who lived in her neighborhood told her friends that while out for her morning walk, she suddenly felt the presence of something terrifying behind her, and she turned to see it was Sandra. Another woman related the experience of going up the escalator at Neiman-Marcus and seeing Sandra descending towards her on the adjacent escalator, smiling at her, which the woman found all the spookier.

CHAPTER 8
AL TEEL, P.I.

While Highland Park society remained mystified by the death of Betsy Bagwell, her widower, Dr. Bagwell, discreetly pursued a private inquiry behind the scenes. Three weeks after the DPD closed Betsy's case, he and his sister Judy met with Chief Medical Examiner Charles Petty. Dr. Bagwell questioned that his wife had committed suicide. Among other things, she'd been making plans, including the immediate task of their evening meal, for which she had set out ingredients just before her death. Dr. Bagwell said he was concerned about "a woman who drove to Love Field Airport with Mrs. Bagwell earlier that day," as Dr. Petty noted in his memo. "This woman was the wife of a patient that Dr. Bagwell had cared for and who'd recently died of lymphoma. Both Dr. Bagwell and Mrs. Bagwell had tried to help the wife of the deceased man over a rather severe emotional problem." Dr. Bagwell said he was considering hiring a private investigator to learn more about her. Dr. Petty noted he thought this could be helpful. He concluded by stating that he could *not* rule out homicide. This indicated he was open to considering the outcome of the private investigation.

SOMETIMES THE best defense is a good offense, and that's when some of Dallas' premier criminal attorneys call on Al Teel. Such was the introductory sentence to a profile of Al Teel PI in *D Magazine*—a popular monthly publication about people and events in Dallas. An Oklahoma native who'd grown up in Monterey, California, Teel spent his formative years working as a cop in Los Altos, then as an investigator for Lockheed Aircraft, and then as a US Postal Service Inspector. In Dallas he built a reputation for being one of the most competent P.I.s in the business. In September of 1982, Dr. Bagwell hired him to investigate Betsy's death, focusing on her last known contact, Sandra Bridewell.

Working in secrecy to avoid alerting Sandra, Teel investigated her past and made intriguing discoveries about the mysterious woman. He learned about the death of her first husband in 1975. David Stegall, a prominent Dallas dentist, had died of a gunshot wound to the head—also from a .22 caliber pistol. The Chief Medical Examiner in 1975 (Dr. Petty's predecessor) ruled David's death a suicide. Seven years later, in Sandra's interview with DPD Detective Coughlin about Betsy's death, she herself brought up her first husband's suicide, claiming that Betsy had inquired about it just before taking her own life. Teel found David Stegall's death suspicious. Among other things, Sandra told multiple people the falsehood that David had an undetected brain tumor when he killed himself. In fact, as Dr. Petty acknowledged, the then medical examiner had *not*, in his forensic examination of David's body, discovered a brain tumor.

Teel assembled a timeline of Betsy's last day and he interviewed the people she'd met in the course of it. He also documented telephone communications between Sandra and members of the Bagwell family, including Dr. Bagwell. Finally, Teel hired an independent forensic scientist in California named John Thornton to analyze the gunshot residue found on Betsy's right hand. The Dallas County trace evidence specialist, I.C. Stone, interpreted this residue as evidence that Betsy had fired the pistol herself. Dr. Thornton—who submitted a report to Al Teel dated August 23, 1983—disagreed. The particles of lead and antimony could have been deposited on Betsy's right hand because of its proximity to the discharging pistol, and not because she herself pulled the trigger.

Teel worked the case for a year and concluded "there is sufficient circumstantial evidence to raise doubt on the Medical Examiner's ruling of suicide and to indicate that unknown person/persons may have been involved in the death." In a letter to Dr. Bagwell dated September 21, 1983, he recommended further investigating the indications that Sandra Bridewell was responsible for Betsy's death, and then turning the matter over to the Dallas County District Attorney. "Sources cognizant of the District Attorney's office feel he would be receptive to a full review of the case," Teel wrote.

Shortly after Teel wrote this letter, he ceased his investigation. The medical examiner did not change the official manner of Betsy's death from suicide to homicide or even to unexplained. The Dallas Police Department did not reopen the case, and though Teel's contacts at the DA's office may have discussed his findings, no prosecution memo was prepared. Teel retained copies of his notes and his letters to Dr. Bagwell, but his investigation and findings would remain confidential for twenty years.

Highland Park society would continue talking and speculating about Betsy's death for decades, but her widower and children remained silent about it. Her closest friends—including the two women with whom she'd lunched at the Dallas Country Club—adopted a policy of strict silence about her death, and they never spoke with the police or press about it. Only their closest friends were even aware of their interactions with Betsy just before her death. What they saw and heard on that fateful day were kept a secret. And so, the mystery of Mary Elizabeth Bagwell's violent death deepened with the passage of time.

CHAPTER 9

THE GRIEVING
PARENTS

Bob and Diana Reardon lived in a beautiful house in Highland Park a few blocks from the Bagwell residence, though the two families didn't know each other. Bob was a successful homebuilder; Diana was a housewife who looked after their five kids. In the spring of 1982, they had to endure the most terrible thing that can happen to parents as their youngest daughter slowly died of leukemia. Decades later, Reardon family friends still vividly remembered the horror of seeing the beautiful little child waste away and groan in pain. Her funeral at St. Michael with a tiny coffin was the saddest thing they'd ever seen.

Because the Reardons were preoccupied with their own catastrophe, they were unaware of the drama around Betsy's death. When Bob was contacted by Sandra Bridewell about serving on the board of her cancer charity, he thought it sounded like a worthy cause and accepted her offer. Apart from him, the board consisted of former Dallas Cowboy Ralph Neely, whose daughter had survived leukemia, and other respected members of Dallas society.

At first Sandra seemed like an elegant lady, but at a board meeting she said something to Bob that struck him as odd. A U.S. Congressman from Ft. Worth was going to attend the meeting and Sandra had misgivings about it.

"He pursued me and was upset when I rejected him," she said. "I'm afraid he's going to bother me, so please stay close to me to discourage him." Bob perceived this assertion to be melodramatic and implausible. And then, at the meeting, the Congressman made no attempt to speak with her. Later Bob discovered it was Sandra who'd attempted to get close to the Congressman, calling his office and scheming to meet him.

After becoming acquainted with Bob, Sandra ingratiated herself with his wife Diana. Following the typical pattern, Diana initially found Sandra charming and fun. But then Sandra started coming over too frequently, showing up uninvited, often bringing one or more of her kids along. It seemed like she was attempting to ensconce herself and her kids in the Reardon home. Bob found it especially jarring when she showed up at his children's athletic games as if she were their mother.

When the first day of camp in August of 1983 finally arrived, things got even weirder. Because the campers were suffering from leukemia, it was necessary to hire mature staff. Thus, the board had found former Camp Longhorn counselors who were in their late twenties and had already completed their university education. Sandra was flirtatious with all of them. She ran the fishing dock, and every morning she invited one of the counselors to join her in driving to a bait shop a few miles away to buy worms. This was obviously an excuse to be alone with the counselor, and her morning ritual came to be known as the "worm run."

One counselor had recently graduated from a prestigious law school and was engaged to be married. Shortly after the camp session, one of the little campers succumbed to leukemia, and the counselor attended the funeral along with Bob and Sandra. At the funeral reception at the home of the child's parents, Sandra said she wasn't feeling well and asked the young man to give her a ride home. Arriving at her house, she invited him into her bedroom. A few weeks later she called Bob and said she was pregnant and expected the young man to break it off with his fiancée and marry her. She claimed to be a devout Christian and wouldn't consider getting an abortion. She wanted Bob to call the young man and talk some sense into him. Bob gave him a ring and asked for an explanation.

"She said she tested positive to a home pregnancy test, so I asked her to go to an obstetrician for an exam," the man explained. "She refuses to do it, so I told her I can't help her." Bob called Sandra back and told her she needed to get examined by an obstetrician, but she refused, claiming the home test was sufficient and that the young man should do the right thing. At this point, Bob made inquiries about Sandra. He was told his situation looked an awful lot like John and Betsy Bagwell's, and that he should distance himself from Sandra. It was imperative that *he* be the one to end the relationship, and by no means give Sandra the impression that Diana had put him up to it. And so, Bob firmly told Sandra that he wished to end his association with her, and he expected her to stay away from his family. Later he heard that, while she was allowed to retain her nominal board position for the Bridewell Foundation, she was told to cease attending camp sessions.

It struck Bob as conspicuous and strange that Sandra was interested in men ten years her junior who were just starting their careers and had no money or property to speak of. This seemed the opposite of the proverbial gold digger who goes for older, wealthy men. What exactly was her game? About six months after Bob ended his association with Sandra, a young man who'd just moved to Dallas made a fateful turn down her street.

CHAPTER 10
A FORTUITOUS ENCOUNTER

As Alan Rehrig later told his best friend, it seemed as though fate had drawn him to the beautiful woman standing in her front yard. He had arrived in Dallas the day before to start work at Nowlin Mortgage, a commercial real estate finance company. One of his colleagues—a guy named Chuck Shealy—suggested he look for a garage or "carriage house" apartment in Highland Park. The idea appealed to him because he didn't want to live in an apartment building. A gardening lover, he was drawn to the tree-lined streets flanked with big yards and flowerbeds.

While on his search, he happened to head down the 4300 block of Lorraine Avenue, and there she was, surveying her flowerbeds with a Mexican gardener. He parked his car, walked to her, and introduced himself. She smiled and seemed pleased to make his acquaintance. It was as though she'd been waiting for him. She said she didn't know of any garage apartments for rent, but if he would return in half an hour, she would give him a neighborhood tour and show him a place where notices were posted.

Alan saw the enchanting lady at a time of transition. A superb basketball and football player—the only to varsity double letter at Oklahoma State

University since 1940—after college he worked as a landman for an independent oil company. He enjoyed the work and was good at it, but in 1984, the price of oil was rapidly falling from its 1980 peak, and he was laid off in a wave of industry downsizing. His old college friend, Phil Askew, suggested he move to Dallas to work for Nowlin Mortgage. Though the Texas petroleum industry was getting pinched, the state's real estate business was booming from loose credit, the deregulation of the Savings and Loan industry, and generous tax loopholes. Baby Boomers had recently taken the helm of Texas banks, and they were more aggressive lenders than the bankers of their fathers' war generation.

For Alan, the job consisted mostly of persuading pension fund managers to invest in commercial real estate developments. His excellent people skills and college athletic stardom would likely appeal to prospective clients. He was also very driven when he had a goal.

"I think you should take Phil's offer," his mother Gloria told him over breakfast one morning. "It will be a fresh start, and Dallas seems like a place of great opportunity."

There he was on the day after his arrival, killing time while the beautiful lady—Sandra was her name—freshened up. After she went into her house, he walked back to his car, where he met an old lady on the sidewalk who gave him some advice.

"Young man, you should stay away from that woman. She's dangerous."

Initially surprised by her assertion, he then attributed it to narrow-mindedness and envy. The old lady was probably just jealous of Sandra's beauty. The notion that this delicate southern belle was *dangerous* seemed crazy.

Thirty minutes later, Sandra climbed into Alan's car, and off they drove for a tour of the neighborhood. A few blocks from her house, she pointed out the Dallas Country Club, where she said she often dined with friends. They then drove down Lakeside Boulevard, where heirs of great oil industry fortunes lived alongside a dammed section of Turtle Creek ensconced in a finely landscaped park. The huge houses and gardens were splendid.

During their tour they became acquainted. Alan told her about his background in Oklahoma and his new job at Nowlin Mortgage. Though

Alan probably didn't realize it at the time, Nowlin occasionally did deals with Rosewood—Caroline Rosewood Hunt's company that had developed the Mansion.

"How old are you?" she asked.

"Twenty-nine," he answered, and though he was too polite to ask her the same question, she volunteered an answer.

"I'm thirty-six," she said, subtracting four years from her true age. "But if you can believe it, I'm already a widow with three children. My husband died of cancer two years ago." Alan found this very sad and wondered how she was managing to raise three kids on her own.

Their drive concluded at the post office and grocery store in the Highland Park Village shopping center a few blocks north of Sandra's house. Both places had notice boards, but neither displayed any for garage apartments. Back at Sandra's house, she told him she'd love to see him again. She said she was about to depart for a week at the Canyon Ranch Spa in Tucson but would call him upon her return. He gave her the number of his cousin's house, where he was staying until he found his own place.

Alan couldn't believe his luck. To have met such an elegant lady, living in such a fine house—surely this was a sign that his move to Dallas had been the right one. The next day he told his friend Phil Askew and the other guys at the office about meeting the beautiful lady in Highland Park, and they all heartily congratulated him.

"Only in town for two days and he's already got a hot date!" exclaimed Dean Castelhano, an industry veteran, originally from New York.

That evening after work, while he was studying finance at his cousin's house, Sandra called. This was a pleasant surprise, because he didn't expect to hear from her until she returned from the Canyon Ranch Spa.

"I just wanted to say how much I enjoyed meeting you," she said. "And I really look forward to seeing you when I get home."

He assured her that he felt the same.

CHAPTER 11
LOVE BOMBING

On warm summer evenings she liked to have sex in her convertible Mercedes with the top down, parked in random places, the risk of being seen heightening the excitement. Once, just before they were about to go out for the evening, a limousine arrived to pick them up. Being with her was vivid and sort of unreal, like being in a movie. Alan had known several girls, but none had been anything like Sandra.

She was a fascinating combination of refinement and sensuality. Her lifestyle suggested she was wealthy, and in the early days of their romance she made some grand gestures such as giving Alan and his co-workers fifth row tickets to Bruce Springsteen's "Born in the USA" concert in Dallas and fourth row season tickets to the Dallas Mavericks, which she said she'd inherited from her deceased husband. She had a worldly sophistication that was new to Alan, and she often made trips to New York, San Francisco, and Europe to go shopping and attend cultural events.

A fabulous cook of gourmet meals, she rarely ate American staples such as hamburgers, which she regarded as junk food. Her favorite place to dine out was the Mansion on Turtle Creek, a hotel and restaurant that had been developed by her deceased husband, Robert Bridewell, in 1979. She bought Alan a tuxedo, which looked smashing on his six-foot frame, and took him to the Mansion whenever the mood struck.

The summer of 1984 with Sandra was one of the most thrilling times of Alan's life, but by August, sober thoughts started intruding into the intoxicating excitement. He was, after all, still in his twenties. Sandra was (he thought) seven years older and had three kids from her first marriage. Though she hadn't mentioned it in their first meeting, she'd been widowed not once, but twice. Her first husband, the biological father of her children, had (she claimed) died of a brain aneurism. She married Bobby Bridewell three years later. He adopted her kids and gave them his name.

Alan also wondered if he would ever attain the social standing to which Sandra was accustomed. New to his career, he was earning a modest salary. How could he ever measure up to her previous husband, an upscale hotel developer and racehorse owner? Maybe it would be better to meet a woman his own age or younger with whom he could start his own family. On the other hand, he loved Sandra's two daughters. Kathryn was a fun and cheerful tomboy. Emily was an angel and the sight of her warmed his heart. Once Emily and Kathryn appeared at his office bearing flowers, and Kathryn told him, "I'm pulling for you and Sandra. We really need a daddy." He didn't know what to make Sandra's oldest child—a boy named Britt, who was often away from the house with friends.

At summer's end, Alan told Sandra he wasn't sure if their relationship had a future, and that he wanted to take a break to think things over. The timing was favorable because he had to make a trip to New Hampshire for a Member Appraisal Institute course at Dartmouth University. The course was dull, and he often found himself thinking about her, with her exquisite white skin and big brown eyes that would gaze at him with desire.

And then, in a strange and thrilling surprise, he saw her in the most unexpected of places. Returning to Dallas, as he was transferring through New York LaGuardia Airport, she appeared before him, walking through the terminal with her daughter Emily. It was, she explained, an amazing coincidence, as they just happened to be returning from a trip to Europe. To Alan, the fortuitous encounter seemed like a sign they were meant to be together, and upon returning to Dallas he resumed his love affair with her. Two months later she got pregnant, and the deal was sealed.

She told him the news right before Phil Askew picked him up to go to a Dallas Mavericks game. In Phil's car on the way to the arena, he broke into tears as he told his friend the momentous news.

"She's pressing for marriage," he said.

"Do you love her?" Phil asked.

"Yes, I do."

"Well, there you go."

The possibility that Sandra was lying about the pregnancy didn't occur to Alan and Phil. In fact, it was impossible for her to conceive because she'd gotten a hysterectomy eight years earlier. In many states, a woman who fakes pregnancy to obtain financial benefits from a man to whom she isn't married is committing larceny by trick or device, a criminal offense. In Sandra's case, she committed fraud in the inducement to marry—a civil offense that may be viewed by courts as grounds for annulment. That Sandra committed this fraud against Alan wasn't technically a criminal offense. Nevertheless, it was a notable expression of her disregard for the truth and her callous decision to treat him as an instrument to be manipulated to provide for her. The deception was part of a larger plan that necessitated telling yet another lie to her new husband after their wedding.

CHAPTER 12
FRIDAY NIGHT LIGHTS

The autumn of 1984, when Alan proposed to Sandra, was a time of great optimism and prosperity in Highland Park. President Reagan was revered by the politically conservative society, and its banking and real estate industries were firing on all cylinders. Above all, the beloved Highland Park Scots football team was having an unexpectedly good season, and there was growing excitement about the prospect of going to the state championship.

Since the 1940s, when Bobby Layne and Doak Walker were local stars, the town had developed great pride in its football team. The entire school (grades 9-12) never had more than about 650 boys to draw from, and rarely did it have any of exceptional size and speed. Throughout Texas, Highland Park kids were regarded as rich, spoiled, and soft, but what they lacked in physical prowess they made up for with brains, discipline, and esprit de corps. Like the great Scottish hero William "Braveheart" Wallace going to meet the stronger forces of Edward II, the Scots filed onto the field with their Highlander Band playing battle hymns on bagpipes.

No one expected HP's 1984 squad, led by quarterback John Stollenwerk, to go to state finals, but after an early season loss to

MacArthur, the victories started piling up. By November, the town was electrified by its team's momentum. If the Scots sustained it, they would challenge the Odessa Permian Panthers on their home turf on December 14. Though four years before the Panthers' 1988 season, immortalized in the book and film *Friday Night Lights*, it was the same era. Highlander Stadium was *the* place to see and be seen in Highland Park on a Friday night.

One Friday in November, Jack Sides Jr. felt the surging energy and excitement around him as he ascended the stairs to his seat. Rising above the cacophony, a female voice cried his name. He turned towards it and saw Sandra Bridewell a few seats down from the aisle. This was a surprise, as Jack had never seen her at a Scots game. His parents had once been close friends of her and her first husband, David Stegall, who'd died in 1975. However, a couple of years earlier, for reasons Jack hadn't understood, his parents had abruptly stopped socializing with her.

"Oh, hello Mrs. Bridewell," he said. She seemed to be in roaring good spirits and very happy to see him.

"Jack, meet my fiancé, Alan Rehrig," she said with a giddy expression.

"Nice to meet you, Mr. Rehrig," Jack said, and shook his hand. He was a nice-looking man with a warm smile. Though Jack didn't give it much thought at the time, later it occurred to him that the encounter had, in some undefined way, struck him as odd. Maybe it was the way Sandra had made such an effort to get his attention, shouting over the din of the stadium. Most of his mom's friends would have smiled and waved at him as he passed, and not gone to such lengths to flag him down.

It wasn't the first time he'd interacted with Sandra in a way that had seemed out of the ordinary. Once he'd done a sleepover with her son Britt at the Stegall house in Greenway Parks. While they were in Britt's room, chatting and laughing, Sandra appeared and told them to pipe down, as she was trying to get some sleep. Her request was normal enough. What got his attention was the fact that she wasn't wearing anything but underwear. Even as a pre-pubescent boy, he was impressed by the sight of her mostly naked body. Now here she was, years later, with her new fiancé at Highlander Stadium. Jack exchanged a few pleasantries with them, and then continued to his seat.

To Alan, Jack probably came across as an exceptionally good-looking and polite boy, and Sandra's apparent friendship with his parents must have seemed indicative of her integration in Highland Park society. And what a cohesive society it was. It seemed the entire town was attending the game, and the spectacle of the Scots winning again seemed to unify everyone into one big happy and proud family. It didn't occur to him that Sandra was feared and ostracized by the people sitting around them.

CHAPTER 13
TILL DEATH DO US PART

After they got engaged, the excitement of their first months gave way to serious considerations. With a new baby on the way, Sandra said she thought it would be prudent to move into a more affordable house until Alan started earning more money. She sold her house on Lorraine and bought a duplex on Asbury Avenue in the neighboring town of University Park. For their budget, they agreed that she would make the house payments and he would cover the other household expenses.

The day before Thanksgiving, Alan called his mother, but before he could get out what he wanted to say, he began to cry.

"What is it, baby?" she asked him.

"Sandra and I are getting married," he finally managed to say.

"Why are you crying?" she asked.

"I guess I'm a bit scared of taking such a big step," he replied.

"Would you like me to come to Dallas to talk about it?"

"That would be great."

Gloria left Edmond that afternoon and drove to Dallas. They met at his office just before dinner. By then he was more composed and spoke of Sandra's great qualities—how beautiful she was and how much he loved her kids.

"How old is she?" Gloria asked.

"Thirty-six," Alan replied.

"Can she still have children?" Gloria asked, wondering if the hasty wedding plans had been prompted by an accidental pregnancy.

"Yes," he said, but didn't mention Sandra's claim to be pregnant.

Thanksgiving was a wonderfully sunny and crisp autumn day. Gloria was given a warm welcome at Alan and Sandra's new home, elegantly furnished with antiques. Her children were delightful, and they hugged her affectionately. Sandra was a gracious hostess and a great cook. Altogether the scene gave the impression of a happy home. And yet, it seemed to Gloria that there was something odd about it. She couldn't help wondering why Sandra wanted her son. What exactly did she see in him—an Oklahoma country boy with no property who'd only just started his career?

Apparently reading her mind, Sandra said, "You know, the first time I saw Alan, I was so impressed by how well put together he was. He looked so sharp in his sports jacket and pressed trousers, and his shoes were brilliantly shined. Then I got in his car and saw how well he took care of it. Later I inquired about Nowlin Mortgage, and I learned it's a top institution."

After dinner, Gloria glanced at the bookshelf in the living room and noticed that among classic works of literature, Sandra had a Bible and books about Christianity.

"We have the same taste in books," Gloria said. "I took the Bethel Bible Study."

"Oh really! So did I," Sandra said.

"I'm comforted to know you're a Christian."

"Yes, and I want you to know that I've taken Paul's advice to the Ephesians to heart. 'Wives, submit to your husbands as to the Lord. For the husband is the head of the wife as Christ is the head of the church.'"

Following Thanksgiving, Alan drove Gloria back to Oklahoma City in her car to keep her company on the long drive. He'd just bought *The Prophet*, by Kahlil Gibran, and he asked her to recite some of the poems about love and marriage. Arriving in Oklahoma City, she dropped him off at the airport, where he flew back to Dallas and his fiancée.

The following Friday, December 7, 1984, Alan's family drove from Edmond to Dallas to attend the wedding, scheduled for the following morning. Gloria's mother, Nana, did not want to go.

"She's too old for Alan and she already has three kids," Nana said.

"She's only seven years older," Gloria said.

"How do you know that?" Nana replied.

"Because Sandra said so. Do you think she would lie about her age?"

"I don't know the woman, so I can't say."

"Well, mom, all I can say is that Alan has chosen to marry her, and he needs our support, so you're going to the wedding." Nana reluctantly agreed.

That evening they had a family dinner at the North Dallas home of Alan's first cousin, Robert Smith and his wife Glady. After dinner, Gloria gave the couple a family heirloom—a teddy bear fashioned from a quilt that Alan's great grandmother had made, with Nana's signature embroidered on it. She hoped that Alan and Sandra would have a child to whom they could pass it down. Nana (despite her disapproval) gave them a silver dinner service. Sandra gave Gloria a potted ivy plant trained in the shape of a heart. The evergreen vine was the symbol of eternity and fidelity.

The ceremony and reception were held at the Mansion on Turtle Creek. Officiating was the Reverend Clayton Bell, Pastor of the Highland Park Presbyterian Church. Son of the famed medical missionary, Nelson Bell, and brother-in-law of the evangelist Billy Graham, Pastor Bell was a national figure in the Presbyterian Church of the U.S.A. That such a distinguished minister wed Alan and Sandra lent great prestige to the ceremony. Sandra was a member of Pastor Bell's congregation, but instead of a church wedding, she wanted to be wed in her deceased husband's hotel.

Sandra looked young, beautiful, and innocent in her white wedding gown, and Alan looked handsome in his fine gray suit. At the reception, held in the same room as the ceremony, he seemed wonderfully happy with Emily and Kathryn sitting on his lap at the table. And yet, again, Gloria sensed there was something strange about the scene. Apart from Sandra's children, only two people attended the wedding on her side— Sissy Carter Alsabrook and her husband Roger. Where were Sandra's other friends? Alan's party of thirty family members and friends were happy to see each other, but the occasion provided no opportunity to meet Sandra's circle. They wondered if she was concerned that her Highland Park society wouldn't approve of her marriage to Alan, with his humble, Oklahoma origins. If someone had told them that—apart from Cissy Alsabrook—Sandra's old friends had dropped her out of fear that she was a murderess, they probably wouldn't have believed it.

CHAPTER 14
THE HONEYMOON IS OVER

A couple of weeks after the wedding, Alan, Sandra, and their three kids came to Edmond for Christmas. At the end of their stay, Sandra was stricken by stomach flu, so she stayed a couple of extra days with Gloria to convalesce after Alan and the kids returned to Dallas. One day she sat in Alan's bedroom, going through his high school yearbooks, asking Gloria about his friends. She was very curious about them, and later surprised Gloria by mentioning a few of their names. She had an exceptionally good memory.

They spoke about Alan's prospects in the year ahead. Sandra had just bought him a leather-bound 1985 calendar made by Alfred Dunhill, and she wanted to mark the birthdays of his family members. With Gloria giving her the dates, she sat at the kitchen table, noting them in the calendar.

"I've been meaning to ask you, what is your birthday?" Gloria asked.

"April 5, 1949," she replied.

Still Sandra mentioned nothing to Gloria about her pregnancy, though she did bring up another important subject.

"Now that Alan has a family, don't you think it would be a good idea for him to buy life insurance?" she asked. Gloria agreed. A few months later, Alan purchased a policy with a $220,000 death benefit.

Nineteen eighty-five would prove to be the climactic year of the Dallas real estate boom before the Savings and Loan Crisis erupted in 1986. Alan greatly wanted to advance and to increase his income, especially with a new baby on the way. Shortly after New Year's Day, disaster struck. One night Alan went to a Mavericks game with Phil Askew, and afterwards they went to Phil's house to work on a presentation. Sandra called and asked to speak with him. She said she'd just left the hospital and had stopped at a 7-Eleven to use a payphone. While he was at the basketball game, she started bleeding and drove herself to the hospital.

"I've had a miscarriage," she said. "It's so terrible. They were twin boys with your red hair, and now they're gone!"

Judy Askew was there when Alan took the call, and she saw the news strike him like a physical blow. She did her best to comfort him, and the next day she prepared a dinner for the Rehrig family and took it to their house in University Park. Sandra answered the door wearing a nightgown and invited Judy in. They put Judy's meal in the refrigerator and then sat in the living room, where some housepainters were working. Judy thought it odd that Sandra hadn't postponed the repainting due to her miscarriage the night before. As she expressed her sorrow about the loss of the twins, Sandra told the painters not to forget the interior panels of the bookshelves. She then said she'd just purchased the most exquisite Italian sheets for the master bed. She was sure Alan would love sleeping in them, but she also knew he would consider them far too expensive, so she hadn't told him the brand. Judy also found this confession rather odd.

Alan had recently written his friend Bill Dodd in Arizona to tell him how much he looked forward to their kids playing together. Now he had to break the news that it wasn't to be. Thank God he hadn't told his mother about Sandra's pregnancy. He hadn't wanted to give her the impression of a shotgun wedding and had therefore planned to tell her later. That he hadn't told her spared her the sadness of knowing about the miscarriage. For his 30th birthday on January 18, they again visited Gloria for the celebration, at which Sandra gave him a beautiful black overcoat. The next day, one of Alan's oldest friends—a lawyer named Ron Barnes—hosted a wedding shower. Ron and his wife Debbie invited their church congregation to their home, and Debbie registered an array of gifts at an Oklahoma City department store.

Returning to Dallas, Alan launched back into work, so he asked Sandra to write the thank you notes. She had a gorgeous hand and seemed to enjoy writing, so it seemed like a reasonable request. She agreed to do it, but he later discovered that she didn't follow through. This was irritating enough, but what really bothered him was her lying about it.

"I can't imagine why no one received a note," she said. "They must have gotten lost in the mail."

"All of them?" Alan asked incredulously.

In a phone conversation with Gloria that spring, he said he'd been bothered by the incident, and though he didn't state it explicitly, he gave Gloria the impression it had caused him to question Sandra's integrity.

To Phil Askew, it seemed that Alan was both in love with Sandra and badly stressed by her. Somehow, she came to dominate him, and a couple of months after his wedding, his cheerful, free spirit was extinguished. Rarely could he go out with his friends anymore. It seemed she kept him on the tightest of leashes. To be sure, she could still delight him. Once on an investor trip with Phil, he opened his briefcase to find her sexy underwear in it—a little reminder of her while he was away. It was a funny surprise and he found it charming.

One weekend that spring, Ron and Debbie Barnes visited Alan and Sandra in Dallas. The weather was beautiful, and one day the four of them went for a stroll from the Rehrig's home to the nearby McCulloch Junior High School, where Alan and Ron shot a few hoops while Sandra and Debbie chatted. As they were walking home the topic of kids came up, and Alan said they were hoping to take another shot at it.

"I'm encouraging Sandra to get into better shape to handle the pregnancy," Alan said. Ron thought the statement was an example of how Alan could occasionally be a tactless clod. Of course, he was sincere. He really believed that Sandra would have a better chance of carrying a child to term if she took better care of herself. The remark reminded Ron that he'd never perceived Sandra to be Alan's type. Before he met her, he'd always dated natural, athletic girls with whom he'd gone hiking and camping and shot hoops. It seemed odd that he'd married this woman who was always dressed like she was going to a formal luncheon. She'd put on weight since their wedding a few months earlier, and in certain lighting she looked considerably older than Alan. His remark about her getting into shape didn't go over well. Ron glanced at her right as Alan said it, and he saw her eyes burn with fury.

In June, Sandra treated Alan and Ron to a weekend of golf at the Garden of the Gods Club and Resort in Colorado Springs. Sandra said she'd inherited her membership from her late husband Robert Bridewell, who died of cancer in 1982. However, as Alan and Ron went to the pro shop to register for a tee time, they were told that Sandra wasn't a member. Upon hearing this, she became furious and marched into the shop.

"I'm Mrs. Robert Bridewell!" she exclaimed, "and I'm still a member." And so, Alan and Ron were given a tee time. Ron wondered if the membership of Sandra's deceased husband was no longer valid. Had the pro shop turned a blind eye to avoid an embarrassing confrontation? That evening, as they were finishing dinner on the patio, another awkward moment occurred when the parents of her deceased husband appeared on the patio and sat at a table near theirs. Their presence made her uncomfortable, and she quickly asked for the check and left without greeting her former in-laws. This was strange. Alan thought she'd had a happy marriage with Mr. Bridewell, so why didn't she wish to speak with his parents?

CHAPTER 15
CALL FROM THE COLLECTIONS DEPARTMENT

Big trouble in their marriage began shortly after their return from Colorado. One day at work, Alan got a call from the American Express collections department. Unbeknownst to him, Sandra had run up the balance on his card to $20,000. This was shocking news. How had she managed to do this? Didn't the card have a credit limit? Yes, the Amex representative said, but his wife, who was also authorized to use the card, had asked for a credit raise. *Twenty thousand dollars*—1985 dollars—was almost as much as he'd brought home in his first year at Nowlin Mortgage. How was he going to pay it? And so, Alan became increasingly stressed about money, which, in turn, dampened his enthusiasm for Sandra and the marriage.

It was during the summer of 1985 that Sandra became friends with her neighbor Margaret (not her real name). During the day, when Alan was at work, Margaret frequently wandered over to Sandra's house and they talked or went out to lunch. Sandra was a great conversationalist and very funny. Margaret occasionally saw Alan on her morning walks as he was leaving the house for work. What she noticed most about him was his warm smile and friendly way of greeting her. His manners were incongruous with Sandra's claim—sometime during the latter half of the summer—that he was not the wholesome guy she'd thought him to be when they'd wed the previous December. He was, she said, stressed about money, and she feared he'd gotten into gambling and owed money to a bookie. She also suspected he'd gotten into cocaine, which could explain his volatile moods. Sandra was, she told Margaret, afraid of Alan.

By the end of October, Alan's financial distress was so great that he contemplated selling his Ford Bronco to retire his car loan at Sherry Lane Bank. He'd initially bought the vehicle outright, but then used it as collateral for a personal loan in the autumn of 1984. One year later, he struggled to make the monthly payments. Sandra told him she would seek a buyer, and on October 27, she said she found one—in Edmond, Oklahoma of all places. That morning, Alan called his mother and said they were headed her way to show the car. When they arrived, Sandra tried calling the prospective buyer but was unable to reach him.

Later that day, while Sandra had a moment alone with Gloria, she proclaimed that Alan's behavior was testing their marriage. He'd become moody, had lost sexual interest in her, and was overstepping in his attempts to discipline Britt. Gloria was a guidance counselor and accustomed to discussing interpersonal problems. However, because Sandra talked so fast without a single pause, Gloria couldn't get a word in edgewise. As the day ended, Sandra still couldn't reach the prospective car buyer, so they decided to leave the Bronco with Gloria to show it to the man (if he finally returned their call). Gloria gave them a ride to Oklahoma City to meet Ron and Debbie Barnes for dinner before catching a flight back to Dallas.

They met at Ron's office and took separate cars to the restaurant. Alan rode with Ron; Sandra rode with Debbie. En route, Alan told Ron he was mystified by Sandra's behavior, her out-of-control spending, and her apparent lack of money, even though she put on the airs of a rich lady.

"Turns out she's four years older than she said she was when we met," Alan said. "Now I'm beginning to question everything she told me about herself. I've never asked to see her financial records, but I'm seriously considering it."

"Both of you should be completely open about your finances," Ron advised.

Meanwhile, in Debbie's car, Sandra said she suspected Alan had gotten into drugs and gambling.

"He's lost sexual interest in me, and I'm afraid he's gay," Sandra said.

The prospective buyer in Edmond never materialized, and on October 30, Alan and Sandra decided to fly back to Oklahoma City to pick up Alan's car. He told Gloria on the phone that he wanted to catch the 6:00 p.m. flight right after work and immediately drive back to Dallas, but for some reason they missed it. Alan then called again and said they would catch a later flight, and he asked her to put the car keys in the mailbox so he wouldn't have to wake her. Gloria could tell from his tone that he was annoyed about the delay, which necessitated having to drive back to Dallas in the middle of the night. A few days later, Alan and Sandra separated. She remained in their home; he moved in with Phil Askew and his wife Judy. Though this seemed to be an overture to divorce, Sandra mentioned nothing about filing. They didn't speak during the month of November.

CHAPTER 16

CRIME AND PUNISHMENT

When Sandra refused to pay back the $20,000 bill she'd run up on his Alan's Amex, he assumed it was from her conviction that it's a man's duty to provide for his wife and children. Because Sandra maintained the lifestyle of a lady of property, Alan didn't realize that she was, in fact, insolvent. Her sale of the Lorraine house didn't put her into the black and she couldn't service the mortgage on her duplex. Nevertheless, her abysmal financial condition didn't deter her from borrowing yet another $20,000.

Somewhere Sandra had met an aspiring theater producer named Josh Lukins who'd started his career in San Francisco and was trying to break into the New York theater scene. In the fall of 1985, he needed money for a new production he was staging Off-Broadway in November, and he hoped Sandra could assist. She introduced him to her contact at the Bank of Dallas who gave him and Sandra an unsecured loan for $20,000 on October 16, 1985. On the same day, Sandra signed a note to Josh, promising that she would pay him back this sum by December 13, 1985, so that he could retire his debt with the Bank of Dallas. In return, Josh granted her a 4% limited partnership share of net profits in his Quantum

Leap Productions, plus a 2% general share of net profits. In addition, Sandra would receive an Associate Producer credit for his latest theater production "in the name of Sandra Bridewell."

Josh's latest production was an ambitious adaptation of Feodor Dostoevsky's novel *Crime and Punishment*, about a young and impoverished law student named Raskolnikov who murders a mean old pawnbroker to steal her money. Right after he commits what turns into a double murder, he is horrified by his actions and crippled with guilt—so much so that he discards the money. He is also appalled to discover that his rationale for committing the crime—to use the old miser's money to help decent people in desperate need—becomes unconvincing. Since *Crime and Punishment* was published in 1866, scholars and philosophers have regarded it as the greatest literary expression of the catastrophe that ensues when the value of an individual life is calculated in terms of its utility. Two of Woody Allen's films—*Crimes and Misdemeanors* (1989) and *Match Point* (2005) were inspired by the novel.

The New York premiere was staged at the Harold Clurman Theater on West 42nd Street on November 17, 1985. On November 13, Sandra apparently realized she had no means of honoring her promissory note to Josh Lukins, which stipulated she pay him back the full $20,000 on or before December 13, 1985. And so, she approached her neighbor Margaret and said she needed to borrow $6,000 to cover household expenses because her other resources were tied up in a New York play. Margaret thought it strange that a woman who couldn't afford to buy groceries was a theater financier, but then again, Sandra was no ordinary woman. It was precisely her quirky, unconventional approach to life that made her so much fun. Margaret loaned her $6,000. A few weeks later, Sandra came to her and said she needed to borrow another $4,000. Altogether, she promised to pay back the $10,000 loan no later than January 14, 1986.

Sandra attended the play's premiere, of which the famous *New York Times* critic Walter Goodman wrote a semi-favorable review. He concluded with the rather neat formulation: *On its own theatrical terms, if it makes sense to consider a stage version of a great novel that way, it has considerable intensity, and the pace never lets up. Its failures are inherent in its ambition. Pay, It Doesn't. CRIME AND PUNISHMENT, by Fyodor Dostoyevsky; adapted by L. A. Sheldon; directed by Maria Mazer with John Van Ness Philip… Presented by Quantum Leap, Josh Lukins and Mr. Philip, in association with Sandra Bridewell.*

CHAPTER 17
ENDGAME

At the time the *New York Times* review was published, Sandra had not filed for divorce from Alan, and they had only been separated for two weeks. Nevertheless, she presented herself as Sandra Bridewell, and not by her married name, Sandra Rehrig. Alan knew nothing about her theater production, but during the month of November, he contemplated the eerie proposition that he didn't really know his wife. Shortly after their separation, he played golf with his old friend Mark Deason at the Colonial course in Fort Worth. They talked about Alan's marital problems. Alan was perplexed about Sandra's behavior, but it seemed to Mark that he was still open to patching things up with her. But then, two weeks later, Mark again played golf with Alan—this time at Las Colinas—and on this occasion it was clear that Alan's feelings about Sandra had changed. Her spell on him was broken and he was ready to get a divorce.

Alan and Mark had been close friends since childhood and had gone to college together. In the past Alan had confided things in Mark that he'd never told anyone else, and so it was on this occasion. Alan had recently made some disturbing discoveries about his wife. For starters, she was four years older than she'd claimed to be. Once he became aware of this major lie, he realized that many other things she'd told him about herself were false or probably false. **Indeed,** he sensed he knew nothing about her apart from the fact that she **had** three children and had been married to Bobby Bridewell for four years. He loved the two girls like his own daughters, and he wanted the best for them, but he was done with Sandra. However, he didn't want to say anything that could cause needless conflict, so he wasn't discussing what he'd discovered with others. He wanted to get out of the marriage as quickly and painlessly as possible.

At the end of November, Gloria bumped into Ron Barnes, and he mentioned the separation. Initially she thought she would let Alan call her when he was ready to talk, but on the evening of Monday, December 2, she could no longer bear the terrible feeling of disconnection from her son, so she called him. He said he didn't want her to think ill of Sandra, but yes, his marriage had been very stressful, and her behavior was often a mystery. They talked for about an hour, and it was clear to Gloria that Alan was thoroughly confounded about his wife and marriage and filled with self-doubt.

"I want you to know how much I love you and that my heart aches for you," she said. "Giving birth to you was the best thing I ever did, and I am so proud to be the mother of such a fine young man."

Sometime during the first week of December, Alan spoke with Sandra on the phone. She didn't invite him to return to their home, but nor did she say she wanted to move forward with the divorce. She said she was afraid he would get half of her property.

"But I don't want half of your property," Alan said. "All I want is my camping equipment and my stereo." As he understood it, whatever property Sandra had before they married, such as her house, wasn't communal anyway, and she hadn't made any money since their wedding, so what was she worried about?

Shortly after this conversation, Sandra saw her neighbor Margaret, to whom she explained that she and Alan were still at an impasse because he refused to go to counseling. Still, she had agreed to meet him at her storage facility because Alan wanted to get his camping gear, and—as

Sandra stated to Margaret—only she had the key to the unit's lock. Margaret advised her not to go alone because, as Sandra had claimed, she was afraid of Alan.

"If you have to meet him there, you should bring someone with you to make sure he doesn't misbehave and that he only takes what belongs to him," Margaret advised.

On December 5, Alan went to a Mavericks game with his old friend Kirk Whitman, to whom he expressed the same bafflement and frustration. He reiterated that he didn't want any of her property, though he did want her to pay him back for the charges she'd made on his American Express card. Lately he'd wondered if she even had any property, and he told Kirk he was going to try to run down some financial data on her. The next day, Friday, December 6, he again spoke with Sandra on the phone, and they agreed to meet on Saturday at the storage warehouse in East Dallas. The next day, Sandra and Margaret went shopping for a Christmas tree and then to lunch at the Greenville Bar & Grill. Sandra didn't mention she was planning to meet Alan at the warehouse at 5:00 p.m.

Saturday, December 7, 1985, was the eve of their one-year anniversary. Sandra had marked it in the leather-bound calendar she'd given Alan with exclamation marks and heart shapes. The weather that day was sunny and unseasonably warm. A seventh birthday celebration was held at the Askew home for their son Jimmy. Alan spent the afternoon playing with kids in the backyard and watching the SMU vs. Oklahoma University football game. As 5:00 p.m. drew near, he went upstairs to his room to freshen up before he departed to the warehouse. However, because it was still warm outside, he wore shorts and a T-shirt, adding only a navy-blue sweater because it would cool off with the setting sun. As he was leaving, Judy met him in the front entrance hall.

"Well honey, it's about to be your first anniversary. I know this is really tough, but maybe things will work out. Let's hope for the best," she said, and gave him a hug and a kiss. Alan hugged her back.

"I'll see you later," he said.

Phil had stepped out to run an errand and returned home right as Alan was pulling out of the circular driveway. The time was around 4:55, which meant he would arrive at the storage warehouse around 5:20. Alan smiled and waved at Phil as he pulled out of the driveway and onto Forrest Lane. Phil waved back. *Good luck, buddy,* he said to himself.

Around 6:15 p.m., Sandra called the Askew house and Phil answered.

"Where is Alan?" she asked angrily.

"What do you mean? He left here an hour ago to meet you at the storage place."

"Well, he's not here and I'm not going to wait any longer. It's just like him not to show."

"Hold on!" Phil exclaimed. "He was definitely going to meet you."

"I'm sure he's off gallivanting around," she replied. "Or maybe he decided to drive to Oklahoma to visit a friend up there. This isn't the first time he's not shown for an appointment." She hung up.

Hours passed and Alan didn't return. Phil wondered what on earth could have diverted him. All routes to the storage unit were safe, and he hadn't had time to stop along the way. Alan didn't come home that night or the next morning, and Phil and Judy grew steadily more worried.

Margaret called Sandra on Sunday morning at 11:00. Emily answered and said her mother was at church and would be home later. Sandra returned Margaret's call around 12:30 and they talked about getting together that evening. At around 7:00 p.m. they went to a showing of *Rocky IV*. Before they walked into the cinema, Margaret noticed that Sandra looked tired and seemed out of sorts. Shortly after they sat down, someone in the row behind her bumped the back of her head, which triggered her to turn and snarl at the woman to watch herself. After the film they went to a pizzeria, and again Margaret was struck by Sandra's exceptionally tired and haggard appearance.

On Monday morning, when Alan didn't show for work, Phil knew something terrible had happened to him, so he called Sandra and broke the bad news. She disagreed with his interpretation. Alan was just being a flake and would eventually turn up. At any rate, she was separated from him, and it wasn't her responsibility. Phil was taken aback by her coldness.

He'd understood that she and Alan were estranged, but not *that* estranged. And obviously she wasn't too alienated to enlist his help in moving things into storage. It was a big favor to ask of him on a Saturday evening. Alan would have preferred to watch the final quarter of the SMU-OU game, and Sandra had a strong, seventeen-year-old son. Phil wondered why she couldn't have scheduled the chore when her son was available to help.

Phil nevertheless persuaded Sandra to let him and Dean Castelhano into the storage warehouse area so that they could look for Alan. The three of them visited the warehouse that day, and Sandra punched in the gate code. Phil and Dean walked the aisles between the concrete and corrugated steel structures, looking for any sign of Alan and yelling his name, thinking that maybe he was locked in one of the storage units.

On that same Monday morning, Gloria Rehrig drove to Tulsa to evaluate a high school counseling program. She'd just taken her seat in the school's library for the meeting when someone told her she had a visitor in the hallway. She stepped outside and saw her niece Cynthia who lived in Tulsa. Cynthia said Al had been missing since Saturday afternoon. She had just heard the news from her brother Robert in Dallas. Sandra had called and told Robert's wife Glady that Al hadn't shown for an appointment at their storage warehouse and that no one had seen him since. Sandra wondered if Alan had made a spontaneous trip to Tulsa to visit Cynthia.

Upon hearing this, Gloria wondered if he'd gone camping. He loved nature and sometimes went into the wilderness to clear his head. With the stress of his marriage, maybe he'd decided to get away from it all. She knew this was probably wishful thinking, because as she drove home to Edmond, she couldn't shake the feeling that something terrible had happened. Arriving home, she spoke with Phil Askew, who told her everything he knew. Phil said he would contact the Dallas police to file a missing person report.

CHAPTER 18

BILL DEAR, P.I.

Dr. Harvey Davisson was a clinical psychologist who specialized in hypnosis therapy for patients suffering from compulsive disorders and addictions. During the eighties he made a name for himself as the go-to psychologist for the wealthy and troubled. His most notorious patient was the Fort Worth oil heir T. Cullen Davis, who was tried for the murder of his stepdaughter in 1976, and then tried a second time two years later for hiring a hit man to murder his estranged second wife and the judge overseeing their divorce case.

Davis, who was thought to be the wealthiest man ever to stand trial for murder in the United States, hired defense attorney Richard "Racehorse" Haynes, who focused on the lack of physical evidence connecting Davis with his stepdaughter's murder. Haynes also skillfully cast the prosecution's key witness—Davis's estranged wife Priscilla—as leading the double life of a Fort Worth high society lady on the one hand, and an addict consorting with cocaine dealers on the other. Davis's acquittals in the two trials were regarded as models of how skilled lawyering could enable a wealthy client to beat the rap despite extremely suspicious circumstances and damning witness testimony. After Cullen and Priscilla divorced, she moved to Highland Park with her son, Cullen,

Jr., and was occasionally seen dining with Sandra at the Mansion. Priscilla was famous for the contrast of her petite figure and gigantic breasts and her habit of wearing a garish gold and diamond-studded necklace that formed the words "Rich Bitch."

Dr. Davisson also treated the troubled children of the wealthy, many of whom were struggling with addictions and associating with the wrong people. As part of his patient workup in such cases, he occasionally used the private investigator William Dear to ascertain what was going on in their lives. On the Monday following Alan Rehrig's disappearance, Bill Dear P.I. received a call from Dr. Davisson.

"I've got a lady here with whom I'd like you to speak right away," Dr. Davisson explained. Dear drove to Dr. Davisson's office. There he met Sandra and was immediately impressed by her lustrous brown hair and big brown eyes. *Wow*, Dear thought, *this is one attractive lady.* Sandra said her husband had disappeared and that she was worried that something had happened to him, and equally worried that whatever had happened to him could also happen to her and her kids. She began to cry as she explained this. Amid sobs she said she was afraid that her husband had gotten into trouble with gambling bookies and drug dealers. Maybe he owed them large sums of money, and they would soon be coming to his home to collect it.

Her husband's disappearance was, she claimed, the culmination of a pattern of troubling behavior that had begun that summer, when he'd started acting moody and stressed about money, which he apparently needed for his cocaine and gambling addictions. Sometimes she'd been mortally afraid of him. Once they'd gone waterskiing at Lake Ray Hubbard. While he was driving the boat and she was waterskiing, she fell in the middle of the lake. Instead of circling around to get her, he motored away, abandoning her to swim a long distance. The nearest shore was grassy and infested with venomous water moccasins, so she was lucky she made it back to the landing alive.

As Sandra expressed her fears to Bill, she struck him as too histrionic. Still, he was intrigued, and he agreed to provide security for her home and to investigate her missing husband. The next day he went to her duplex and was impressed by her elegant antiques and art. It was a beautifully decorated place, replete with freshly cut flowers. All its contents—from her Neiman-Marcus clothing to the designer luggage he saw in a closet—were of the finest quality. Strange that such a refined Park Cities lady had married a man who'd been associating with dangerous criminals.

On the same day Dear visited Sandra's duplex, Gloria Rehrig called the DPD and was directed to Officer Joe Murdock, who assured her the DPD would keep an eye out for Alan. Gloria asked him to visit Sandra's house and look at the alley entrance to the garage—not visible from the street—to see if Al's Bronco was parked there. She also requested that he ask Sandra if Al's camping gear was in the garage or in their storage unit.

Officer Murdock agreed to perform these tasks, and a few hours later he called back. He said he'd visited Mrs. Rehrig at her home and that she'd accompanied him to the warehouse. Alan's Bronco was nowhere to be found, but his camping gear was in the storage unit. Officer Murdock assured Gloria that Sandra was a very nice lady. He saw no reason to suspect that she had anything to do with Alan's disappearance.

Right after Gloria spoke with Officer Murdock, Sandra called her.

"Why did you ask a Dallas policeman to come to my house?" she asked furiously.

"I asked him to check to see if Al's camping gear was missing," Gloria replied.

"You could have asked me," Sandra said.

"But you haven't been helpful at all. Phil told me you didn't even want to file a missing person report."

"I haven't seen Alan in over a month, and he was living with Phil, so I think Phil should file the report. I can't believe you called the police, Gloria. I'm so hurt." She hung up.

CHAPTER 19

"SOMETHING HAS HAPPENED TO ALAN."

The next evening (Wednesday, December 11) at 10:30, two Oklahoma City police patrol officers were cruising South MacArthur Boulevard, just north of the Will Rogers Airport, when they spotted a Ford Bronco parked in a dirt lot next to an electrical substation. They checked it out and found it locked. Shining a flashlight into the driver's side, they saw a dead man in the vehicle. Upon closer inspection, they saw the corpse was clothed in athletic shorts, a T-shirt, and a Navy-blue sweater. The man had been shot twice—once into the right side of his chest and once in the back of his head. No weapon was found in or near the car. The officers found no wallet or car keys, but robbery didn't appear to be the motive because the dead man was still wearing a good watch, and the culprit had abandoned the car when he could have dumped the body and driven away.

The dead man had been rolled from the driver's seat towards the center console, and his head and upper body had fallen backward into the back seat. His legs were lying in between the front seats. Altogether it appeared that someone had shot the man while he was sitting in the driver's seat, then pushed him out of the seat and onto the floorboard so that the culprit could drive the car to the place where it was found. The position of the driver's seat indicated it had been moved forward for a driver who was considerably shorter than the dead man. That the dead man was wearing athletic shorts, a T-shirt, and a light sweater indicated he had dressed for much warmer weather than the current weather in Oklahoma City, which was below freezing. A severe cold front with snowfall had moved in two days earlier. The ground around his car was covered with snow free of footprints.

The registration and Texas plates indicated the car belonged to Norman Alan Rehrig, a resident of Dallas. An OCPD officer called the Dallas Police Department to inquire if the man was missing. Indeed, a missing person report had been filed with the DPD just two days earlier. Because no photo ID was found with the dead man, the police couldn't be certain he was Norman Alan Rehrig. And so instead of performing an in-person notification of next of kin, a DPD officer called Norman Alan Rehrig's house to inquire about his whereabouts. Sandra answered the phone, and after introducing himself, the DPD officer asked: "Was your husband wearing shorts and a Navy-blue sweater when you last saw him?"

"Yes," she replied. "Has something bad happened to him?"

"I'm afraid so, ma'am," the officer replied. At this point Sandra apparently became so distraught that she said she couldn't bear to hear anymore.

"Please call his friend Ron Barnes," she said, and gave the officer Ron's number. Though puzzled by her response, the officer thought that maybe she didn't want to hear bad news from a stranger. The officer called Ron Barnes and explained that Alan had been found dead and that his widow had requested that he be notified first. Ron then called Sandra to break the news. She seemed upset, but Ron found it strange that she didn't ask a single question about what had happened or where Alan had been found. Later that same night, Phil Askew was awakened by a call from Sandra.

"Something has happened to Alan," she said. "You will soon be hearing from the police." Phil got up to get dressed, and soon a Dallas police officer called and notified him that Alan had been found dead.

That night Gloria struggled to fall asleep and finally nodded off sometime after midnight. She was awakened the next morning by someone entering the house and she sat up in bed.

"Al, is that you?" she yelled. Her sister Winifred entered her bedroom.

"Oh, Glo, they've found Al," she said.

"Is he alive?" Gloria asked.

"No. He's been shot. He's dead."

Ron Barnes entered the bedroom.

"I'm so sorry, Glo," he said, his voice quivering. He then told her that Alan had been found dead in his Bronco in Oklahoma City, and that he'd been murdered. *Murdered.* The word struck her with shock and despair. In an instant the life she'd always known was shattered, and she knew she would never be the same again.

Phil Askew did his best to comfort Sandra. She asked him to give her a ride to the home of David and Debbie Thomkins, where her daughter Kathryn was staying. Both David and Debbie were there when they arrived, as was Kathryn. Sandra told them that Alan had been found dead. She then swooned towards David and sobbed, "No one will ever love me again!" Kathryn was devastated and bewildered.

"No! No! Not again!" she exclaimed, breaking into tears.

CHAPTER 20
ALAN'S FUNERAL

All day long, Gloria received condolence calls from friends and associates. A conspicuous exception was Sandra. Gloria finally called her. She seemed strangely curt, as though she had little time to talk.

"We need to schedule his funeral," Gloria said. "We'd like to have a memorial gathering in his honor on Friday evening and his burial on Saturday. Can you make it?" Sandra said she could.

She and her children arrived at the Will Rogers (Oklahoma City) airport on Friday the 13th of December. Ron Barnes picked them up, and per the request of the Oklahoma City police, he took her to the station for an interview with detectives Steve Pacheco and David Shupe. They found her demeanor oddly flirtatious.

"Do you think I'm pretty?" she asked coquettishly. They also thought it conspicuous that during her entire time in the station, she never took off her elegant ladies' gloves. She told the OKC detectives roughly the same story she'd told Bill Dear—that is, she feared Alan had gotten into drugs and gambling and had been killed by a criminal to whom he owed money. She claimed she'd been afraid of him, especially after an incident that summer. While riding tandem on a jet ski, she fell off in the middle of the lake. Instead of circling around to get her, Alan motored away, leaving her to swim a long way back to shore. She was, she said, lucky to have made it back to the landing alive.

Despite being afraid of him, she went alone to meet him at the storage warehouse in an isolated industrial area on the evening of December 7. Alan, she claimed, failed to show for their appointment. She then called Phil Askew to ask where he was, and then returned home. That evening she went out with a doctor from Austin named Alan Frank and his wife Barbara. They watched the late showing of the film *White Nights*. She returned home around 1:00 a.m., went to sleep, and then got up for Sunday service at the Highland Park Presbyterian Church. When asked if she knew why Alan's vehicle and body were found in Oklahoma City, she said she believed his old friend Mark Deason in Edmond was his cocaine dealer. Maybe, on that Saturday evening, Alan felt the need for a fix and drove to Oklahoma City.

During her interview, Phil Askew arrived at the station to give his own. After waiting for a while in the hallway, he peeked into an open office, where he saw an officer watching a video monitor of Sandra talking with the detectives. Phil introduced himself and the officer asked, "Do you think she's capable of murdering her husband?"

"She's weird, but I think it's a big leap from weird to murderer," Phil said.

"She just told the detectives she suspects that her husband was gay and having an affair with you."

"What!" Phil exclaimed. "Did she really say that?"

"Yes, she did."

"Well, I can assure you it isn't true."

"Don't worry, they don't believe her."

The detectives had begun the interview thinking they would have plenty of time to go over everything with Sandra, but then, abruptly, she said she needed to tend to her husband's funeral preparations.

"Please feel free to visit me in Dallas if you'd like to talk some more," she said in a friendly tone. The detectives thanked her for the invitation, but they also asked her to pass by the station again before her return to Dallas after the funeral. She said she would do so and left the station.

From there, Ron Barnes took Sandra and her kids to the funeral home. To clothe her dead husband, she'd brought one of his old suits instead of the new suit she'd bought for him during their marriage. She then chose the cheapest casket on display, remarking, "Alan would want it that way. He wouldn't want to burden his family." When it was time to settle the bill for opening the grave and the casket, she said she'd forgotten her wallet and checkbook. This was so awkward that Ron Barnes interjected that he would cover the cost.

That night, Gloria went to the funeral home to view Alan's body. She held his face and hands and stroked his hair. He was so cold and stiff, but it was still so hard for her to believe that he was dead. How terrible that she would never be able to embrace him again and that he'd never have his own children to hug. Suddenly she was overcome with guilt that she'd encouraged him to take the job in Dallas. It was a bitter irony that, while Alan had often chosen not to take her advice, he had on that occasion.

The funeral was held the next morning at the First Christian Church, where Alan had attended service since he was a boy. Sandra didn't want to ride with Alan's family in the limousine to the chapel, but in a separate car. She and her kids were therefore the last of his family to enter and take their seats at the front. Gloria greeted them as they walked in. Sandra was wearing a full-length mink. Britt was wearing the beautiful overcoat Sandra had given to Alan on his thirtieth birthday.

Kyle Maxwell, the Rehrig family minister, conducted the service and eulogy. He'd known and loved Alan for most of the murdered man's short life. At one point he became so emotional that he struck the pulpit with his fist, and the jolt caused his glasses to fall from his face to the ground.

"Make no mistake," he said. "One person pulled the trigger, but a terrible thing like this can only happen as a result of good people doing nothing."

With the limousine parked in front of the church and everyone watching, Sandra couldn't avoid riding with Alan's family to the cemetery. It was bitterly cold, and a tent had been erected over the gravesite as a shelter from the icy wind. At the conclusion of the burial service, Sandra and her children hurried to the limousine, as she apparently wished to avoid further contact with Alan's friends and family. Gloria and Alan's brother

Phillip remained in the tent to thank everyone for coming, and then went to the limousine for the ride back to the church. As they took their seats, Sandra remarked that one of Alan's old friends wasn't properly dressed.

"I'm sorry he doesn't meet your standards," said Phillip Rehrig. "He's a man of limited means." *Who is this woman who dodges the bill for her husband's funeral and then criticizes one of his old friends for being poorly dressed?* Phillip wondered as they left the cemetery. *Who in the hell does she think she is?* Arriving back at the church, she and her kids quickly ate a lunch prepared by some of the congregants and then caught a ride to the airport. Breaking her agreement with the Oklahoma City Police detectives, she didn't pass by the station for a second talk. On the plane back to Dallas, some of Alan's friends who'd attended the funeral saw her flirting with a passenger.

CHAPTER 21

THE ANONYMOUS CALLER

That evening, after the funeral, Gloria sat in her kitchen, talking to her sister Winie, trying to make sense of the disaster that had befallen her son and herself. The phone rang and she answered.

"May I speak with Gloria Rehrig?" a woman's voice said.

"This is she," Gloria replied. The woman said she was calling from Dallas, where she had known Sandra for a long time.

"Many years ago, we were friends, but then I began to see her for what she really is, and I separated from her. When I heard your son had been murdered, I felt compelled to call you."

The woman explained that when she and her friends had learned of Sandra's marriage to Alan, they had been very concerned about him. They figured that because he was new to Dallas, he didn't know about Sandra's past.

"What past?" Gloria asked the woman and gestured to Winie for a pen and something to write on. With Gloria taking notes, the anonymous woman proceeded to tell a story so strange and shocking as to be scarcely believable. She began with Sandra's first husband—a dentist named David Stegall. Somehow, the woman knew that Sandra had told Alan that David had died of a brain aneurism.

"In fact, he was shot in the head," she said. "The authorities ruled it a suicide, but I'm afraid they got it wrong." The woman then proceeded to relate a litany of outrageous acts for which Sandra had fallen under suspicion. Her daughter Kathryn had once been rushed to an emergency room after ingesting an overdose of prescription medication. Sandra claimed the child had fished the pills out of the trash, but Kathryn's pediatrician found the incident suspicious and wondered if Sandra had wanted to get rid of her daughter or if it was a case of Munchausen by Proxy. The anonymous caller knew from reliable sources that Sandra had seduced and blackmailed married men. One of her tricks was to persuade them to co-sign a bank loan, and then threaten to expose the affair if they didn't pay it off.

After she married her second husband, Bobby Bridewell in 1978, she seemed satisfied, but then he was diagnosed with terminal cancer, and she treated him callously during the final months of his life. At the same time, she became friends with his doctor, and a couple of months after Bobby died, the doctor's wife was shot in the head. Her last known contact was with Sandra, but the Dallas authorities ruled her death a suicide. Sandra was, the woman said, extremely manipulative and had an astonishing ability to get away with things.

By the end of the conversation, Gloria figured her son had never known his wife. Sandra had shown him a mask that had concealed the reality of her character and motives. He had apparently glimpsed cracks in her mask, but he never saw the real Sandra. The closest he came was perhaps during the last second of his life.

CHAPTER 22
ATTORNEY'S ADVICE

The anonymous caller proved to be the first of many who'd known Sandra in Dallas. Each had her own story to tell, but the pattern was the same. Initially they'd found her charming, but with experience, they realized her charm concealed a ruthless and dishonest character. Many of the callers insisted on maintaining their anonymity because they were afraid of her.

On the Monday following Alan's funeral, Gloria received a call from Phil Askew, who reported yet another strange occurrence. Sandra had just turned up at his company offices and said she needed to look in Alan's desk. Dean Castelhano watched as she walked into Alan's office, went behind the desk, and opened the drawers.

"Here they are!" she exclaimed and held up a couple of credit cards. "I thought he'd left them in his desk."

Phil Askew, who'd briefly stepped out, entered the office just in time to see this performance. He looked at Dean and the two men exchanged an amazed look. Sandra then put the credit cards in her purse and left. Only later did Phil and Dean realize how improbable it was that Alan had left his credit cards in his desk. Then they remembered that Alan's billfold was missing from his body, which meant that the culprit had taken his credit cards. Had Sandra just created a pretense for how they came into her possession so that she could use them?

Detectives Pacheco, Shupe, and Mitchell arrived in Dallas to begin their investigation. They too had spoken with the anonymous woman and were aware of the two previous shooting deaths that had been ruled suicides. Per standard procedure and courtesy, they visited the Dallas police department homicide unit, where they met the detective who'd investigated the death of the cancer doctor's wife. Detective Coughlin assured them that—according to the medical examiner—the woman had committed suicide. The three detectives then proceeded to Sandra's house in University Park. They thought they were accepting her invitation to visit her in Dallas to continue the conversation they'd started in Oklahoma City. She opened the door with a big surprise.

"I'm sorry," she said, "my attorney has advised me not to speak with you." Detective Pacheco explained that they'd come to Dallas to find her husband's murderer and that they were hoping she would be able to assist them. Implied in his statement was the question: why don't you *want* to help us find your husband's murderer?

"Sorry," she said. "I have to follow my attorney's advice." She also refused to provide fingerprint and hair samples, even though these could enable the detectives to exclude her as the donor of prints and hair fibers found in Alan's Bronco. That she didn't want to provide her fingerprints may have accounted for why she wore gloves during her entire interview at OCPD headquarters just before the funeral.

Sandra's lawyer was Vincent Perini, one of the most formidable criminal defense attorneys in Dallas. Following their attempt to interview Sandra in Dallas, the OKC detectives received a letter from Perini, demanding they cease their attempts to talk to Sandra and her children. And so, with no help from the Dallas police or the victim's wife, Pacheco and Mitchell were left to their own devices in Dallas—a city with which they were completely unfamiliar. For a workspace, Phil Askew offered them a conference room in his company offices. Because Sandra was the beneficiary of Alan's life insurance policy and because she refused to cooperate with the police investigation, she became the prime suspect. The detectives' initial task was to reconstruct her movements just before and after Alan's disappearance. She had already stated that Alan had *not* made it to their appointment at the storage warehouse—that she had not seen him at all on the evening of his disappearance. Thus, the objective of the OKC detectives was to find evidence that: 1). Alan had made it to the storage facility. 2). Sandra had been with Alan or in his car between his disappearance and the discovery of his body. 3). Sandra had travelled to Oklahoma City and back to Dallas between Alan's disappearance and the discovery of his car and body.

Based on Sandra's interview in OKC, the detectives assembled the following timeline:

5:15 p.m.: Sandra arrives at warehouse.

5:15 to 6:10 p.m.: Sandra waits for Alan at warehouse.

6:15 p.m.: Sandra finds payphone on Northwest Highway, calls Askew residence.

6:30 p.m.: Sandra goes shopping for Christmas items at Neiman-Marcus.

7:00 p.m.: Sandra arrives back at her house.

8:45 to 9:00 p.m.: Sandra drives to the Dallas home of Barbara Frank's mother, where Barbara and her husband, Allen, are staying during their weekend trip to Dallas (they reside in Austin).

9:00 p.m. to 1:30 a.m.: Sandra goes out with Allen and Barbara Frank to a movie and late dinner.

1:30 a.m.: Sandra drops off the Franks, then drives home to her place about 15 minutes away, arriving home around **1:45 a.m.**

Barbara Frank told Detective Pacheco in an interview on January 7, 1986:

> I don't know what's so complicated about this. We were with SANDRA from approximately, oh, I don't know to tell you the truth. I can't even remember. We talked to her on the phone around 6:00 p.m. to verify what movie we were going to see and what time the movie was, and all that kind of stuff. We talked about 20 minutes or more, then we hung up. She got to my

mother's house, maybe at, I don't know, 8:30 to 9:00 p.m., and we were out until 1:30 a.m. or later. We went to a movie, ate and then we came home, sat in the car, and talked and visited and that was it.

Mrs. Frank was very defensive of Sandra, whom she described as "the most fine, kind, good person, good human being I have ever met in my life." Her husband, Dr. Frank, was uncooperative about answering the detectives' questions about their time with Sandra that evening. No murder weapon was found in Alan's car, and Sandra claimed to have gotten into the car on Friday, December 6, to retrieve a Christmas gift for Emily that Alan had left in a bag on the back seat. And so, the detectives focused on finding witness testimony linking Sandra to the murder.

CHAPTER 23

A PARALLEL INVESTIGATION

While Sandra refused to cooperate with the OCPD detectives, she seemed eager to assist Bill Dear in finding Alan's killer. She emphasized that Alan was into gambling and drugs. She also feared he was gay. The thought had initially occurred to her because of his strong preference for sexual intercourse from behind. Her therapist, Harvey Davisson got the same impression of Alan during their joint therapy sessions.

"Harvey also thought he was a homosexual and he warned me to watch out for Alan making a play for my seventeen-year-old son Britt," she said.

On December 18, Bill Dear visited Phil Askew's office, and arrived as Phil was having a conversation with OCPD detectives Pacheco and Shupe. As Dear walked into the conference room, he struck Phil as aggressive. He told the detectives that Alan had gone bad and was hanging around with bad people.

"My client was afraid of him," Dear said. Pacheco asked Dear if his client knew the identity of the bad guys with whom Alan was consorting. Dear replied that he'd just started his investigation. Phil remarked that Dear would be hard-pressed to find a single person who shared Sandra's suspicions of Alan, who had many colleagues and friends who could vouch for his character and clean living. He had never missed a day of work, and all his colleagues loved him.

A few weeks later, Dear realized that Phil was probably telling the truth. By all accounts except Sandra's, Alan Rehrig had led the routine life of a finance professional, went to the occasional Mavericks game, and played golf on the weekends. His recent stress about money could be explained by the fact that he was being hounded by American Express collections to pay $20,000 of charges his wife had run up on his card without his knowledge at the time of transactions. He spent the last day of his life at his boss's house, where he'd been living for a month, playing with his boss's son and other kids on the boy's birthday. He was last seen alive on a Saturday evening, and the toxicology section of his autopsy report showed no alcohol or any other substances in his blood. In response to his wife's assertion that he was gay, the pathologist had swabbed his body for spermatozoa and found none.

No, it appeared there was nothing to Sandra's claim that Alan had been hanging around with criminals. More likely she was trying to fabricate an alternative hypothesis to explain his murder. Her histrionic affect—her lamentations of how terrible it was, and how she was afraid for herself and her children—also seemed false. He found it especially jarring when he visited the storage warehouse with Sandra. As he then discovered, it was Alan's storage unit. The young man had rented it shortly after his arrival in Dallas in 1984 and started sharing it with Sandra after they married. She easily accessed it and didn't need to refer to a note when she opened the combination lock. Dear asked her about it, and she told him that, after she and Alan became estranged, she put her own lock on the door to prevent him from accessing it without her permission and presence. This was especially strange, given there was little if anything of value that belonged to Sandra in the unit. Putting her lock on the door was simply to impede Alan from gaining access to *his* personal property without going through her.

As Christmas drew near, Sandra sensed she was losing credibility in Dear's eyes.

"You've got to believe me, Bill," she said in that pitiful, pleading way of hers that he suspected was part of her "little girl lost" persona that provoked chivalrous instincts in so many men. *I'm just a helpless woman in desperate need of a big strong man like you*, was her persistent message. Her beauty and overt sexuality appealed to men's lust; her professed need for their strength and competence appealed to their egos.

To be sure, she was a desirable woman, and he was tempted when she came onto him. In an interview decades later, he said he'd contemplated yielding to temptation "for professional reasons, to ascertain what it was precisely that gave her such power over men." After an internal struggle, his instinct for self-preservation prevailed.

"I think it would help your credibility if you took a polygraph test," Bill suggested just before Christmas. She agreed, and on December 23, he took her to a polygraph examiner's office. Per Sandra's request for moral support, Margaret accompanied them and waited in the car while Sandra and Bill Dear went into the building. A while later they returned to the car and Sandra was crying.

"I can't believe I failed!" she sobbed.

"You're not supposed to talk about the results!" Bill exclaimed. He hastened to add that the polygraph isn't always accurate, and he suggested that Sandra get some rest and go for a second exam. The failed lie detector test made Margaret wonder about her charming neighbor and friend. She didn't accompany Sandra to the second exam on December 30, again expressing a deceptive response to two questions: 1). Do you know anything about Alan's death? 2). Did you kill him?

While Vincent Perini blocked the cops for Sandra in Dallas, Mack Martin did the same in Oklahoma City. Martin was a junior associate in the law firm of D.C. Thomas, who was widely regarded as the best defense attorney in Oklahoma City. After Sandra retained Vincent Perini, he contacted Mr. Thomas to make sure she would have representation in the event she was arrested and extradited to Oklahoma. Martin informed the OKC police that Sandra was Alan Rehrig's heir, and therefore had a claim to the murdered man's vehicle. Thus, the police needed to perform their search, bag whatever evidence they found, and return the vehicle to Mrs. Rehrig. The police complied with Mr. Martin's request and released the car to Sandra's representative, William Dear P.I., who drove it back to Dallas wearing a respirator against the smell of decomposition. As the Bronco was of no use to her, she sold it to Dear, who said he wanted to use it for his training seminars. She pocketed the money and submitted Alan's outstanding car loan to his estate.

The more Dear observed Sandra's conduct and investigated her past, the more he suspected she had murdered Alan Rehrig.

"Don't be surprised if it turns out that she was involved," he told Harvey Davisson, her therapist. Davisson was a strong advocate for Sandra, who was especially concerned about Britt speaking with school counselors or police officers. On January 15, 1986, he wrote a letter to Highland Park High School attendance coordinator, Cecil Homes, in which he stated, "Britt is being treated for a severe adjustment reaction to recent trauma. Please excuse all of Britt's absences from November 26, 1985 through the present date."

Dear believed that Vincent Perini was also going the extra mile for Sandra.

"Be careful of your client," he advised the attorney.

Gloria was unaware of this apparent rift in Sandra's team. She marveled that Alan's widow was counseled by a flamboyant private investigator, two high profile criminal defense attorneys, and a prominent psychotherapist to deal with the troubles that beset her after Alan was murdered. Gloria wondered why, instead of carrying on with these expensive professionals, Sandra didn't just cooperate with the police. Later, when her abysmal financial condition was revealed, Gloria wondered how she'd paid for their services.

CHAPTER 24
REVELATIONS

In January of 1986, two reporters for the *Dallas Times Herald*—Linda Fibich and Hugh Aynesworth—contacted Gloria for an interview about her murdered son and she answered their questions. Their story appeared on the front page of the Saturday, January 18, 1986, edition under the headline "Banker's mysterious slaying stuns two cities." The report was lengthy and thorough; the reporters had done much research. On the report's second page, Gloria read the statement that Sandra was "40" at the time she met Alan. *Was she really forty, and not thirty-six, as she'd told Alan?* Gloria called Linda Fibich to inquire about this, and she said they had determined Sandra's true age from reliable records.

Later that day, Gloria received a call from Sandra.

"I just saw the newspaper article," she said. "I can't believe that you, my own mother, talked to those reporters."

"What do you mean? Why wouldn't I talk to them?" Gloria replied.

"Because this is so hurtful to me and my kids. They didn't know their father committed suicide. Imagine how they feel to learn it from a newspaper?"

Gloria didn't know what to say. It was no secret among Sandra's old friends that her first husband had shot himself. How could she have kept this from her kids for a decade? This also didn't explain why she'd lied to

Alan about it. She could have told him in confidence.

"Please don't try to make me feel guilty for talking to the reporters," Gloria said. "You haven't cooperated with the detectives who are trying to solve Alan's murder. Instead, you have hired criminal defense lawyers and remained silent. A person with nothing to hide wouldn't do that." Sandra hung up.

Shortly after this conversation, Gloria received a letter from Alan's friend, Bill Dodd, in Arizona. Bill told her that at the end of 1984, Alan had written him a letter about his new life with Sandra and the coming of their first child. Enclosed was Alan's letter. As Gloria read it, she could hear her son's voice:

12-27-84

Merry Christmas! H.N.Y.!

Hi Y'all, I hope you all had a wonderful time. Did any family come out?

We had Christmas in Edmond with everybody there. Lots of laughs and good times. It was special having Sandra and her (my) kids with us (Rehrigs & Smiths) for our 1st Christmas. Everyone loves her & the kids (Britt-16, Kathryn-14, & Emily-11). ...

You know, with some of my dating experience since high school, it's been hard to realize or believe that someone truly loves me; man-woman, wife-husband, no matter what. But she does, and so do the kids. And I love her & the kids. We are thrilled about having a baby (I hope it's a boy—all of my family has only girls). Just wish we could share this with everybody else. We will announce it next month I guess. ...I'm ready and willing to be a poppa, and can't wait. Sandra is also ready. But having to keep it quiet and then make plans for a 'quick' wedding had me confused. Now that we have gotten married & been sharing our life together, we know we did the right thing. We love each other (and want more babies!). It's hard for me to explain the confusion and doubt I felt. I think now it was a combination,

89

first of all, of fear (can I do it? Am I man enough to accept the responsibility of husband and father of 3 kids, whew!). Past experiences, guilt that mom is now alone, and ego and selfishness—difficulty in putting someone else first, their feelings and needs.

Having known each other only 6 months, we are still getting to know each other. It's been fun. We had a good time in New Orleans—our hotel was super and the seafood terrific. San Francisco was beautiful—the stewardess on the plane gave us a bottle of champagne just because we looked like we were 'in love.' Then we showed her the wedding pictures!

There have been adjustments to make, but they have been healthy ones. About the only thing I don't like about her is that she can't run. I need somebody that will run w/me on the beach. She is pretty good at running from store to store shopping though! Are the kids athletes? Kathryn a little bit, Emily more of a ballerina, and Britt has bad knees. So you see I'm really pulling for a boy, twins would be perfect.

We had a good time at the wedding and took lots of pictures. My brother was best man. ... It was scheduled to start at 11:00, Sandra was late (punctuality is not one of her traits) but it all worked out fine. Work is going well. Phillip was happy with the year—now he wants to have a better one in 85. He is beginning to give me more responsibility, so I am feeling more like a contributor around the office.

Here's to a great and fulfilling 1985, with happy times and healthy baby boys and girls, and a chance to work out enough so I will be able to dunk it again! I'll be talking to you three soon. I love you.

Al

Now Gloria understood that he hadn't told her about Sandra's pregnancy so that she wouldn't think his wedding had been forced by it. But what happened to the pregnancy? She   called Phil Askew, and he told her about the evening in January of 1985 when he and Alan had gone to a Mavericks game. Afterwards, when they were at Phil's house, Sandra called from a 7-Eleven payphone and said she'd miscarried twin boys who had Alan's red hair. Gloria was thunderstruck. Babies conceived in the fall of 1984 and miscarried in January of 1985, *and they already had red hair on their heads.* How could Alan have been so naïve? Had she fabricated the pregnancy to trap him into marrying her?

Spring's arrival in Edmond was a vivid reminder of time's passage. Three months had elapsed since Alan's burial on that icy cold day in December, and still the Oklahoma City police said nothing about arresting Sandra. A feeling of dread grew in Gloria. She understood that murder investigations are complex, and that the standard of proof is high. But what more could the Oklahoma City police do that couldn't be done in the first three months? Two more months passed, and still no word from the detectives about making an arrest. On Thursday, May 29, she got a call at her office from Protective Life Insurance, from whom Alan had purchased his policy. Earlier she'd written a letter to the company, explaining that her son had been murdered and that the policy's beneficiary had not been cleared of suspicion. The representative explained that, because the beneficiary had not been arrested, the company would soon have to pay her the death benefit. Because Alan Rehrig's estate was indebted, a portion could be paid to the estate. However, because Sandra had been appointed administratrix, she would have some discretion in how the funds were used.

"What is your deadline for making the payment?" Gloria asked.

"Tomorrow," the representative replied.

Gloria hung up and called Alan's lawyer friend, Ron Barnes, and explained the situation. He quickly found a probate attorney in Dallas named David Wise. An hour later, Gloria, her son Phillip, her sister Winifred, and Winifred's husband Robert Smith, were on the road to Dallas, where they met Mr. Wise. He filed an application to the court for Sandra to provide a full accounting of the Estate's assets and liabilities and to remove her as administratrix. He also hand delivered a letter to the insurance company's Dallas office on that day, giving notice that Alan Rehrig had been murdered and that the beneficiary of his life insurance policy was the prime suspect.

Gloria and her family remained in Dallas for ten days to search for additional witnesses and clues. They printed flyers illustrated with a photograph of Alan (standing with Sandra and Gloria), a photograph of his Ford Bronco, and the text:

DID YOU SEE THIS MAN AND/OR THIS BRONCO ON SATURDAY, DECEMBER 7 OR SUNDAY, DECEMBER 8, 1985? A $10,000 reward was offered for information leading to an arrest and conviction. Informants were directed to call the Oklahoma City Police Dept. homicide unit.

They posted the flyers in the Highland Park Village and Snider Plaza shopping centers, in all the gas stations between Phil Askew's house and the warehouse in Garland, and in all the gas stations between Dallas and Oklahoma City and back on Interstate 35. Later they went to Sandra's house. She wasn't home, so they parked across the street and waited in their car for her return. A while later, a black pickup truck stopped in front of her house and, to their surprise, Sandra got out of it. As the truck pulled away, Philipp Rehrig got out of their car. Sandra saw him and dashed to her front door, but Phillip stopped her from shutting it, and Gloria hurried to the door behind him.

"I can't believe you put those flyers all over the Village!" she said furiously.

"We're trying to find Alan's murderer. Why don't you help us?" Gloria asked.

"Alan and I were separated, and I don't know anything else."

On this same trip to Dallas in June of 1986, Gloria met Frank and Percye Monroe, the parents of Betsy Bagwell. They had been confounded by the cursory investigation of their daughter's death. They didn't believe that Betsy had been suicidal, but the police and medical examiner had insisted that her death was a "textbook" suicide. They'd been further confounded by a rumor that Betsy could have left a suicide note that John Bagwell destroyed because he considered suicide shameful and a poor reflection on his marriage. Their confusion was dispelled when they heard that Alan had been murdered. At that point, they had no doubt that Sandra had murdered him and Betsy. Frank was the former superintendent of schools, and when he heard that Oklahoma City police detectives were pursuing their investigation in Dallas, he contacted the Highland Park High School principal and requested that the detectives be granted full access to the Bridewell children during school hours. Sandra caught wind of this and withdrew them in the middle of the spring semester and moved them to the San Francisco Bay Area.

Gloria also spoke with Dallas women who'd known Sandra in the seventies and early eighties. The best informed was the anonymous caller after Alan's funeral. Gloria met her in her beautiful home. Though forthcoming with information, the lady insisted that her identity remain a secret. Years earlier she had found Sandra delightful, but over time, with experience, she became afraid of her. Fear turned to terror after the death of the doctor's wife, Betsy Bagwell. The lady had no doubt that Sandra had murdered Betsy but had somehow gotten away with it. And if she could get away with murdering Betsy, she could get away with anything.

The lady felt terrible for Gloria, and the two women had a long talk. At one point, Gloria mentioned her suspicion that Sandra had intentionally gotten pregnant to trap Alan into marrying her.

"I can imagine her pretending to be pregnant," the lady said. "But a real pregnancy was out of the question, because Sandra got a hysterectomy in 1977." The lady was certain of this because she'd accompanied Sandra to the hospital for the procedure. This was shocking news, and Gloria would often think about it in the years ahead. Her son had gone to his grave without knowing that his marriage was a lie and a trap.

CHAPTER 25

DEATH OF AN
INSURANCE SALESMAN

On Thursday, June 19, 1986, a big, front-page story appeared in the *Park Cities News* under the headline: **Victim's relatives search for witness, clues to help police solve murder case**. The report was illustrated with a photograph of Alan Rehrig standing with his mother Gloria and his wife Sandra. The article didn't state that Sandra was the prime suspect, but the circumstances reported indicated that she was. The article also mentioned the peculiar fact that "Sandra Rehrig is communicating with the police through her lawyer, Vincent Perini of Dallas."

Though Sandra was in California, preparing for her move to the Bay Area, she was aware of the story because its reporter had interviewed her. The *Park Cities News* was a small, community newspaper, but it was thoroughly distributed in the Park Cities. All the ladies who'd become acquainted with Sandra since she'd moved to Highland Park in 1978 were soon talking about it.

A conspicuous feature of the report was the prominent role it attributed to Alan's aunt and uncle, Winifred and Bob Smith, who "were in town last week to open the Alan Rehrig Investigation and Reward Fund at the Sherry

Lane National Bank. A Reward of $10,000 for information leading to the arrest and conviction of the killer will be paid out of the account."

"Nothing like this has ever happened to anyone in our family before," Bob Smith said. "We are not wealthy people; we have nothing to hide. But we will not stop until justice has been served."

Assisting their effort was Bob's son, Robert Dale Smith II, who also lived in Dallas with his wife Glady and their three children. Even before Alan's death, Robert had gotten a bad vibe about Sandra. To him, she seemed false, and he sensed that she was using Alan. Maybe she thought he had the potential to become a big earner. Maybe she just wanted him to pay household bills. To be sure, Robert was biased because after a few interactions with her, he noticed signs in her demeanor that she looked down her nose at him and his family, apparently considering them to be Oklahoma rubes. But this gave added urgency to the question: why did a woman of her upper class marry Alan?

After Alan's funeral, Robert became mortally afraid of Sandra. He didn't articulate why he regarded her with such dread, but his family and friends sensed it. Normally a lighthearted and jocular man, he seemed anxious and oppressed. Sandra wasn't the beneficiary of his life insurance policy, so she didn't have an obvious motive for harming him or his children. Still, Robert wasn't taking any chances. His job as an insurance salesman gave him a more flexible schedule than that of his wife, who worked at a mortgage company. Every afternoon when his children got out of school, he picked them up, took them home, and instructed them to do their homework. Upon leaving to return to work for a few hours, he locked the doors and told them not to open them for anyone apart from their parents.

One day, after Alan's funeral, Robert went to Pockets Menswear on Greenville Avenue to buy some shirts. While he was talking with the salesman, he saw, through the front window, Sandra drive into a parking space in front of the shop.

"Oh, good Lord, I'm scared to death of that woman," he said to the salesman, and hurried out the store's rear entrance. Later that day his friends Bill and Nina Raef popped by to say hello, and he told them he feared he was being followed by someone—perhaps someone in league with Sandra. He was visibly shaken as he related the occurrence.

Robert had a hunch that Sandra might have taken out additional life insurance policies on Alan, so he made a trip to Austin to visit the Texas Department of Insurance to try to trace other policies she may have purchased. He couldn't find any others, but a department spokesman told him that, in theory Sandra could have purchased a thousand-dollar policy in all fifty states and it would never show up in their records.

One day Robert accompanied Alan's old friends Ron Barnes and Bill Gustafson to collect Alan's things from Sandra's duplex. Sandra had coordinated the pickup with Ron, but Robert was still concerned that it was a dangerous situation in which she or a male accomplice might do something treacherous. And so, while Ron and Bill went inside to fetch Alan's things, Robert stood in the driveway with a .44 magnum. He held it close to his legs so that passing cars and pedestrians wouldn't see it, but he had every intention of using it if the need arose.

On July 3, 1986, the attorney David Wise filed an application at the Dallas County Probate court to have Sandra removed as Administratrix of Alan's estate and to be replaced by Robert Dale Smith II. Robert accepted the responsibility, but it heightened his fear of Sandra. His children didn't understand what their father had been appointed to do, but his oldest child—a twelve-year-old boy named Robert Matthew (who went by the name Matthew)—sensed it made his father nervous. One day Matthew fetched his father's briefcase from his car, parked in the driveway. Matthew was surprised by its unusual weight.

"What are you carrying in this thing?" he asked.

"A .44 magnum in case you know who comes around," Robert replied.

Around this time, Robert and his friend Bill Raef went to a gun range to sight a new deer rifle that Robert had recently bought for Matthew. On Sunday evening, July 13, he sat at the kitchen table, cleaning the weapon as his daughters, Courtney and Heather and their friend Robin Raef entered the kitchen. They grabbed a snack and lingered for a while chatting.

"Would you kids mind going somewhere else?" Robert said. Robin glanced at him and saw he'd disassembled the rifle and was cleaning the bore. This didn't strike her as strange, as she'd often seen her father do the same. What was notable was Robert's annoyed expression. Though just a ten-year-old child, she too had noticed that Mr. Smith had recently seemed irritable. Robin was Heather's best friend and frequently spent the night at the Smith house.

The next morning, Monday, July 14, Glady Smith went to work while Robert stayed home to look after the kids and work in his home office. At 11:30 am, he visited Glady at her office and returned home at 12:30. Courtney, Heather, and Robin were again hanging around the house, and around 2:00 p.m., he again asked them if they would go somewhere else to play. Robin called her mother, Nina, to request that she pick them up to go swimming in their neighbor's pool. Nina agreed and soon arrived. Popping into the house, she briefly spoke with Robert, who struck her as being in a serious mood, as though he were trying to concentrate on something. She collected the girls and took them to the pool.

After they left, only Matthew remained in the house, playing video games in his room. Robert asked him to return a bicycle that belonged to one of his sister's friends, who lived two miles away. Matthew did as he was told, and about an hour later, returned home to discover he was locked out. The hide-a-key in a flowerpot on the front porch was missing. Neither his father nor his father's car was anywhere to be seen. Matthew went to a neighbor's house and called Glady at her office. She told him to play in the neighborhood until she came home.

At 5:10 p.m., Glady returned from work to discover that her electronic garage door opener didn't function. She parked in the driveway, went inside, changed clothes, and then went for a walk in the neighborhood. Matthew came home, and at around 6:45 p.m., Nina Raef brought Courtney and Heather home from the pool. Glady instructed the kids to stay at home while she went for a glass of wine at the Raef house between about 7:00 – 8:00.

At 8:05, Glady returned home and painted the exterior of the garage door. Robert still hadn't come home, but it wasn't till about 10:00 that Glady became concerned. She called his boss, with whom she believed

Robert had an evening meeting. The boss's wife said their meeting had been postponed. Only then did Glady decide to investigate the closed garage. Because the back door was locked, she used a flashlight to look through one of the garage door's windows and saw Robert's car parked inside. She then called the Raef house and asked Bill to come over to assist. He broke into the back door. With Glady and the three children following him, he entered the garage and immediately saw—through the station wagon's windshield—Robert in the driver's seat, slumped to the left with the top of his head pressed against the driver's side window. With this one glance, Bill knew that his best friend was dead, so he did an about-face and herded Glady and the three kids back out of the garage. Realizing that something was terribly wrong with their father, they screamed and tried to rush to the car.

"No, you shouldn't see it!" Bill yelled above their screams and pushed them back into the house. The former college football player was big and strong, and Glady was petite, so he held her by the waist with one arm while he dialed 911 with the other. After he reported the incident, he called their pastor at the nearby Presbyterian Church, who rushed over to be with the family while officers from the Dallas Police Department and Medical Examiner's Office inspected Robert.

They found him sitting in the driver's seat, wearing his seatbelt. Lying across the car's bench seat, its muzzle still pressed against Robert's right side, was the Ruger .243 hunting rifle he'd recently gifted to his son Matthew. One shot had been fired into the right side of Robert's torso. A suicide note was found on the windshield that had apparently been authored by the dead man. Based on this note and a sample of his handwriting provided by his widow, the Dallas County Medical Examiner ruled his death a suicide.

CHAPTER 26

THE PROBATE ATTORNEY

Damn, there he is again, thought David Wise as the black Ford pickup truck seemed to come out of nowhere and get on his tail. Every morning the probate attorney rose early and drove from his house on Frankford Road to the Cooper Clinic to exercise, and every morning he was tailed by the same black pickup truck. In the darkness and the glare of the truck's headlights, he couldn't read its license plate, but it was clearly the same vehicle every morning. At 5:00 a.m. there was no one else on the road, so it didn't seem possible that this convergence of their vehicles was just a fluke of their daily commute. No, the pickup driver was deliberately following David to rattle his nerves.

It just so happened that this daily occurrence coincided with David learning about Sandra Bridewell—the adversary of his client, Gloria Rehrig. Within the space of ten years, three young and physically healthy people had wound up shot in the head after getting close with Sandra, and she was the last known contact of all three. And then Alan Rehrig's cousin was fatally shot eleven days after he was nominated as Sandra's successor administrator of Alan's estate.

The OKC detectives Steve Pacheco and Ron Mitchell didn't conceal their suspicion that Sandra had murdered Alan for the life insurance. Like David, they had great sympathy for Gloria Rehrig, and they seemed dedicated to making their case. They said they would be happy to testify in probate court that Sandra—the beneficiary of Alan's life insurance— was suspected of murdering him.

David often marveled that he'd gotten involved in such a dramatic and apparently dangerous case. At the time he'd received the call at the end of May, he'd thought it was just a matter of giving the insurance company notice that Sandra was a suspect for Alan's murder. Because Alan had died in debt, the insurer had gone ahead and paid $102,000 (of the $220,000 total death benefit) to his estate. This sum, and the debts that Sandra had submitted to the estate for payment, were in bitter dispute. And now David was being followed by someone trying to intimidate him. After a week of this daily occurrence, he started carrying a .357 Magnum in his briefcase. He then began to worry about his wife and kids and decided it would be best if they stayed with her parents in Virginia until the dispute with Sandra was resolved.

Initially David believed he could easily show the probate court a preponderance of evidence that Sandra had played a role in Alan's murder. But then, to David's surprise and dismay, Judge Nikki Deshazo told him in a prehearing conference that he would have to prove it beyond a reasonable doubt. David protested that theirs was a civil dispute over a life insurance payout, not a trial in criminal court. Deshazo replied that because he was alleging murder, the burden of proof in *her* court would be beyond a reasonable doubt.

"We will appeal," David said.

"So be it," she replied.

Judge Deshazo's assertion—which struck David as arbitrary and out of bounds—was just one of many perplexing aspects of the case in which everything seemed to go Sandra's way, and against Gloria Rehrig. This was in spite of the fact that Sandra was widely regarded with grave suspicion and even feared by many people in her community. The totality of circumstances indicated a high probability (well over 50%) that she had murdered her husband for his life insurance. Even though she was, by her own assertion, estranged and separated from him at the time of his death, she applied to the probate court to be appointed administratrix of his estate and became so on January 14, 1986.

She then proceeded to submit to the estate all the debts that she had incurred—without Alan's permission or even knowledge at the time of the transactions—during their marriage. These included her unauthorized charges on Alan's Amex and Visa cards, a jewelry purchase at Neiman-Marcus, and a long unpaid bill for a golf weekend at the Garden of the Gods Resort in Colorado Springs from the summer of 1985. At the time of the trip, she had acted as though it were a treat for her husband. She also submitted her legal bills to the estate, plus a $5,450 fee for her services as administratrix. On the asset side of her inventory, she did *not* include her investment in the play *Crime and Punishment*, which was technically community property. She also omitted Alan's Ford Bronco from the asset column, though she included the associated car loan in the debt column.

After Judge Deshazo said she would impose the beyond a reasonable doubt standard of evidence, David submitted a Second Amended Application on September 6, 1986, in which he notified the court that, according to OKC Police Detectives Steve Pacheco and Ron Mitchell, "evidence will be presented to the Grand Jury in Oklahoma City in November 1986 sufficient to indict Sandra Rehrig for the murder of Norman Alan Rehrig and that such indictment is imminent."

On September 26, 1986, David received notice from one of Sandra's attorneys that she would resign as administratrix. However, this was a Pyrrhic victory because the initial $102,000 life insurance payment had already been used to pay debts that Sandra had incurred and lawyers' fees. Moreover, though Sandra had agreed to resign as administratrix, she maintained her claim to the remaining ($118,000) of Alan's life insurance. Unless she was soon indicted, she could press her claim for it.

What happened next was stupendously perplexing. First, Sandra made a permanent move to California without leaving a forwarding address. Then November came and went with no grand jury proceedings to indict her. Gloria inquired at the DA's office and was told that a grand jury probe was unnecessary because federal investigators had taken an interest in the case and would likely seek a federal indictment. In December 1986, the FBI opened an investigation of Sandra's activities, during which it also examined Robert Smith's death. One day an investigator visited the Smith residence and spoke with his widow, Glady. He told her he was examining the possibility that Robert's death was linked to Alan Rehrig's.

When Gloria and Phillip Rehrig heard about this, they contacted the FBI investigator and asked why he thought the deaths might be linked. The investigator replied that Robert's right-hand position, as it was visible in the death scene photographs, was inconsistent with the proposition that he'd fired the rifle. His statement raised Gloria's hopes that the FBI was on the cusp of making a breakthrough in their investigation of both deaths, but she never again heard from the investigator.

During Gloria's trip to Dallas in June of 1986, she spoke to Sandra's former neighbor Margaret who had, since Alan's death, become afraid of her erstwhile friend. Among the many surprising things that Margaret told Gloria was the fact that—so far from being a lady of property—Sandra was often strapped for cash. Her financial condition seemed to fluctuate wildly. Sometimes, such as in mid-October 1985, she claimed to have no money at all. But then, in mid-December, she bought a new BMW equipped with a fancy cell phone. In January she booked a ski trip to Santa Fe, invited Margaret and her son to join, and footed the entire bill. They stayed in the historic Santa Fe Hilton that had once belonged to Sandra's deceased husband, Bobby Bridewell. How Sandra came into her fresh cash supply was anyone's guess.

Unbeknownst to Margaret and Gloria, Sandra obtained a $25,000 unsecured loan from the Bank of Dallas on December 20, 1985. A month later, she got yet another unsecured loan from the Bank of Dallas for $40,000. Had Margaret and Gloria known about these loans, they would have wondered how on earth Sandra had persuaded a Bank of Dallas loan officer to lend her—a woman of zero credit—*any* money, much less two unsecured loans totaling $65,000. The $40,000 loan she obtained on January 21, 1986, was especially remarkable, given that, just three days earlier, she was repeatedly mentioned in a front-page *Dallas Times Herald* story about her murdered husband. Even the most obtuse reader could surmise from the report that she was a suspect.

Sandra made no payments on the loans and moved to California. Ultimately the Bank of Dallas submitted a claim for her unpaid debt to Alan's estate because, in the words of its Intervenor's Petition to the probate court: *Defendant is hiding and the attorney representing Defendant, David Whitehead of San Francisco, California, states he has been instructed not to disclose her whereabouts or the whereabouts of her assets.*

CHAPTER 27

KNIGHT IN SHINING ARMOR

If any of the men who came and went from Sandra's life deserved the epithet Knight in Shining Armor, it was Mr. David Whitehead. The 1971 Stanford Law School graduate was an attorney of great distinction and a prominent member of San Francisco society. He became Sandra's legal representative after she moved to the Bay Area in the summer of 1986, and he provided counsel in her disputes with Gloria Rehrig and the Bank of Dallas. In February of 1987, the Bank of Dallas requested an order of dismissal with prejudice of its Intervenor's petition and offered to pay the cost of its intervention. Somehow Sandra had managed to settle her "matters in controversy" with the bank. Its request for dismissal with prejudice was reminiscent of Mr. Big's request in 1978, which makes one wonder about Sandra's relationship with the bank officer who gave her a $65,000 unsecured loan.

On June 15, 1987, David Wise took an oral deposition from Sandra in San Francisco. He had developed his questions from his own investigation and his conversations with Oklahoma City detectives Steve Pacheco and Ron Mitchell. Though the detectives hadn't shown him their case file, they'd told him about some of the clues they'd found despite Sandra's refusal to talk with them. As Mr. Wise entered the law offices in which the deposition was scheduled, he was introduced to David Whitehead. Sandra had not yet arrived, and as they sat at the conference table, waiting for her, Mr. Wise studied her attorney. His bland appearance belied his strength as her lawyer. He was doing a great job for Sandra.

"I guess you sleep with one eye open," David said half-joking. Mr. Whitehead gave him an indignant look but didn't rise to the bait. Sandra entered and took her seat. *So, this is the great seductress,* Mr. Wise thought. Certainly, she was a pretty woman, though her beauty was marred by large circles under her eyes, suggesting she hadn't slept well. For the most part, Sandra and her attorneys did a good job of evading his questions. She frequently claimed not to remember certain details. After all, nineteen months had elapsed since the events in question. Her attorneys frequently objected on the grounds that Mr. Wise was being argumentative. Nevertheless, her answers to a few of his most pertinent questions were implausible and contradictory of other statements she'd made in the past. Two of her answers hinted at scenarios that the OKC police detectives had apparently never examined—at least not with any rigor.

Sandra ultimately prevailed against Gloria's legal action to prevent her from receiving the rest ($118,000) of Alan's life insurance payout. Mr. Whitehead helped her to achieve this by threatening to sue Gloria for libel if she didn't drop her action. He claimed Gloria had made false and libelous statements about Sandra in the probate court (a public forum) and to the Dallas press. These statements, he claimed, had defamed Sandra's character in her community, inflicting grave damage to her and her children.

Gloria was already struggling to pay her attorney's fees. The prospect of now having to defend herself against a libel suit struck her with dread and despair. She wrote to a few prominent men in Dallas and Oklahoma, explaining that her son had recently been murdered and his wife was the prime suspect. By means of legal action she could no longer afford to pursue, she was trying to delay the insurance payment to the suspect until the crime was solved. Now she was being threatened with a libel lawsuit. If she lost it, she would be compelled to pay damages and the suspect's legal fees, which would ruin her altogether. She asked each of the letter's recipients (known to be benefactors of various worthy causes) if they would assist her in seeking justice for her murdered son. None of the men replied, though Ross Perot's secretary was kind enough to answer with a note regretting that Mr. Perot could be of no assistance. And so, Gloria dropped her action to block the insurance payment to Sandra. To protect herself if Mr. Whitehead carried out his threat to sue her for libel, she declared personal bankruptcy.

Gloria had long been a faithful Christian. She knew that evil existed in the world, and that there was always, in the heart of every woman and man, a spiritual struggle between good and bad. But until Alan's murder, she'd always believed that if good people pursued truth and justice, they would ultimately prevail. In the year 1987, her faith in this was sorely tested. She often thought of the woman who'd called on the night of Alan's funeral. She too was a Christian who believed in the ultimate triumph of truth. And yet, by her own admission, she was terrified of Sandra, whom she believed could get away with anything. There was always someone to pay her bills, forgive her debts, and provide her with a legal defense. What could explain her mysterious power?

CHAPTER 28

THE BLACK WIDOW OF HIGHLAND PARK

I sat in in the Highland Park High School cafeteria, about to eat a "chicken cutlet" dressed in dubious light brown gravy, when my friend Tyler sat down next to me.

"Have you seen this?" he asked and held up a copy of the May 1987 edition of *D Magazine*. I looked at the cover and saw in bold print:

DEATH AND GOSSIP
IN HIGHLAND PARK

Sandra Bridewell, elegant and seductive, seemed tailor-made for Dallas high society. But something happened on her way up the social ladder. Her first two husbands died. Her third husband was murdered. Then, the police and FBI began asking questions: Could there be another, darker side to the beautiful widow—or is she the victim?

"What the hell?" I said, my mind racing to comprehend what I was reading. "Do the cops think she whacked her husbands?"

"Dude, it's totally crazy. You gotta read it." I studied his face, trying to ascertain his thoughts. Tyler was usually so keen to express his opinions.

"Can I borrow your copy?" I asked.

"No, but you can photocopy it." This I did, and during my afternoon classes I managed to read snippets, but each teacher saw I wasn't paying attention to her and interrupted my reading by asking me a question. And so, for the first time in my student life, I went straight to the school library after the day's final class to read my photocopy of the *D Magazine* article. It was an extraordinary tale of Sandra's rise and fall in Dallas society, recounting the apparent suicides of David Stegall in 1975 and Betsy Bagwell in 1982, as well as the murder of Alan Rehrig in 1985. An eerie feeling swept over me as I thought of Sandra—the snow white-skinned beauty gazing at me with her big brown eyes while we talked in her kitchen.

In my early teens, I'd often visited her house, one block down from my family home on Lorraine Avenue, because her daughter Kathryn and I were friends. The place had a formal, museum quality about it, with no lounging room for Kathryn and her two siblings, so we usually sat in Kathryn's bedroom, listening to music, and talking. Kathryn was a bold and adventurous tomboy with a broad sense of humor. At the age of thirteen, when I felt awkward and shy around girls, she was a notable exception. She had a wonderful candor, and I could talk to her about anything.

It was sometime in the summer of 1983 that I first met her mother. Sandra happened to be home during one of my visits, and I chatted with her in the kitchen while she prepared something. Straightway I sensed she was different from other moms. It wasn't just her striking beauty—her white skin that contrasted with her big brown eyes and lustrous brown hair. Nor was it the way she was so perfectly dressed and made up, even though she was working in her kitchen. Certainly, these contributed to the effect she had on me, but there was something else about her that captured my attention. Maybe it was her graceful movements and soft, girlish way of speaking. I guess all these qualities produced an exceptionally feminine presence. While most of my friends' mothers seemed old and harried by their kids, she was youthful and relaxed.

Kathryn mentioned that her mom often made trips to New York and Europe, which gave her a glamorous air. It seemed she was always enjoying herself.

Occasionally I saw her driving down our street or pulling into her driveway in her blue Mercedes 380SL convertible with the top down. Seeing her in the sexy two-seater, I thought she was the most dashing mom I'd ever seen. It didn't occur to me that other moms didn't drive such a car because it was unsuitable for hauling kids. To me, she looked like Mrs. Hart in the popular TV show *Hart to Hart*, who drove the same model and had the same haircut. Years later I learned that Sandra's maiden name was Powers, the surname of the actress who played Mrs. Hart. Sandra looked every bit as stylish.

During a conversation on a subsequent visit, she engaged me in a way I'd never experienced before. She asked me questions and seemed to find my answers genuinely interesting, gazing at me with her big brown eyes while I spoke. The way she talked to me made me feel significant. I think I felt that, with her, I was on the cusp of having a grownup conversation with a woman, and not merely exchanging pleasantries with a friend's mother.

I didn't know at the time that Sandra was the most notorious woman who'd ever lived in Highland Park. When I met her in 1983, she was widely suspected of murdering her first husband, a dentist named David Stegall, as well as Betsy Bagwell. That no one had ever breathed a word about this to me would later strike me as strange, because my parents knew just about everyone in Sandra's past.

My mother had heard rumors about Sandra, but in 1983 she had little time for gossip because she was busy raising four boys and caring for her parents, whose lives had been terribly affected by my grandmother's cancer. She didn't know that I was often at the Bridewell house and that I found Sandra fascinating. In those days before cell phones, parents in our community didn't track their kids' movements. We played all day in the neighborhood and came home for dinner.

About a year after I became friends with Kathryn, she started looking less tomboyish and more like a pretty girl, and other boys noticed her. One of them was my friend Mark. He was the best athlete in our class, excelling at every sport, but especially at football. Our star tailback, he flattened anyone who tried to tackle him, often running up the score to dizzying heights. This gave him a special status in our community, and even the men of our fathers' generation showed him exceptional respect. One day in early June of 1984, right after school recessed for the summer, Mark was over at my place for a swim. Realizing that Kathryn lived right up the street, he suggested we pay her a visit. She happened to be at home and seemed happy to see us.

"Hey guys!" she said with her usual bright smile and cheerfulness.

"We were just swimming at John's house and thought of you," Mark said. She invited us in, and we sat in the kitchen, drinking cokes and chatting. After about fifteen minutes I went to the bathroom, and when I returned, Mark and Kathryn were gone. I figured they were off somewhere kissing, so I decided to stay put and wait for them to return. I stood there wondering what it would be like to kiss Kathryn and was surprised by her brother Britt entering the kitchen. He was tall and handsome, with his mother's brown hair and eyes. Three years older than me, I'd rarely seen him and never really talked with him.

"Oh hey, Britt," I said, a bit jarred by his sudden appearance, as I hadn't been aware he was in the house. Without saying a word, he hit me in the face, and then followed with more punches. I managed to get my guards up, but I was too shocked and intimidated by the much bigger boy to fight back. Somehow, I managed to push him away for long enough to bolt for the kitchen door. I ran into the back yard, so scared that I didn't notice that Britt wasn't pursuing me.

"Hey John!" I heard Mark's voice. "Where are you going?" I turned to see him and Kathryn standing by a tree, where they'd apparently been kissing.

"Kathryn's brother just attacked me!" I exclaimed. "We gotta get out of here!" He looked at the closed kitchen door, then back at me, confused. A distressed look appeared on Kathryn's face, and in the awkward silence, we made the decision to leave. We exited through the backyard gate and into the alley. On the way back to my house, I told Mark what had just happened.

"What's his problem?" he said. "You weren't the one kissing his sister. Did he say anything?"

"Not a word."

"I'd love for him to try that shit on me. I'll drop kick his ass down the street."

Later I thought about how strange this incident was. I'd been in many schoolyard fights, including a couple with Mark. Once I'd accepted that I was a big notch below him in the pecking order, he became affectionate, even protective of me. These fights had a ritualized quality. They started with exchanging insults, then pushing, then a bunch of poorly thrown punches until someone was knocked down, which usually signaled the end of the fight. Britt's attack had a different quality. It was as though he were assailing an alien intruder in his home, and not his sister's friend. Above all it was his silence that was disturbing. His only communication was the cold fury in his eyes, which seemed to express hate. But what had I done to make him hate me? I thought maybe he was still angry about the death of his father from cancer a year earlier and felt overly protective of his sister. Maybe, because he lacked his father's natural authority, he felt he had to use violent intimidation against boys with dishonorable intentions—that verbal warnings weren't enough. Highland Park in 1984 was a socially conservative place in which a girl's reputation could be easily ruined. Only later did it occur to me that maybe Britt had acted under the mistaken impression that I was *already* having improper contact with his sister, and not merely fantasizing about it.

In any case, I got the message, and never visited Kathryn again. Occasionally I bumped into her on our street, but the incident seemed to mark the end of our carefree friendship. A few months later, her family moved from their house on Lorraine Avenue to the neighboring town of University Park, and I saw her less and less. And then, abruptly it seemed to me, her family moved to California, and I lost touch with her altogether.

Reading the *D Magazine* piece, I realized that, at the same time— possibly the same day—I was violently ejected from Kathryn's home, Alan Rehrig made a wrong turn down our street. Until the moment I read the sensational story, I'd taken for granted that no serious crime ever happened in Highland Park. For years our police department's chief occupation had been chasing me and my rowdy friends for our pranks. In the years 1980-85, I was the worst kid in the neighborhood, and after a while, whenever an incident was reported of a boy throwing mud balls at cars, riding a motor-cross bike at blistering speeds through lawns (and on one occasion through the Highland Park Village Safeway) or climbing onto a girl's balcony at night, the HP cops didn't even bother pursuing me, but simply went to my parents' house, where they were invariably greeted by my mother. I believe they enjoyed these incidents because my mother was beautiful and charming.

The only time the HPPD was seriously provoked was when I threw a Molotov cocktail into a residential street. Because I only put a small amount of gasoline into a small Coke bottle, I didn't anticipate the alarming size of the firebomb. Though no person or property was damaged, it was a major incident that sparked a major investigation. Suspicion didn't initially fall on me because the crime seemed out of my league, but then the investigator found a witness who'd seen me running down a neighboring alley right after the explosion, and my goose was cooked. The police and fire chiefs, and my parents, wanted to know what the hell was wrong with me.

"How did you know how to build this incendiary device?" the chiefs asked in a solemn interview with me and my parents at the station.

"From the movie *Escape from New York*," I replied. "Snake Plisskin threw one at some bad guys who were coming after him."

"I see," said the Fire Chief.

"Do you have any idea how dangerous that is to yourself and others?"

"I do now," I said.

I believe the consequences would have been far worse if it hadn't been for my mother, who said all the right things about being extremely concerned. She understood that my thrill-seeking and impulsive behavior were very disturbing character traits in an adolescent boy. Throwing a firebomb onto Arcady Boulevard in the middle of Highland Park was outrageously beyond the pale. Clearly, I might have been a bad seed, headed down a bad path. But even at that time, I sensed the two chiefs were animated with an old-fashioned sense of chivalry towards my distressed mother, and by the end of the meeting, they were downright friendly.

Maybe I flatter myself, but I don't think that my misbehavior was motivated by a desire to harm. I was an extremely curious boy with a compulsive desire to explore and to test boundaries and rules. Already at the age of ten, I occasionally jumped freighters on the Katy Railroad that divided Highland Park from Dallas and rode them for a few miles north or south to see what lay outside of my small world. I sensed that adults craved order, and that this craving governed their lives. Highland Park was a place of property, and property seemed to signify everything that adults wanted. Displaying it demonstrated their status. To me, all the arrangements of the adult world were devoid of excitement. Only decades later did I understand that many adults in Highland Park also found their lives boring and stultifying. They too yearned for excitement, but their circumstances wouldn't allow them to indulge their desire—at least not publicly.

My Molotov cocktail stunt was probably the most disorderly thing to happen in Highland Park since Bonnie and Clyde knocked off the Texaco station on the town's south boundary in the thirties, and it enhanced my outlaw reputation. And yet, as much as I was given to performing dangerous stunts, I found murder incomprehensible. In my mind, murder only happened in poor neighborhoods and in movies. *Murder.* Again, I thought of the beguiling Sandra. The suspicion that she had murdered one or more people seemed unfathomably strange.

I finished reading the *D Magazine* piece and reviewed the photo illustrations. None of the pictures of Sandra did her beauty justice. One image was a family portrait of her with her third husband, Alan Rehrig, and her three kids, lying together on a lawn. Kathryn, with her impish grin, looked charming; her younger sister Emily looked angelic. Britt looked as handsome as ever and uncharacteristically sweet. It was a contrived picture of a happy family (later I would learn it was taken for a Christmas card). It reminded me of a similar portrait of my family, taken years earlier, and I wondered if the same photographer had done both jobs. That everyone was wearing a sweater indicated it was taken in the fall of 1984, just a few months after I'd last seen Sandra. I studied the image of Alan Rehrig. He was a handsome young man, and I thought it strange that I'd never seen him.

Just as strange as Alan Rehrig's murder was the purported suicide of Betsy Bagwell three years earlier. Her son Andrew was in the class above me, and though I didn't really know him, we had mutual friends. Vaguely I recalled someone talking about his mom's death, but I'd never heard that Sandra was her last known contact. Dr. John Bagwell was my grandmother's oncologist. She'd been diagnosed with oral cancer in 1980—the same year in which Bobby Bridewell was diagnosed with lymphoma. When I got home from school, I showed my mom the *D Magazine* article and asked her about Betsy's death.

"Betsy's friends always said that Sandra had something to do with it, but the medical examiner insisted it was suicide."

"Why didn't you ever tell me about that?" I asked.

"I figured it was probably just gossip. I was never close with Betsy, and I don't know Sandra at all, so I never paid much attention to the talk."

"What do you know about Betsy's husband?" I asked.

"He was always very sweet to mother. Once he made a house call and brought her chocolate chip cookies. But I can't say that I really know him. Now that I think about it, there's something sort of enigmatic about him."

The May 1987 *D Magazine* story about Sandra Bridewell made a huge stir in Highland Park and left a lasting impression on me. One of the many intriguing elements of the story was the absence of the Dallas police and DA's office from it. As the report made clear, within our community, Sandra was widely suspected of involvement in the shooting deaths of two husbands and a prominent doctor's wife. However, this suspicion had prompted little response from law enforcement. Following the deaths of David Stegall and Betsy Bagwell, Dallas police officers had taken statements from Sandra, but these had been subjected to little scrutiny. Three years later, Alan Rehrig's murder was investigated entirely by Oklahoma City police detectives. Even though Sandra became the prime suspect, and even though Alan's shooting death strongly resembled Betsy's, it did not prompt the DPD or medical examiner to reexamine the earlier deaths. This struck me and many others as strange. *Very strange.*

The report mentioned that Sandra was, at the time, living "in a spacious apartment near the San Francisco Yacht Club, over-looking the

Bay." It also mentioned the FBI "has joined the murder probe and is looking not only at the Rehrig murder but deep into Sandra's clouded past." I figured she must have been keeping a low profile in San Francisco. Surely, with state and federal investigators looking at her, she wouldn't dare do anything else that could get her into trouble.

PART II
WANDERING SPIRIT

CHAPTER 29

BELVEDERE

Elizabeth Merrill was an elegant lady who lived in a beautiful home in Belvedere, on San Francisco Bay just northeast of the Golden Gate. Her husband, John Merrill, was a partner in the legendary architectural firm Skidmore, Owings, & Merrill, which his father had founded. One day in the summer of 1988, Elizabeth met the most delightful woman at a luncheon at the Francisca Club—the oldest ladies social club in San Francisco. Sandra Bridewell was her name, and as Elizabeth would later recall, "I thought she was beautiful, gracious, gentle, and kind. Just extraordinarily feminine."

Around the same time, at a function hosted by the Guardsman—a charitable organization for helping at risk youth—a lady named Cindy Abbott met Sandra and was charmed by her lively conversation. She had a marvelous way of expounding on all manner of topics with knowledge and enthusiasm. Both Elizabeth and Cindy felt a strong desire to be with Sandra and to help her establish herself in the Bay Area. They knew nothing about her past, and because they perceived her to value her privacy, they didn't inquire about it. The most notable detail that Sandra volunteered was that she'd twice been widowed; both husbands had died of cancer. To both women, she said she wanted to meet someone new.

One night in August of 1988, Cindy Abbott hosted a dinner party to which she invited Sandra and her friend Dennis Kuba, a lawyer from Santa Rosa who'd recently separated from his wife. Dennis was captivated. As Sandra engaged him in conversation, everyone else in the room seemed to vanish. Her big brown eyes were mesmerizing, and she often leaned close to him and touched his elbow to emphasize a point. Upon hearing he was an equestrian, she revealed an extraordinary knowledge of horses. Instantly he felt what he later described as "an incredible attraction" to her.

Mr. Kuba started taking Sandra out for dinner dates. Unbeknownst to him, she was also seeing another married man—an insurance executive from Southern California named Thomas Finney—whom she'd met at a party in Belvedere. Though happily married, Finney found Sandra fascinating. Despite being a newcomer to the Bay Area, she already seemed to know everyone and was welcome in all the right households and clubs. Talking with her, he found her dark eyes hypnotic.

Sandra's Belvedere apartment next to the Yacht Club was furnished with beautiful antiques and original oil paintings that gave the impression she was a lady of property. It therefore came as a surprise when she asked Dennis and Thomas for large sums of money. She claimed she lived on a trust set up by her husband who'd died of cancer. Though it contained considerable assets, they weren't entirely liquid, and funds were only distributed to her twice a year. Settling in Belvedere and enrolling her children in private schools had resulted in unexpectedly high costs. Being bereft of her husband and raising three kids on her own was often formidably difficult. Sandra told her sad story with great affect. How could Dennis and Thomas say no?

During this same period, a film producer named Antony Michaels met Sandra at the home of some friends in Belvedere. And then, by a delightful coincidence, he began bumping into her all over town. Later he would describe these fortuitous encounters with her in unexpected places as "the weirdest, most pleasant sensation."

"Each time I felt as if I had come away the recipient of some miracle. She was like an angel, except she wasn't boring or goody two-shoes. She was beautiful, and she was the epitome of womanhood. She knew it and didn't mind if you knew it, too." Dimly he was aware that he wasn't exactly Sandra's type and that maybe, in her eyes, his wealth enhanced his attractiveness. But surely, he thought, this couldn't be her primary motive because, in her taste and manners, she herself had such a strong air of wealth.

They enjoyed picnicking and art galleries, and then one day he flew her to a film premiere in Los Angeles in his private jet. Upon their return, on their final descent to San Francisco, Sandra surprised him with a teary-eyed confession.

"No one has been this kind to me in years, but there's something I have to tell you." She was, she explained amid sobs, in deep financial trouble, with creditors hounding her for the rent and her children's school tuitions. And so, Mr. Michaels agreed to give her a $10,000 loan. Two weeks later she asked for another $5,000. When she asked him a third time, he told her they needed to work out a repayment plan, and she hung up on him. About fifteen minutes later she called him again and told him she was pregnant.

"Well, that's funny," he said, "because I've had a vasectomy." His anger got the better of him and he told her to get lost. She did as she was told, taking his fifteen grand with her.

In January 1988, Mr. Finney heard about Mr. Kuba, and contacted him. They discovered that in their relations with her, they'd been perfectly interchangeable. Each had found her irresistibly vulnerable, the tears welling up in her big brown eyes and rolling down her milky white cheeks as she told them stories of her hardship. Both had felt an irresistible desire to help the damsel in distress. She'd taken Kuba for a total of $24,000, and Finney for $75,000, much of it from his retirement account. Later the two men learned of yet another man, a San Francisco lawyer who'd helped Sandra with her legal problems and had apparently loaned her over $300,000 when she'd moved to Marin in early 1987.

One by one, Sandra had dumped the men without paying them back. From the standpoint of strict utility, this was a rational decision, because she had reached her credit limit with all three. Remaining with them would have subjected her to demands for repayment, while there was apparently no end to the suckers in the Bay Area. Dennis Kuba and Thomas Finney were married men, and as they knew well, married men aren't supposed to loan money to women outside the marital community. If money had been such a concern for them, they wouldn't have loaned it to her. She told Finney that if she paid him any of the money it would contribute to his divorce. If he wanted to see his money, he could divorce his wife and live with her.

On the other hand, Dennis was still a friend of Cindy Abbott in San Francisco, and he knew residents of Belvedere as well. Speaking with people in the tight-knit community, he learned that he wasn't alone in perceiving the elegant Southern belle to have a ruthless side. Women in the community whom she'd initially charmed became wary of her when they detected signs she was interested in their propertied husbands. As Dennis later recalled, "The way to cause a stir in Belvedere was to mention her name at a party. The crowd would immediately hush and at least four or five men would look nervously around the room."

In the spring of 1989, copies of the famous *D Magazine* article "The Black Widow" arrived in the mail at several homes and offices in the Bay Area from an anonymous sender. Even those who'd already taken a dim view of Sandra were thunderstruck by the story of her two husbands and a friend shot to death. Was she a serial killer like the Theresa Russell character in *Black Widow*—a film that had appeared in cinemas at the same time Sandra arrived in Marin County? Or was she just a serial seducer and grifter who'd become the subject of vicious gossip among Highland Park ladies, as some quoted in the article suggested?

The report's circulation in the Bay Area caused a stir and emboldened Dennis Kuba and Thomas Finney to file lawsuits against Sandra for fraud. It also prompted the *San Francisco Chronicle* to publish a major feature titled "Mystery in Marin" in its July 12, 1989, edition. Local news channel KRON-TV broadcast an eight-minute segment on her adventures in San Francisco and Dallas. The FBI renewed its investigation of Sandra, now focusing on the suspicion of illicit banking practices. One day an investigator contacted Cindy Abbott. Referring to the *D Magazine* passage on the death of Betsy Bagwell in 1982, he said, "If you took Betsy Bagwell and put her in California, you are Betsy Bagwell."

At this point, ladies in Dallas started receiving calls from their friends in the Bay Area inquiring about Sandra. The documentary television shows *Inside Edition* and *Current Affair* began researching her story. One segment was scheduled to broadcast on October 17, 1989. That evening, dozens of women who'd known Sandra in Dallas and San Francisco eagerly awaited the show and were shocked by its postponement due to the Loma Prieta earthquake, which killed 63 and injured 3,757. A few months later Geraldo did a segment on Sandra and invited Gloria Rehrig and OKC detective Ron Mitchell to participate. Gloria calmly asked the audience, "If Sandra didn't murder my son, why has she never cooperated with our efforts to find out who did?" Fireworks ensued when one of Sandra's friends (with the alias "Jean") called into the show and parroted Sandra's claim that Alan was probably murdered because he'd gotten into drugs and didn't pay back his dealer. Detective Mitchell vehemently rejected her assertion. He assured the audience that he'd done a thorough background check on Alan and found nothing to substantiate Sandra's claim that he'd been an indebted drug user.

Dennis Kuba ended up dropping his lawsuit against Sandra, but Thomas Finney got a default judgment. However, as he soon learned, it was one thing to win a judgment and quite another to collect it. Faced with bad press in the Bay Area, Sandra did what she would often do in the years ahead—*disappear.*

The advent of the nineties marked a new phase in her life during which she frequently moved. She started calling herself by her middle name, Camille, after her adoptive mother who'd been killed in a car accident when Sandra was three. In each new place she invariably met a man who supported her until he realized that he was being exploited. Dawning awareness triggered curiosity about Camille's true background (as distinct from whatever story she offered), and this often resulted in the discovery of the *D Magazine* story. And so, like Caine in the Book of Genesis, Sandra seemed doomed by her nature and reputation to wander, a fugitive from her past and from the fresh trouble she got into as she wandered from place to place. Throughout her drifting, she never gave up hope that she would someday meet a fabulously wealthy man who would take care of her in high style for the rest of her life.

In 1992 she lived in Palo Alto, California and made frequent trips to San Francisco. At a party in the city, she met a venture capitalist who was married. Sandra's two-year affair with the man ended when his wife discovered it through a private investigator. To keep his business in San Francisco and placate his wife, he moved Sandra (in 1994) to Boston. Sandra agreed on the condition that he covered the cost of a $3,000 per month apartment on Beacon Hill for six months.

Three months later she called him and told him she was three months pregnant and intended to take the child to term, which necessitated an extension of his support. Six months after that, she called him again and claimed she'd just gone into labor and was headed to the maternity ward. Though the newborn would go straight into adoption, she wanted another six months' rent to help her get back on her feet in Boston—yet another condition to which he agreed. Only later did he learn from his wife's P.I. that Sandra was fifty years old and had had a hysterectomy fifteen years earlier. His reaction was one of disbelief. How was this possible? In every conversation he'd had with her about the pregnancy and delivery, she had sounded perfectly convincing.

Even at fifty, Sandra could still pull off the old pregnancy trick she'd used to deceive Alan Rehrig and others, but as the nineties ticked off and she showed the inevitable signs of age, she apparently recognized the limitations imposed upon her by time and mortality. Finding herself in the back third of life, she knew she needed much greater help to make her dreams come true. Facing the harsh parameters of the human condition, she did what millions have done throughout history. She turned to religion.

CHAPTER 30

A PROVERBS 31 WIFE

Dr. Joseph Dandridge was a cardiologist who lived in San Antonio. In the year 2000, he found himself looking for a new path in life. Three years earlier, his marriage of twenty years had collapsed, and the divorce had left him depleted and in search of spiritual renewal. He wanted to learn more about Christianity, and he thought that doing some kind of ministerial or missionary work could give him a new sense of purpose. And so, in May of 2000, he attended a two-week conference on the "Prophetic Church" at the Wagner Leadership Institute in Colorado Springs. According to its Mission Statement, the institute is part of the network of international apostolic training centers established to equip the body of Christ for Kingdom ministry (Ephesians 4:11-12).

The conference began with trainees joining for a prayer. The instructor asked the students to face each other in pairs and clasp each other's hands. Dandridge turned to the woman standing next to him and looked into her big brown eyes that seemed to dance. She had a lovely, warm smile, and as she clasped his hands, he instantly perceived in her an extraordinary sweetness. Her name was Camille Bridewell. Originally from California, she was a widow with three children. Already a minister and missionary who'd been mentored by Marilyn Hickey, she was attending the conference as part of her ongoing apostolic training.

In the days that followed, Dandridge often marveled at Camille's extraordinary charisma. Afire with dedication to spreading the love and wisdom of Christ, she was a prophet in her own right, adept at speaking in tongues. On one occasion he witnessed her exorcise a demon from a long-afflicted man.

She told Dr. Dandridge she was seeking the man who would be her Boaz—the kind and gentle farmer in the Book of Ruth. For her part, she wanted to be a "Proverbs 31 Wife"— the perfect woman described by King Lemuel's mother, who advised her royal son to avoid the pleasures of wine and sensual women. Instead, he should find a woman of exceptional virtue. Camille knew the verses by heart.

> She brings him good, not harm, all the days of her life…
> She watches over her household and does not eat the
> bread of idleness…
> Many women do noble things, but you surpass them all…
> Charm is deceptive and beauty is fleeting, but a woman
> who praises the Lord is to be praised.

After the conference, Camille visited Dr. Dandridge in San Antonio, and in September he proposed marriage. She set about planning the occasion at the Broadmoor Hotel in Colorado Springs. The lavishness of the event, which ended up costing $60,000, revealed that she was also passionately interested in the material world. They wed on October 8, 2000, in front of about thirty guests, including her daughter Emily, who made a special trip from Maui with her boyfriend, courtesy of Dr. Dandridge. It was a beautiful ceremony, and Sandra looked lovely in her white wedding gown, but that night was a grave disappointment for Dr. Dandridge, because his new bride spurned his advances in the bedroom.

Getting married seemed to transform Camille from a tender lady into what Dr. Dandridge perceived to be a witch. Prone to sudden and violent bursts of negative emotion, she lurched from anger to coldness, and demeaned him with harsh criticism. Sometimes his new wife seemed to have multiple personalities, as if she were possessed by a demon that occasionally emerged when she was angry. She also had a mania for shopping and travelling to tony places and staying at expensive hotels and spas. After returning from a Marilyn Hickey retreat to South America, she launched into redecorating his home, but then seemed to lose interest in the project. She formed a nonprofit ministry called Willing Hearts, purportedly for doing charitable works, and she asked Dr. Dandridge to take out a home equity loan to fund it. When he refused because he couldn't afford it, she screamed at him.

He did, however, agree to purchase a life insurance policy with a $100,000 death benefit. As his marriage progressively came to resemble hell, he wondered about the prudence of this. One night she unexpectedly sweetened and set about cooking a fine meal. This was a surprise because, far from being a Proverbs 31 wife, she was rarely at home and almost never cooked. And then it hit him just before she served the beautiful dinner: *maybe she was about to poison him for the life insurance.* Still, he couldn't bring himself to refuse the proffered meal.

After a miserable holiday season, Dr. Dandridge entered the New Year at his wit's end. His marriage was a constant source of terrible stress that was making it increasingly hard to function. One day in January he met with a friend and pastor named Mike McLean in whom he confided his troubles with his wife. Pastor McLean perceived him to be so distraught as to be in danger of committing suicide. It occurred to him that maybe Dr. Dandridge had not really gotten to know Camille before he married her. He made inquiries into her past and discovered that she had not been mentored by Marilyn Hickey, nor had she done any missionary work, but had merely gone on a few of Hickey's cushy organized tours to places of religious significance. The revelation inspired Dandridge to dig further, and he soon discovered that Camille was a full ten years older than she'd claimed to be. Somehow his initial inquiry failed to uncover the most troubling feature of Camille's past— namely, that she was a suspected serial killer.

At the end of January of 2001 his tortuous cohabitation with Camille ended when she took his brand-new Ford Expedition SUV and prized coin collection and disappeared. Unbeknownst to him, she had invited her daughter Emily, who still lived on Maui, to meet her for a reunion in San Jose, California. She told Emily that the new SUV was hers, and she didn't mention that she'd left her new husband. For a couple of days, they visited some of their old stomping grounds around Palo Alto, where they'd lived in the early nineties, before Sandra moved to Boston. Emily then proposed that they drive up to Marin County to visit her brother Britt. Sandra said that her relationship with Britt was strained, so Emily visited him by herself. She was happy to see her brother, but also disturbed by his stern advice.

"You really shouldn't be hanging around with mom," he said. He then explained that it was time for Emily to understand what she'd been too young to realize when they were growing up—namely, that their mother was extremely destructive. To illustrate his point, he said that, on an excursion to a lake in the summer of 1985, Sandra had asked him to run over their subsequently murdered stepfather, Alan Rehrig, with a jet ski while making it look like an accident. This was a shocking revelation, and it seemed to resolve the cognitive dissonance that Emily had long felt about her mother. She deeply loved Sandra, who'd often been a wonderfully loving mother. However, for years, Emily had been unable to reconcile Sandra's tenderness with her disturbing behavior on several occasions. Her brother's words caused her to realize that her misgivings had arisen from the terrible reality that Sandra was destructive and deceptive.

Returning to Palo Alto, Emily questioned Sandra about what was going on in her marriage to her new husband, and about the SUV she was driving. Sandra was evasive, which prompted Emily to call Dr. Dandridge.

"Do you know that my mom has your car?" she asked.

"Yes, because she stole it from me," he replied. Emily then confronted her mother with this discovery. Sandra replied that she'd left Joseph because, she claimed, he was an abusive gay pedophile. How many times had Emily heard her mother say such things about a discarded man? She especially remembered the lawyer in San Francisco who'd been so devoted and helpful, only to be dumped by Sandra with the remark that he was gay.

Emily felt a strong desire to do the right thing, so she called the local police and reported that her mother had stolen her stepfather's car. She gave the police the address of the house where Sandra was staying, and then called her with the aim of keeping her on the phone until the cops arrived. When a patrol officer knocked on Sandra's door, she realized that Emily had set her up.

"You betrayed me!" she growled over the phone, her voice dropping an octave. Sandra told the police that because she was Dr. Dandridge's lawful wife, the vehicle was community property, and she'd been within her rights to use it for visiting her daughter. They'd found her argument hard to refute, and they could do no more than notify Dr. Dandridge of the car's location. His prized coin collection, comprised of over 100 ounces of gold, was irrevocably lost, having been liquidated by Sandra, who'd spent the cash. Upon his return from California, he petitioned the Bexar County court to annul the marriage. Around the same time, he received calls from collection agencies. His wife had, unbeknownst to him, taken out several credit cards during their brief marriage and charged vast sums for merchandise and services.

When Dr. Dandridge married Sandra, he had zero consumer debt and owned a large amount of gold. Four months later he had $150,000 of credit card debt and no valuable personal property. In just a quarter of a year, his marriage to a woman who professed to be a "Proverbs 31 Wife" had resulted in a $200,000 loss. As disastrous as it had been, at least he'd made it out of the marriage alive—a notable distinction from Sandra's previous three husbands.

CHAPTER 31

THE MISSIONARY

Like Mother Teresa, the missionary had felt directed by the Lord to serve the poor and sick in India. In December of 2003, after eight years of caring for orphans in that fascinating country, she was finally returning to San Francisco. Seated next to her on a connecting flight from Atlanta was a woman named Michelle. As the two fell into conversation, Michelle mentioned that she owned a business in Sonoma. This was a remarkable coincidence, because the missionary was herself headed to Sonoma to seek land for the next phase of her life's mission—to teach children from Third World countries sustainable organic farming methods.

Michelle was charmed and awed by this woman who'd led such an extraordinary life of adventure and service following the death of her husband from cancer twenty years before. He'd been a wealthy hotel investor, and upon his death, the woman—Camille Bridewell was her name—had felt the call of service to others. And so, she had founded her Willing Hearts Ministry and wandered the earth, helping those less fortunate. She lived on a trust set up by her deceased husband, but its funds were available for distribution only twice per year. Until the next distribution, she would have to figure out a way to make ends meet.

Upon their arrival in Santa Rosa, Michelle lodged Camille in a hotel for a few days and put her in touch with a lay minister who had a job opportunity for Camille. Ninety-two-year-old John Retter, a well-to-do local resident who lived on a small ranch with his wife Charlotte, had recently fallen and fractured his hip. This injury was accompanied by renal failure, which obliged him to make frequent trips to a dialysis clinic. In exchange for providing home care and driving Mr. Retter to the clinic, Minister Bridewell would receive room and board and $100 per week.

About a week after Minister Bridewell moved in with the Retter family, Charlotte Retter began to suspect the minister was trying to ingratiate herself with John. On a few occasions, she overheard Camille tell him that she loved him. Indeed, the missionary had succeeded in gaining the old man's affection. Unbeknownst to his wife, he was already planning to increase Camille's meager weekly salary by a considerable sum. After a few days of growing suspicion, Charlotte asked to see Camille's identification and Social Security Card. When Camille refused to present these, Charlotte fired her.

Camille then contacted Steve Retter, John's son from a previous marriage, and told him stories of Charlotte's cruelty to his father. His stepmother was, she explained, a gold digger who didn't love his father and was only interested in his estate. Steve found Camille so persuasive that he agreed to let her stay in his own home. His perception of her only began to change when, late one night, she logged onto his wife's personal computer without permission.

One day Camille showed up at the dialysis clinic during one of John's appointments and demanded to see him, becoming angry when the clinic staff refused to grant her request. Charlotte Retter called the Sonoma County Sheriff's Department, which opened an investigation. Detective Mestrovich went to the home of Steve and Karen Retter to interview Sandra, who vehemently proclaimed that the detective had been duped by Charlotte Retter. Mrs. Retter was, Sandra claimed, possessed by the devil and jealous of Sandra's relationship with John.

Two days later Detectives Mestrovich and Spencer followed up with a second interview from which they concluded that Minister Bridewell was a confidence woman. Because she'd fallen under suspicion before she'd committed a crime, she was not placed under arrest. However, the dialysis clinic reported her to Adult Protective Services. And as Detective Spencer concluded his Incident Report:

> I believe that Camille Bridewell actively seeks people that she could ingratiate herself with and then take their property. I also believe that if Camille's actions were not found out, she would have succeeded in taking sizeable assets from John Retter.

CHAPTER 32
CAPE FEAR

The small, slender woman with long raven hair and pale skin had a way of fixing you with her big brown eyes. Her face bore the signs of age, but she was still sprightly. When she walked around seventy-seven-year-old Sue Moseley's house, barefoot, wearing a simple dress, she had a girlish way about her. Sue often marveled at how quietly she could move. Sometimes, while sitting at the kitchen table reading or preparing something to eat, Sue would turn her head and there she was!

"Where did you come from?" Sue would ask.

"I just thought I'd come down to say hello," she would reply, an impish grin on her face, her eyes twinkling. How, Sue wondered, did she walk down the stairs from her bedroom so noiselessly?

Her name was Camille Bowers, and she was an itinerant missionary who'd recently wandered into North Carolina. One day in the summer of 2006, a man driving through the little town of Pinewood saw her standing in front of the grocery store with a couple of tattered bags, apparently homeless. He stopped to ask her if she needed a lift somewhere.

"God bless you," she said in a voice that was oddly girlish for a woman her age (she appeared to be in her late fifties). She said she worked for evangelical charities that delivered food and medicine to needy people all over the world. She was in between missions, and in fact she did need a place to stay. Her story was strange, but her intense, friendly gaze and her smile—warm and intelligent with a hint of playfulness—evoked sympathy and trust.

And so, like the Good Samaritan in the Bible, the man offered to help her find a place to stay. He took her to an antique shop owned by a Baptist pastor. Surely the pastor knew someone who could use some company for a while, especially from such a compassionate Christian woman. He was right. Sue Moseley's sister Audrey—also an elderly lady who lived alone—sometimes browsed at the shop, and she welcomed Camille's company. As she was recovering from a recent eye surgery, she could use a live-in companion to help around the house (beyond the chores performed by her cleaning lady).

After living with Camille for a few weeks, Audrey began to think that there was something strange about her. She couldn't quite put her finger on it, but she felt it. Camille's candlelit communions with God, alone in her room, sipping red wine that symbolized the blood of Christ, seemed a bit too intense. There was something eerie about her mysticism, as though she wasn't so much worshipping God as attempting to harness His favor and power. Audrey also sensed a conspiratorial quality in Camille's relationship with the cleaning lady. It seemed that Camille had somehow seduced the weak-minded woman and formed a secret bond with her. Audrey perceived the two women were scheming—to do what, she couldn't say. And so, one day Audrey blurted out what her intuition told her, even though her intellect couldn't support it.

"I think you're a witch," she said. Camille acted insulted and withdrew to her room.

A few days later, Audrey and Camille visited Sue at her beautiful house in Saint James Plantation—a gated community near Southport. Like Audrey, Sue was convalescing from a recent health problem, in her case an abdominal surgery that had gone septic. Cured by antibiotics, she was still weak from the ordeal. To make matters worse, her daughter Nancy—recently divorced and living with her—had just been in a terrible car accident that had hospitalized her with severe trauma. Shortly after

Audrey and Camille arrived, Sue mentioned the accident and the difficult recovery that lay ahead for Nancy.

"The poor girl!" Camille explained. "I feel called upon to visit her in hospital. May I borrow your car?"

"Yes," Sue answered, too surprised to know how else to reply. Camille asked for directions and then drove off in Sue's car.

Upon her return about an hour later, she said she felt called to care for Nancy and Sue during this trying period in their lives before she embarked on her next mission to Africa.

"I could do the household chores and help you take care of Nancy in exchange for a place to stay," she suggested.

Sue was charmed by the proposal and accepted it without hesitation. Her sister Audrey didn't (at that time) express her suspicion that Camille was a witch, and Sue didn't share her sister's perception. At least not yet. On the contrary, her first impression of the missionary was that she was a perfect southern belle—as dainty, soft-spoken, and graceful as a woman could be. At church two days later, Sue's congregation at Bethel Baptist in Southport got the same impression. Camille's warm smile and attentiveness seemed to embrace everyone, and everyone was delighted by the new addition to their flock. After the service, Camille engaged the pastor in conversation about the gospel he'd cited in his homily, and he was impressed by her knowledge of it.

Like many people in Brunswick County, Sue Moseley believed in the gospels. They weren't just stories about people who lived thousands of years ago, far away from North Carolina. They were the living truth. When the preachers at church or on the local radio stations recounted the teachings of Christ and his disciples, she could picture them and hear their voices.

Hope, redemption, salvation—concepts that appeal to anyone who has ever seriously contemplated the facts of suffering and death—are especially appealing to people for whom life is often hard and distressing. Until well after the Second World War, the coastal lowlands of Brunswick County North Carolina were a place of rural poverty, oppressed by sweltering heat in the summer and blasted by hurricanes in the fall. Southport lies directly across a narrow sound from Cape Fear, named by sailors afraid of running aground its lee shore that projects into the Atlantic.

At seventy-seven, with her recent surgery and complications, Sue couldn't help feeling a little afraid of what lay ahead for her. Her sons Neil and Jimmy occasionally expressed their fear that she was getting too old and frail to live alone, and they made no secret of their belief that she should sell her house and move into an assisted living facility in Charlotte. But Sue loved her home, and she had worked hard to acquire it. In 1949, she had gone to nursing school in her native Richmond, Virginia and specialized in the rehabilitation of injured workers. Her house was the fruit of her many years of labor and her marriage, and she wasn't about to sell it. Since 1995, when she'd moved in, Southport's beauty and mild winters had drawn wealthy northerners in search of a retirement or vacation home, and housing prices had shot up. By 2006, Sue's property with a lovely view of the Inland Waterway was worth a small fortune.

Though determined to maintain her independence, she was grateful for Camille's help with chores, grocery shopping, and cooking. The missionary was also excellent company, enlivening the house with her cheerful spirit. She often sang and did little dances in the kitchen while she prepared meals. Sue found her delightful. In the evenings they sat on the porch, and Camille regaled her with colorful stories about her wanderings. Since her husband had died of cancer twenty years earlier, she'd chosen a life of austerity and service, even though she'd inherited a fortune from him. For years she'd wandered the world's poor regions, taking care of hungry and sick children. She wasn't afraid of the discomforts, dangers, and diseases of the undeveloped world. She loved the adventure and spoke of exotic people, landscapes, and animals. Often, she'd witnessed miracles, such as the time she'd encountered a poor woman in Somalia who'd been born with no eyes or even eye sockets. For weeks Camille had prayed for her, and then one morning the woman walked into the village with a lovely set of eyes.

Astonishing was her knowledge of the Bible. Sue often read the Bible, but her knowledge of the Good Book was a fraction of Camille's. It wasn't only that she spent so much time studying her well-worn copy, whose margins she had filled with notes. She also had an extraordinary memory. Upon hearing an anecdote or the name of a person or place, she never forgot it, and could later instantly recall it.

Though Camille sometimes fasted and could go for several days without food, she wasn't altogether abstinent. She had a weakness for expensive red wines, which she often drank at sunset. Sue marveled at how she could sink an entire bottle without appearing to get drunk. And good Lord was she interested in men! Every morning when she came down from her bedroom on the second floor, she was already beautifully made up, and she was conspicuously friendly to most of the men she encountered. She seemed to take special fancy to Ron, the security guard at St. James, and often lingered at the gate to chat with him with that winning way of hers. Twice while running errands in Sue's car, she ran out of gas and called Ron for help. He was happy to oblige, bringing a gas can—enough to get her to the filling station. Sue wondered if maybe it was a ruse to be alone with him, away from his post.

In a similar fashion she seemed to go out of her way to talk to some of the more prominent men in the church congregation, and she often asked Sue about a particular man. What sort of character did he have and what did he do for a living? Whenever she got curious about someone, she researched him on the internet, often staying awake late into the night. After a while, some of the women in the congregation revised their view of Camille. Her initial interest in everyone had, with time, shifted to a focus on the men. She was, it seemed, an aggressive flirt.

She also seemed to take special interest in Sue's son Jimmy, who lived in Charlotte but occasionally visited his mother. He too found Camille charming, and he was glad his mother had a live-in companion, but he felt the missionary came on a bit strong. During one of his visits, he woke up in the middle of the night and saw her standing next to his bed in her nightgown. Coming out of sleep he was startled by her unexpected presence, and she appeared to be staring at him.

"I thought you might like some company," she said.

"No thank you, I'm quite tired," he replied.

Jimmy didn't want to make trouble for Camille and therefore didn't tell his mother about the incident. Camille was, after all, still a relatively young and attractive woman, so it was only natural that she was interested in men. Clearly his mother enjoyed her company and valued her help around the house. Sue was a tolerant person and considered Camille's minor vices to signify little compared to her dedication to Christ. Indeed, Camille was sorely disappointed when her organization cancelled her mission to Africa because of a cholera outbreak.

"I'm not afraid of cholera! Tending to the sick is what we're supposed to do!" she exclaimed. Sue was glad she was going to stay for another couple of months.

The trouble began after Nancy was released from hospital. Soon it became apparent that she'd developed a dependency on the post-operation pain medication she received, and her addiction seemed to change her personality. She was increasingly out of sorts, moody, and disoriented. And then, in a shocking breach of trust, she wrote a check on Sue's account at CVS pharmacy.

Camille emphasized to Sue that Nancy had indeed grown untrustworthy, and that as tragic as her condition was, such behavior was intolerable. Drug users, Camille explained, are entirely focused on acquiring drugs, and will do anything to get them, no matter how immoral.

"I fear that Nancy and her boyfriend are scheming to get your money," she explained.

A little while later, Sue received a notice from the Social Security Administration that someone calling from her phone number had recently attempted to change the bank account receiving her monthly Social Security payment but had been unable to provide her passcode. Suspecting Nancy, Sue called the Brunswick County Sheriff's Department. Detective Marty Folding visited her while Nancy was away, and he placed a recording device on her phone. However, before he had a chance to follow up, Sue concluded (on the advice of Camille) that Nancy couldn't be trusted to live under the same roof. And so, as heartbreaking as it was, Sue asked her daughter to leave and find another place to stay.

With Nancy's departure, and with Sue's three sons living in distant cities, Camille became Sue's primary social contact and confidant, doing much of the cooking and cleaning, and serving as Sue's secretary, picking up and sorting the mail, driving her to Wilmington to stock up on household supplies, and giving her little daily reminders about her schedule.

Prior to her car accident, Nancy had divorced and vacated the home she'd shared with her husband. During her marriage, she'd accumulated many possessions, including antiques she'd inherited from her deceased father and gifts from her mother. These she had put in a storage facility in Wilmington. Sue had agreed to pay for the storage until Nancy found her own place. In January, Camille advised Sue to stop paying for the storage unit. As Camille pointed out, it was a significant monthly expense, and it wasn't Sue's responsibility. Nancy couldn't afford it, so one day she called her mother and explained that she and a friend with a truck were headed to the warehouse to remove the contents. When she and her friend arrived, they were surprised to find Camille waiting for them with the final month's bill for the storage unit.

"I told your mother not to pay this because it's not her responsibility," she said. "You need to pay it before you can remove your things." As Camille had evidently expected, Nancy didn't have any money. Fortunately, her friend did, and was able to settle the bill.

"After we load this stuff, we'll pass by my mom's house to pick up some clothes in my closet and my silver dinner service," Nancy said to Camille. But then, when Nancy and her friend arrived at Sue's house, they found her clothes sitting on the front porch in trash bags. Camille had already packed them up and wouldn't let Nancy into the house to see her mother. Notably, her silver service was not among the bagged items. Camille told her she could come back and get it on another occasion, but at that moment her mother was so upset that Nancy needed to leave right then and there.

Sue was indeed upset, but not only with Nancy. In principle she understood Camille's insistence that she be firm with her daughter and cease enabling her destructive habits. And yet, increasingly Sue perceived that Camille was too harsh, unforgiving, and extreme. Above all, she seemed to be totally lacking empathy for Sue's maternal pain.

"What if this happened to your child?" Sue asked her. "Would you really be so tough with one of your children?" Sue's question was part of her shifting perception of the missionary. It seemed odd how Sandra strictly forbade Sue from entering her bedroom, even though it was part of Sue's house. Once Sue walked into her room to talk to her, and she raised her voice and said, "Please don't come in here! This is my private space!" This seemed like an overreaction, and it gave Sue the impression that Camille was hiding something. She also insisted that all lights in the house be turned off at night. This went against Sue's habit of burning a light in the living room, near the entrance, but Camille wanted the house to be in total darkness after bedtime.

Sue began to get the impression there was something mysterious about the missionary, and it made her feel uneasy. One morning Camille offered to take charge of her daily medication regimen.

"To make sure you remember to take all of them properly," she said.

"That's not necessary," Sue replied. "You know I was a nurse for many years." The proposal wasn't alarming, but it still didn't quite sit right with Sue. Shortly after this incident, Camille announced that she would depart on a missionary trip to India at the beginning of February but planned to return to Southport at its conclusion. Indeed, she'd grown so fond of Southport that she'd decided to acquire her own house in the community. Sue and Camille visited a local realtor named Jack Vereene. Camille told him she wanted a big place with enough rooms to house all six of her children for family reunions. When they weren't visiting, she would use the house for missionary activities such as teaching the local people organic farming methods.

Mr. Vereene had a listing for a six-bedroom, plantation style house right on the Intracoastal Waterway for $2.7 million. Camille said it was just what she was looking for.

"Would you like me to put you in touch with a lender?" Mr. Vereene asked.

"That won't be necessary," she replied. "I'll pay with cash."

Mr. Vereen thought there was something odd about the missionary. She insisted she wanted the house and would pay cash for it, but she repeatedly dodged the question of earnest money. It wasn't unusual for prospective buyers to fantasize about owning a house they couldn't afford, but the discrepancy between the missionary's assurances and her lack of anything to show she was qualified seemed extreme. And generally, there was just something strange about the woman and her relationship with Mrs. Moseley. Who was Camille Bowers?

He did a web search of "Camille Bowers Missionary" and on the first page of the search results he saw a 2004 *Dallas Observer* report titled "Seductress of the Saints" about a woman named Camille Bridewell who had, for years, wandered the country, introducing herself as a Christian missionary who was in between trips abroad. With her charm and extraordinary knowledge of the Bible, she had ingratiated herself with vulnerable people. As the reporter, Glenna Whitley, memorably put it, "She seeks out the devout, the compassionate, and the weak–people starved for love, sex, companionship or a connection with God and the supernatural." Under the guise of needing temporary lodging, she had then moved in with her successive victims and gained access to their credit cards and bank accounts. When her victims realized they'd been deceived, Camille would disappear and move to a different state.

Though several people had told their stories to Glenna Whitley, few had reported Camille to the police. Considering themselves lucky to be rid of her, they'd reckoned it was best just to get on with their lives. It had also seemed unlikely that the police would be able to find her even if they tried. However, in the year 2004, detectives at the Sonoma County Sheriff's Department had investigated her for trying to scam a ninety-two-year-old man after moving in with him to serve as his home care provider.

About halfway through the report, Vereene came to a passage detailing how, in 2004, Camille had tried to acquire a $3.7 million property in rural Marin County by fraudulent means, including a forged letter from a financial advisor on Morgan Stanley letterhead. Most alarming was the report's repeated references to the fact that the missionary Camille Bridewell, AKA Sandra Bridewell, was suspected of murdering her third husband. The *Dallas Observer* report wasn't illustrated with photos of Sandra Bridewell, but a web search for her name led Mr. Vereene to the famous 1987 *D Magazine* article illustrated with several images of her. Though the photos had been taken when she was much younger, there could be no doubt that Sandra Bridewell was the woman living with Sue Moseley who called herself Camille Bowers. Upon seeing this, Mr. Vereene called the security guard at St. James Plantation.

CHAPTER 33

NEMESIS

Brunswick County Sheriff's Department Detective Jayne Todd investigated the identity and activities of Sue Moseley's home caretaker. After speaking with the security guard at St. James Plantation, she read the 1987 *D Magazine* article "The Black Widow" and the 2004 *Dallas Observer* article "Seductress of the Saints." She then called Glenna Whitley, who provided a thorough briefing on Sandra's modus operandi. Over the years, Glenna had become a clearinghouse of information about the missionary. Her periodic reports, easily accessible online, had been an albatross around Sandra's neck, often exposing her identity and true colors to those who'd encountered her. In so doing, Glenna had spared numerous people from enduring incalculable psychological and financial damage, and it's possible she had even saved lives.

Her reporting on Sandra began in 1989, when she got a job at *D Magazine* and inherited Skip Hollandsworth's "Black Widow" file following his departure to *Texas Monthly*. One morning in 1991, during an editorial meeting, the receptionist walked into the conference room and told Glenna that an urgent phone call had just come in from a man who desperately wanted to talk to someone about Hollandsworth's feature. Glenna left the meeting and took the call in her office. The man explained that he was a resident of Tucson but was visiting friends in Dallas. That morning, on the nightstand in their guest bedroom, he saw the *D Magazine* cover story about Sandra.

"Is it true?" he asked frantically.

"Skip Hollandworth is an excellent reporter, and the piece was thoroughly vetted by an attorney," Glenna replied. "Mrs. Bridewell has never threatened legal action against us."

"My God," he said, and then explained how he'd met this woman, who called herself Camille, at the swimming pool in his condominium. A whirlwind romance had ensued, and now she was living with him.

"With you, as in your condominium?" Glenna asked.

"Yes, what should I do?" the man asked.

"Tell her to leave," Glenna said. "As you can see from our report, living with her is risky." The man said he would indeed ask Sandra to vacate his home. Later Glenna learned that this had prompted a dramatic scene in which Sandra refused to leave. She holed herself up in one of the condo's bedrooms, called her daughter Kathryn—who was also living in Tucson at the time—to whom she claimed her new boyfriend was threatening her with violence. Kathryn armed herself with a frying pan and went to the condominium, where a standoff was taking place between her mother—hiding in a locked bedroom—and the condo's owner, who was telling her to come out of the room and leave. A confrontation ensued in which Kathryn menaced the man with the frying pan and then persuaded her mother to leave.

Just as Glenna had advised the Tucson man eighteen years earlier, she emphasized to Detective Jayne Todd that Sandra was potentially a mortal danger. Jayne then called Sue Moseley's son Jimmy and told him she was getting a warrant to search his mother's house. Sue was staying with Jimmy in Charlotte while Camille the missionary was on a trip to India, so the timing was ideal. Camille's room was on the second floor of Mrs. Moseley's house. The room contained little of interest; however, set into one of its walls was a closet door that led to a storage room in the house's eaves, where Jayne found piles of mail addressed to Minister Camille Bowers and to Mrs. Sue Moseley. Most notable was a Bank of America statement addressed to Sue.

By a stroke of luck, Camille had given Ron, the security guard, a photograph of herself—wearing a V-neck sweater that showed her lovely white skin—as a Christmas gift. Equipped with this photograph and the Bank of America statement, Jayne visited the merchants at which the charges had been made. Three of the shopkeepers remembered a slender brunette wearing a colorful long skirt and headscarf that looked sort of Indian, which gave them the impression she was a hippie. To one of them she mentioned she was a Christian missionary about to embark on a trip to India. After hearing their descriptions, Jayne showed them the photograph of Sandra, and they identified her as the woman who'd made the charges.

Jayne told fellow Detective Marty Folding about her investigation, which reminded him that he'd never retrieved the recording device he'd placed on Mrs. Moseley's phone a few months earlier. At the time, it was her daughter Nancy who'd been under suspicion, and Camille had been present during his visit. Luckily, she hadn't seen him mount the device on the phone in Mrs. Moseley's bedroom. Marty and Jayne obtained the recordings from the phone company and listened to them. The first call was of Camille talking with a friend to whom she said, "It went very well with the detective." The next noteworthy call was from Ron the security guard checking on Sue, as he had seen some cars that he didn't recognize pulling into her driveway the day before and he hadn't seen any lights in her house that night.

"The first one was a detective," Sue said. "It's about Nancy. They're all afraid that there's going to be something violent with someone around this house, so they're warning us to just be very, very careful." Then there was a call from Sue to a flooring company in which she explained that she'd just installed a new burglar alarm and would need to be at home when the carpenter arrived. As Jayne later discovered, Sandra had encouraged Sue to install the alarm to prevent Nancy and her boyfriend from breaking in.

Following this was a long conversation between Sue and another elderly lady she called "Granny." Granny wanted to make a new quilt, but her scissors were too dull, so Sue volunteered to bring over some sharp ones. Sue then spoke happily about her new puppy.

"His name is Joshua!" she said proudly.

"Well God bless him," Granny said. "That's a good name!" Both ladies laughed.

"Yeah, sometimes I can't remember his name and I think of the walls falling down," Sue said, alluding to Joshua's account of Jericho's fortified walls collapsing by an act of God.

"Well tell me something, where is Nancy?" Granny asked.

"Honey, I don't know." Sue then went on to give an account of Nancy's problems and conflicts with the law because of her addiction.

"I just can't do this anymore," she said, her voice quivering. "Camille and I thought we might run by your house for a little while."

"Well darling I'll be right here. Be glad to cry with you."

"I've done enough of that. I went to church, and I'd heard all this stuff and I just broke down while we were singing and I just got up and left."

"Well honey you can't help it and it's good for you."

After this call, Sandra made the most remarkable call on the tape—to the Social Security Administration's office in Wilmington. She reached a recorded voice, which instructed "Please tell me briefly the reason for your call."

"Automatic draft payments, change of bank," Sandra's voice replied.

The battery died on the recording device before the call ended, so it was only later that a Social Security Administration Investigator was able to discover what had happened. Sandra, and not Nancy, had placed the first call to try to change the receiving bank of Sue's social security payments, but had been unable to do so because she didn't know the correct password. However, after Nancy moved out, Sandra set up Sue with an online banking account. For her passcode, Sue proposed the name of one of her deceased dogs, and she mentioned to Sandra that she *always* used the name of one of her deceased dogs for a passcode. This prompted Sandra to take another crack at calling Social Security to change the receiving bank account. However, the passcode for her Social Security account was named after a different deceased dog than the one Sue had proposed for her online banking account. And so, Sandra's second attempt at rerouting Sue's Social Security benefit was also thwarted.

Jayne thought about the perfidy of it. Using an alias, Sandra had presented herself as a pious servant of God to gain Miss Sue's trust, then she exploited Miss Sue's frailty, then she exploited the disaster of Nancy's car accident and substance abuse, and then she alienated Miss Sue from her own child by painting Nancy as a lost soul, given to ruthless greed. In fact, it was she, Sandra Camille Powers, who was the predator—the most dreadful wolf in sheep's clothing that Jayne had ever encountered.

Jayne obtained arrest warrants for the credit card charges and working together with Officer Harry Inch of the Charlotte Mecklenburg PD, she set up a sting to arrest Sandra upon her return to Charlotte from India. However, a few days later, a meeting was convened in the office of Brunswick County Sheriff Ron Hewitt, attended by DA Rex Gore and Assistant DA Brooke Leland to review the evidence. Both the Sherriff and the DA doubted that Jayne's discoveries warranted arresting Sandra. The $2,000 sum was small potatoes, and her entire case hinged on the alleged victim's assurance on the telephone that she hadn't authorized the charges. District Attorney Gore didn't think it was enough for his office to pursue the matter.

"You can't just let her go!" Jayne exclaimed, breaking into tears. "She'll keep victimizing others like Miss Sue, and next time she may do far worse before she's detected." With these words, she rose and hurried out of Sheriff Hewitt's office. A few minutes later, Assistant DA Leland appeared in her office.

"I agree with you, and I went to bat for you," she said. "If you can persuade Mrs. Moseley to make a recorded, in-person statement that she didn't authorize the charges, you can keep the warrants and proceed as planned."

Jayne understood the bureaucratic nature of law enforcement, with its procedures that left little room for personal feelings of justice. The determining factor in how property crimes were handled was the sum of money stolen, not the moral quality of the transgression. Sandra's web of lies and deceit, her feigning of affection to gain trust and exploit vulnerable people—these weren't punishable offenses unto themselves, but the means to committing them. So far, all that Jayne could prove was that Sandra was a petty grifter who'd made about $2,000 of unauthorized charges on Sue Moseley's credit card by representing herself as Sue and forging her name. However, her attempt to reroute the Social Security payments showed that her intent was to plunder far more, and that her scheme may have included becoming an heir to Sue's estate.

Jayne's sense of justice was reminiscent of the old chivalric code of combatting villains as a way of life, and not merely as a profession. This code found popular modern expression in *The Lone Ranger* and other stories about lawmen on the American frontier. She'd been raised in the Christian faith, and though she wasn't overtly religious in her manners and speech, she believed in the struggle of good vs. evil. She'd once arrested and jailed her brother for burglary, and unbeknownst to her boss (and cousin) Sheriff Ron Hewitt, she was assisting an internal affairs investigation of his abusive and possibly criminal conduct. Truly she was never one to turn a blind eye.

Sherriff Hewitt's increasing megalomania offered one clear advantage with respect to Jayne's investigation of Sandra. Once he realized that the subject was a figure of great media interest, he changed his tune about pursuing her. Her forthcoming arrest would generate great publicity, and he quickly warmed up to being in the spotlight as the lawman that finally put the notorious Black Widow of Highland Park away. Once he consented to serving the arrest warrants on Sandra, he gave Jayne unlimited time and resources to work the case.

The next resistance Jayne had to overcome was from two of Sue Moseley's sons, who wanted to drop the matter because of the unwelcome media attention and the stress it was creating for their mother. Jayne knew from studying Sandra's past that the families of other victims had drawn the same conclusion, which had enabled her to escape unscathed and move on to her next victim.

"She needs to be stopped now," Jayne said to Sue's sons. "She will be prosecuted even without your blessing."

Jayne sought no glory for herself, knowing full well that if she made her case against Sandra, it would be Ron who gave the press interviews. She was also happy to help detectives in other counties and states to make a case against Sandra for crimes the wandering missionary had committed in their jurisdictions. Jayne contacted potential witnesses in South Carolina, Georgia, and Arkansas, and then passed on the information to local agencies.

During the last week of February, Sandra called Jimmy's house and spoke to Sue. She implied that she was calling from India. In fact, she was calling on a Blackberry phone (that she'd purchased using Sue's credit card) from Rock Hill, South Carolina, just twenty-six miles south of Jimmy's house in Charlotte.

"Did you save a lot of souls?" Sue asked.

"Oh yes, mission accomplished!"

Sandra said she would arrive in Charlotte on March 2 and would be happy to catch a taxi. Jimmy proposed meeting at Dean & Delucca café, as he would already be in that neighborhood for an earlier appointment. And so, the trap was set.

At the appointed time, Jimmy sat at a table in the coffee shop, reading the paper. Near the entrance sat a group of Charlotte plainclothes police officers posing as customers. Uniformed officers assigned to serve the warrant were waiting outside in unmarked cars. Like Jimmy, the undercover officers occasionally glanced at the front door, waiting for Camille to arrive. She was characteristically late, and Jimmy's mind began to wander. He then felt a tap on his shoulder and turned to see Camille, standing next to his table, smiling at him. Her sudden appearance—having entered through the café's back service entrance—scared the devil out of him, and he almost jumped out of his seat.

"Oh, hello Camille," he said loudly, hoping to draw the attention of the cops who were looking at the front entrance and still hadn't seen her.

"Hello Jimmy," she said. "How are you?"

"Very well," he said, folding and rolling his newspaper. "Please sit down and have a coffee." Finally, a cop glanced in his direction, and Jimmy gestured with the newspaper towards Camille. The officer spoke on a concealed radio to the officers outside, and they stormed into the shop and surrounded her while Officer Harry Inch read her Miranda rights. For over a quarter of a century, Sandra Camille Powers had been suspected of committing multiple crimes. Now, for the first time in her life, she was arrested and put into handcuffs. A local news crew had caught wind of her impending arrest and captured footage of her being walked out of Dean & Delucca and placed in a police car.

"Do you wish to make a statement?" a reporter asked her.

"I know my rights and I want a lawyer," she said. At Jimmy Moseley's house, Sue took great satisfaction in watching the news footage of Sandra's arrest. She too had read the *D Magazine* and *Dallas Observer* pieces. To think that Camille had presented herself as a devoted servant of the Lord to deceive and steal—truly it was the height of wickedness.

CHAPTER 34

THE BRUNSWICK
COUNTY JAIL

Jayne stood behind the check-in counter of the Brunswick County Jail and watched Sandra as she was brought into the facility. Her appearance starkly contrasted with the images of the girlish looking bride that Jayne had just seen in the *D Magazine* report. It wasn't just that she was twenty-three years older. Her face and body were gaunt, as though she were undernourished. Her personal belongings were also strikingly incongruous with how she was depicted in the magazine. In addition to her large handbag and green suitcase, she had two large, stuffed trash sacks. The elegant Dallas socialite had become a bag lady.

"We need to inventory your possessions," Jayne said to her. "Please give me your handbag."

"You can't go through my handbag," Sandra said.

"Yes, I can. Please hand it to me or the jailers will take it from you." Sandra complied, but objected again when Jayne emptied the purse's contents onto the counter.

"What are you doing?"

"Inventorying your possessions and collecting evidence," Jayne said, holding up a JC Penny Rewards Mastercard and a Peebles dress shop card, both bearing the name Sue S. Moseley. She glanced from the credit cards to Sandra, whose face became impassive, her eyes staring at her antagonist with cold fury. In Jayne's twelve years in law enforcement, she had dealt with aggressive male offenders, including a spectacular psychopath, and she had grown accustomed to their intimidation tactics. But never had she come face to face with such a piercing gaze, and she felt the hair on the back of her neck stand up. She thought of her grandmother Lena, who'd often told her that when it came to assessing people, she should always listen to her gut.

"Your gut will always tell you when you meet an evil person," she'd said. "Don't question it; just get away." Right then and there, Jayne felt morally certain that Sandra had murdered her third husband.

"I understand that you didn't always call yourself Camille Bowers," Jayne said. "You used to go by the name Sandra Bridewell, didn't you?"

"Bridewell was my husband's name. He died in 1982."

"For a while you went by the name Sandra Rehrig, after your third husband, Alan Rehrig."

"I don't know who that is."

"Really? You don't remember your third husband?"

"I don't know what you're talking about."

"What about your first husband, David Stegall?"

"No. My husband was Robert Bridewell."

"Well, I just spoke with your daughter Emily, and she thinks that her father was your first husband, David Stegall."

"You spoke with Emily?" Sandra said, her eyes lighting up.

"Yes." The news seemed to lift her spirits.

"Please hand me your Bible," Jayne said, referring to the book that Sandra was holding in her hands.

"You can't take my Bible," Sandra said.

"Yes, I can. You can hand it to me, or the jailers will." Sandra handed over her Bible. Jayne flipped through it and was astonished by what she saw. Between the Holy Book's pages were inserted glossy color advertisements of fancy cars and handbags and stately looking houses from architectural magazines. She had also scribbled marginalia on many of its pages and altered many of its passages by scratching out certain words and replacing them with her own.

"I'm going to need to book your Bible as evidence. We will issue you another one during your stay." Again, Sandra protested, again to no avail.

After the inventory was complete, Jayne escorted her to the jail's common room. As they reached the entrance, she stopped and turned to Sandra.

"I will go ahead and register you to receive calls from your daughter Emily." Upon hearing this, Sandra reached out and touched Jayne's elbow. It was a move she'd often made over the years to create a feeling of intimacy and trust, and it had often been highly effective. With Jayne it had the opposite effect, instantly giving her the heebie-jeebies.

"I'll let you know when to expect Emily's call," Jayne said, reflexively pulling her arm away and opening the entrance to the women's unit. Sandra entered what would be her grim home for the coming months.

In fact, Emily had told Jayne she wanted nothing to do with her mother. For as she revealed—and as was confirmed by the Social Security Administration—Sandra had, years earlier, stolen her social security number, obtained credit cards in her name, and then destroyed her credit. That a mother would do such a thing to her child was incomprehensible. Jayne was herself a mother of two children, aged seventeen and twenty, and the mere thought of exploiting and harming them struck her as the height of depravity.

Another notable item found in Sandra's purse was a foreclosure notice for Sue Moseley's house in St. James Plantation. As Jayne discovered, Sue's monthly mortgage payments were automatically drawn from an investment account her deceased husband had set up for her. Three months earlier, Sandra had changed the receiving bank account from Sue's mortgage lender to a Wells Fargo bank account in Sue's name and to which Sandra had access. The result was that Sue's mortgage was in arrears and the lender was about to foreclose on her house. Jayne called Jimmy Moseley and asked him to check Sue's mailbox for additional notices, and there he found the Second Notice. He then made the three delinquent payments, thereby saving his mother's house from foreclosure.

In yet another strange twist, Jayne discovered that Sandra had, for months, maintained a second residence at the house of Venida (the cleaning lady of Sue's sister Audrey) in Rock Hill, South Carolina. She had stayed there the entire time of her purported trip to India. Her passport had expired in 2005, which marked the end of her international travel. A search of Sandra's room turned up additional credit cards and bank statements that belonged to Sue Moseley. During her sojourns in Rock Hill, Sandra had dined out, shopped, and gone to beauty spas under the assumed named Camille Moseley, though she continued signing the credit card receipts with the name Sue Moseley.

CHAPTER 35

THE MEANING
OF MALICE

Shortly after Jayne placed Sandra's possessions in her office, the Sheriff's Department cleaning lady pronounced that the stuffed trash sacks contained pure evil, and that she wouldn't clean Jayne's office until they were removed. This was remarkable because she had no means of knowing to whom they belonged.

"Why do you think they're full of evil?" Jayne asked her.

"Because I feel it every time I walk past your door," she replied. Normally Jayne would have dismissed such talk as ridiculous superstition, but in this case, she wondered if Sandra had something like an evil aura that was conspicuous to some people but imperceptible to others. Generally, it seemed that women were far quicker to see it than men. Gloria Rehrig, the *Dallas Observer* columnist Glenna Whitley, and the P.I. Carrie Huskinson all perceived Sandra to be an odious predator.

Men, on the other hand, were susceptible to Sandra's manipulative charm, and Jayne was opposed to male detectives being left alone with her. If any man in the department could handle her, it was Marty Folding—a great detective and a rock-solid guy—and he was given the assignment of interviewing Sandra. Still, at times Jayne worried that even Marty would fall under her spell. He was the first to admit that she was persuasive. In fact, she was the most persuasive suspect he'd ever met. She perfectly presented herself as a helpless and bewildered woman who'd loved Sue Moseley with all her heart. One day she told Marty a hypothetical motive for why Sue had turned against her and made false accusations.

Back in January, getting all that stuff together for Nancy, and Sue would get really angry. And she'd say, 'What if this happened to your child? What if this was one of your children? What if you were in jail? You were in prison? ... And she was just coming at me about that. ...Even when I told her that it was the best way for Nancy to get help. And so Donna, a friend of mine, who ... she's a dog groomer, she knew Sue, that's how I met her. She had this dream one night. And it was Sue in a room, more haggard looking, and more aged looking I guess than she is, and that she was coming at me like this. And Donna said it was like a warning dream, and it was like Sue wanted to do me harm ... And she imparted it to the Lord because she didn't understand what the meaning of the dream was, and the interpretation was that it was the spirit of malice. ... The Lord had shown her that it was ... a family issue, about malice. She didn't really know all the meanings of malice, so she looked up the meanings and she wrote them down from the dictionary ... and she gave that to Sue and we prayed about that. But malice meaning, 'wanting to do harm or wanting someone to suffer like they had suffered.' So, I thought at that time that it might be directed at me. ... Anyway, still, I love her, I love the family, and I want the best for all of them.

Marty knew that Sandra had taken a grain of truth about her disagreement with Sue and spun a big lie around it. All the same, she told the story with such amazing emotional affect that he reckoned she was either the greatest actress in the world or she herself believed what she was saying.

Marty pretended to be sympathetic to her plight in the hope she would slip up and reveal something or contradict herself. While Jayne was pitiless, Marty was kind, gentle, and all ears. Listening to Sandra, he often had to remind himself of her long history of suspicious conduct and the fact that she remained the sole suspect for the murder of her third husband. He'd familiarized himself with the circumstances and read the autopsy report. Sitting with Sandra in the interrogation room, looking at her feminine face and listening to her oddly girlish voice, it was eerie for him to ponder the possibility that she'd shot the young man at close range. He wondered if she would do the same to him if she had a pistol and knew she could get away with it. Intuitively he sensed that she would.

During her time in Southport, Sandra had made friends with a few people who kept the faith that she'd been unfairly arrested. They believed that Sue Moseley had, because of cognitive decline, forgotten that she had authorized Sandra to make the disputed charges. Shortly after her arrest, Sandra called a woman from the county jail to request certain products (especially bottled water) and to ask favors. Amid sobbing fits, she made assurances of her innocence, but also of her belief that there was divine purpose in her arrest. For as hard as her mission was, she knew that the Lord had sent her to the jailhouse to save souls.

Quickly she assembled a following of women to whom she preached in the day room. She had a rival preacher—another inmate named Martha Farmer who'd recently murdered a rival for her boyfriend's affection. Martha didn't possess Sandra's knowledge of the Bible, but she had a natural aggression and strength that gave her a leadership aura. Sandra's flock consisted mostly of women arrested for drug possession. Martha appealed to a tougher set whose criminal behavior wasn't purely a function of addiction. The two women frequently argued about the meaning of Jesus's statements to his disciples and of his Parables. Occasionally when the debate got heated, Martha turned ad hominem.

"You're a phony minister and a murderer," she said. "I know a murderer when I see one."

CHAPTER 36

"GOD BLESS YOU, SANDRA."

One day Jayne purchased a greeting card for Sandra. In it she wrote "God bless you, Sandra" and signed it "Alan R." The card was delivered to Sandra in a manila envelope containing other mail. Jayne watched her on the closed-circuit video as she opened the package in her cell. When she read the card from "Alan R." she flew into an apoplectic rage. In a voice that dropped an octave, she screamed curses while she tore the greeting card into tiny pieces that she flushed down the toilet.

About a week later, Jayne did the same trick with a copy of Sandra and Alan Rehrig's wedding certificate, witnessed and signed by Pastor Clayton Bell. This time the fury unleashed was even more spectacular. For what seemed like an eternity, Sandra tore and tore again the piece of paper until it was reduced to tiny specs, which she then gathered and again flushed down the toilet. It seemed that a demon dwelled in her who emerged during these irate episodes.

Jayne was horrified and fascinated, and her investigation came to occupy most of her waking hours. Often, she stayed up late at night, after her husband had gone to sleep, sifting through the documents in Sandra's possession when she was arrested. Sandra was an obsessive-compulsive writer of notes, scribbling them on random scraps of paper, post-it sticky notes, and ruled binders.

Another one of Jayne's projects was studying Sandra's Bible, trying to decipher the meaning of the marginalia and what it revealed about the author's mind. Sandra had mentioned to Sue Moseley that the Bible had belonged to her late husband, Robert Bridewell, and that she'd carried it with her ever since his death in 1982. Many of the notations were so small they could only be read with a magnifying glass. A common theme throughout her writings was her desire for money and possessions, and her belief the Bible was a talisman for obtaining them. Many of the passages that spoke of rewards for the faithful were altered to designate Sandra as the recipient. The glossy images of high-end consumer products, inserted into the pages, were the specific benefactions she sought. She really seemed to believe that God—the Creator of the Universe—could be induced to bless her with a champagne-colored Lexus and a pair of Jimmy Choo shoes.

Jayne reckoned the Bible would be of great interest to psychologists, but she could find nothing in the marginalia that seemed to hint at criminal acts or penance for them. The Bible did, however, contain one thing that was of possible forensic value. Across one of the pages was what appeared to be blood spatter, apparently deposited as the book was lying wide open. Jayne imagined a scenario in which Sandra sat in the passenger seat of a car with the Bible open on her lap, pretending to read it. With the Holy Book still open in her lap, or perhaps placed open on the dashboard, she could have drawn a pistol from her purse and shot someone sitting in the driver's seat, causing back-spatter onto the Bible's page. It was a hypothetical idea, but Jayne reckoned the substance should be analyzed. If it was indeed blood, perhaps it would yield a DNA sample, which could be compared with a sample of Alan Rehrig's DNA or that of his mother and brother.

CHAPTER 37
PASTOR YOUNCE TO THE RESCUE

Around the time that Jayne was analyzing Sandra's Bible, an evangelical minister named Lee Younce was returning from a retreat in the Grand Canyon to his home in Marion, North Carolina. Passing a newsstand in the Phoenix airport, he saw a tabloid newspaper with a front-page story about Sandra's arrest. Perusing it, he saw she was a Christian missionary who'd purportedly done work in Third World countries to feed and care for orphaned children. This made her a kindred spirit, as Mr. Younce himself ran a Christian charity called Operation Feed-a-Child, and he too had had a brush with the law that had resulted in a fraud conviction in Florida. As he would later proclaim, the Lord drew him to the tabloid newspaper, and gave him the mission to rescue Sandra from her unjust incarceration.

And so, shortly after his return from the Grand Canyon, he drove to Southport, retained an attorney, and petitioned the court to lower Sandra's bond to a sum he could afford. A bond reduction hearing was scheduled, which prompted Jayne to redouble her efforts. As luck would have it, she had already found evidence of additional crimes. Most notably, Sandra had cancelled Sue's Met Life insurance policy. Because

Sue had made premium payments for years, the cancellation entitled her to a $1,460 payment. Sandra, who had assumed the job of retrieving the mail every day, intercepted the check. She had then gone to Sue's local Bank of America branch and performed a clever trick.

Over four months, she had often accompanied Sue to the bank to make deposits and withdrawals, subtly presenting herself to the tellers as Sue's caretaker and advisor. Sandra would do most of the talking, but on a couple of occasions, Sue asked the teller about her recent bank statements, as she hadn't received them. To this, Sandra had quickly interjected, "Yes you have! They're in the big jar on your desk." Over time, the tellers got the impression that Sandra was completely in charge of Sue financial affairs. She reinforced this impression by sometimes going to the bank alone and making deposits for Sue. On these occasions she invariably said something to the teller about Sue's memory declining. Thus, when Sandra presented herself at the bank with the Met Life check, endorsed with Sue Moseley's signature, she acted as though she were cashing it for Sue. She did the same trick two other times with checks from Sue's personal account, signed and endorsed with Sue's signature. Jayne obtained copies of the checks and the bank video surveillance of Sandra cashing all three. Her forgery of Sue's signature was almost perfect. And so, Jayne obtained warrants for forgery and uttering a forged instrument, and then waited until the bond reduction hearing to serve them on Sandra.

Jayne's strategy was to make the case that the defendant was a flight risk, not only from the charges against her in Brunswick County, but also because the Oklahoma City Police Department had reopened its investigation of her possible murder of Alan Rehrig. Sandra had a history of abruptly moving from state to state and changing her alias. With the possibility of a murder charge being filed against her in Oklahoma City, Sandra would be incentivized to disappear.

The only problem with Jayne's strategy was the unresponsiveness of the OKC police. First Jayne contacted OKC cold case investigator Kyle Eastridge and requested that he examine all of Sandra's possessions and her Bible for references to Alan Rehrig's murder. Though it was a long shot, maybe there was something in her writings that could yield a fresh lead. That the suspect was in the county jail afforded a unique opportunity to interview her.

After sending e-mails and leaving voicemails for Eastridge and receiving no reply, Jayne called his lieutenant to make her request. A couple of days later she received an e-mail from Kyle Eastridge that contained a cartoon image of a buzzard sitting on an icicle encrusted tree limb—the symbol of the OKCPD Cold Case Unit. The implication—which Jayne found hilariously funny—was that she was akin to a buzzard for bothering him and going over his head to his lieutenant.

Switching tactics, Jayne called Gloria Rehrig and suggested she petition District Attorney David Prater to reopen the investigation of Alan's murder. Gloria drafted the petition, got the members of her church congregation to sign it, and then submitted it to the DA's Office. This seemed to work, because shortly thereafter, Kyle Eastridge finally called Jayne.

"Why are you doing this?" he asked her.

"Because I need you to reopen your case, not only because it should be reopened, but also because it will help me to keep her in jail until her trial instead of posting bond and disappearing. Getting the victim's mother involved seems to be the only way to get things done." Kyle agreed to reopen the case, and he sent Jayne an e-mail to confirm it. Shortly thereafter, he and DA's Office investigator Mike Burke made a statement to the *Daily Oklahoman* that, considering Sandra's arrest on felony charges in North Carolina, they were going to reexamine her as the suspect for the murder of Norman Alan Rehrig.

Sheriff Hewitt invited a local news crew to attend the bond reduction hearing, and for dramatic effect he led them through the county jail and into the adjacent courthouse. Jayne had already taken her seat when they arrived. During the hearing, she argued that Sandra was a flight risk, especially considering the Oklahoma City police had reopened their murder investigation in which she was the prime suspect. Moreover, Jayne had discovered evidence of additional crimes that Sandra had committed against Sue Moseley, and she was ready to serve the warrants on the defendant. The hearing went into recess, Sandra was taken to a holding cell, and Jayne served her the warrants. Judge Ola Lewis responded favorably to Jayne's argument. Instead of reducing Sandra's bond, she raised it to one million dollars.

It was the first time Pastor Lee Younce's desire to spring Sandra from jail was frustrated, but it wouldn't be the last. While he was in Brunswick County, he took Sue Moseley out to dinner at a fine restaurant and offered to repay her for the funds Sandra had stolen. He also emphasized that forgiveness was the essence of the Christian faith. Sue replied that she'd already forgiven Sandra, but this didn't change the fact that she posed a danger to society and therefore needed to be incarcerated.

"You never know what a woman like her is going to cook up," she said.

CHAPTER 38
"YOU BETRAYED ME."

To keep the case in the spotlight, Marty and Jayne issued a press release to the national media, informing newspapers and television stations from Marin County to New York that they had arrested the notorious Black Widow of Highland Park, and were seeking all witnesses of her criminal conduct over the years. Immediately Jayne started receiving calls and e-mails from people all over the country who'd encountered Sandra and had felt deceived and defrauded by her.

The news that she'd been arrested and that OKC detectives were taking another look at her for the murder of her third husband prompted *DATELINE* to broadcast an episode (on August 6, 2007) on the story. Especially significant was the contribution of the OKC police detective Steve Pacheco, who declared his belief on national television that Sandra had murdered Alan Rehrig. Only Sandra had the motive—the large life insurance death benefit. The circumstances of Alan's death and her uncooperative behavior indicated that she was the culprit. Detective Pacheco hypothesized that, after murdering Alan at the storage warehouse, she placed his vehicle, containing his body, in a storage unit. She then went out with her visiting friends to create an alibi. Later she returned to the warehouse in the middle of the night, drove the Bronco to Oklahoma City, dropped it near the airport, and caught the first flight back to Dallas that morning.

Gloria's petition and renewed media interest in the case seemed to have the desired effect, and the matter was scheduled to be brought before the Oklahoma multi-county grand jury in November of 2007. Subpoenas were issued to Sandra's three children, and Kyle Eastridge flew to Raleigh to interview Sandra. She was initially friendly and waived her right to have counsel present. However, once the detective started asking her questions about Alan Rehrig, she changed her mind and said she didn't wish to speak without counsel. After the aborted interview, Eastridge took Sandra's Bible from Jayne into his custody and flew back to Oklahoma City. A while later Jayne left him a voicemail, asking him if he'd gotten the apparent blood spatter in the Bible analyzed. She never heard back from him.

Because Sandra had used Sue Moseley's social security number to obtain credit cards in her name—just as she'd done to her own daughter years before—Jayne and Marty were able to persuade a Social Security Administration investigator to examine Sandra's activities all over the country. However, in the end, the US Attorney General's Office in Raleigh Durham decided to seek an indictment only for Sandra's offenses against Sue Moseley. A federal grand jury was convened, and Sandra was indicted. A few days later, Marty and Jayne transported her to a preliminary hearing at the Raleigh federal courthouse.

Marty drove, Jayne sat in the passenger seat, and Sandra sat in the back seat, her hands cuffed, her ankles shackled. After they got onto I-40 north of Wilmington, Sandra leaned forward, stuck her head between the front seats, and said, "How are y'all doing?" Her closeness gave Jayne the creeps, and she commanded Sandra to lean back. Sandra complied, and then engaged Marty in a friendly conversation. As always, he was happy to chat with her. *Does she really believe that Marty is on her side?* Jayne wondered. At the hearing, Marty testified about his findings under Sandra's watchful gaze. He hadn't been taken in by her. His sympathetic demeanor had been just an act. As he said in his testimony, there could be no doubt that the accused had ruthlessly deceived Sue Moseley to steal her property.

"You betrayed me," Sandra said to Marty after the hearing, at which point she was taken into custody by federal authorities in Raleigh. Because their local women's detention center was full, she was transferred to the Edgecombe County Jail in the town of Tarboro.

CHAPTER 39

"GOD IS MY WITNESS AND VINDICATOR."

The basement jail of the Edgecombe County Courthouse was a grim place of concrete and steel that smelled faintly of sewage. Sandra Camille Powers shared a cell with four other inmates. The slender, sixty-three-year-old woman with white skin and long dark hair stood in a tiny visitation booth. On the morning of September 16, 2007, I walked to the other side of the glass partition and looked at her for a moment before I spoke. Her delicate face and lovely small hands had aged. Long gray roots of her once lustrous raven hair were telltales of six months she'd spent in pretrial detention without hair dye. Her new residence in the squalid county jail was a long way from her elegant home in Highland Park, where I'd last seen her in the spring of 1984, but she maintained an air of dignity with her erect posture and calm composure.

"Hello Sandra, do you remember me?" I asked. Her big brown eyes gazed into mine, apparently searching me, and her memory, for recognition.

"No," she said. "Who are you?" She spoke with the same girlish voice that had charmed me twenty-three years earlier.

"I'm John Leake—Sam and Kathy's son. I grew up down the street from you on Lorraine. I was a friend of your daughter Kathryn and I occasionally talked with you in your home."

"No, I don't remember you." Her expression seemed to say *I'm sorry that I don't, but I'm still glad you came.* She looked at me calmly, sizing me up. Dimly I was aware that she probably saw me more clearly than I saw myself, for she was skilled at quickly assessing people. I sensed she wasn't impressed.

"Well, I remember you," I said. "I've come here because I'd like to hear your side of the story."

"My side of the story will come out in due time."

"I hope so, because what's been written about you so far—"

"The gossip and slander of hypocrites," she said. "Lies that have hurt me and my family."

"Why have you never given an interview to tell your side of the story?"

"I see no need to do that. God is my witness and vindicator."

"So, the truth will be told in your trial?"

"That's a matter for my lawyer," she replied. "I have very good representation."

"So, the allegations of your misconduct with Mrs. Moseley are false?" I asked, holding her eye contact. She hesitated and blinked.

"Uh, yes, I am innocent."

"Okay, well, thanks for talking to me," I said, at a loss for how to proceed.

"I didn't have a choice," she replied with the same calm, matter of fact tone.

"You have to present yourself to whomever shows up?"

"They don't tell me who's coming. They just say that I have a visitor."

"Thanks anyway," I said lamely.

"Thanks for visiting me," she said. "God bless you."

CHAPTER 40

THE HEARING

Carol Younce, the wife of Pastor Lee Younce, had filed a motion for the release of Sandra into her custody until her trial commenced. The day after I visited Sandra in jail, a hearing was held in the Raleigh Federal Courthouse to examine the motion. It opened with a statement from Sandra's lawyer, who argued that the court had no reason to believe that his client was a flight risk or a danger to the community. Mrs. Moseley lived on the opposite side of the state and had no reason to fear Ms. Powers. Most significantly, Ms. Powers had no criminal record.

Carol Younce took the stand. Her charming dress and bright red lipstick struck me as more suitable for a cocktail party than a court custody evaluation. She seemed distressed, apparently on the verge of tears, as she said it was senseless for Camille to languish in jail. In Mrs. Younce's custody, Camille would experience the dignity of hard work for Pastor Younce's Operation: Feed-A-Child, and she would certainly appear for her trial.

A federal prosecutor examined the pastor's wife.

"Mrs. Younce, why have you and your husband taken such an interest in the accused?"

"Last April, we were in an airport, returning from a ministerial retreat in the Grand Canyon, and as we passed a newsstand, we saw a report

169

about Ms. Powers' arrest. When we saw her photo, the Lord directed us to help her."

"Did you read the report?" the prosecutor asked.

"Yes."

"What did it say?"

"It was mostly about her background. It mentioned that one of her husbands had died of cancer, which I thought was very sad."

"Did it mention the suspicion that she had played a role in the deaths of two other husbands and the wife of a prominent doctor?"

"Yes."

"Were you aware of your husband's criminal record when you married him?"

"Yes."

"Did he tell you anything about his offense?"

"No, it happened a long time ago and we don't discuss it."

I studied the profile of Mrs. Younce's husband, who was sitting a few feet from me. The wiry, tough-looking man wearing a huge silver ring and gold bracelet didn't look like a Christian minister, even by the strange standards of the American South. I knew that he passionately wanted to get Sandra out of jail. He had paid for her attorney, tried to get her bond reduced, and had offered to pay restitution to Sue Moseley. I wondered why he was so keen to help Sandra. In her younger days, she had bewitched men with her sex appeal, but this had faded. What was it about her that had so inflamed Pastor Younce's desire to spring her from jail?

The testimony concluded and the judge stated his ruling. The motion was plainly absurd. The court had "zero reason" to believe that Mrs. Younce would have any sway over the defendant or that the defendant would appear for her trial. *Motion denied. The defendant would remain in pretrial detention.*

As we were leaving the courtroom, I approached Sandra's would-be savior.

"Mr. Younce, may I have a word with you?" He gave me a contemptuous look and said "no." I sheepishly followed him out of the courtroom, toward the elevator. Suddenly losing my nerve to stand with him in the car, I stood to wait for the next one. Just as the elevator door was closing, he looked directly at me and then raised his right arm to point at me, causing the door to jolt back open.

"John Leake—spelled L E A K E—son of Katharine and Sam Leake, grew up on Lorraine Avenue in Dallas!" he said accusingly.

"That's me," I said, trying to conceal my shock. He stepped out of the elevator and towards me. Under his hounds-tooth jacket he wore a black T-shirt that clung to his sinewy torso.

"You presented yourself to Ms. Powers under false pretenses! You introduced yourself as a former neighbor, when in fact you're an author."

"I am a former neighbor *and* I'm an author. I told her I wanted to hear her side of the story. Why do you think she won't tell it?" His expression softened, and he adopted a friendly tone.

"The press has thrown her under the bus, so she's reluctant to talk to reporters."

"I'm not a press reporter. I work hard to get the truth, and I always seek both sides of a story. I've heard Mrs. Moseley's side of the story. Now I'd like to hear Sandra's." He studied me for a moment and said, "Let's go for a walk."

We exited the courthouse, and he turned to face me.

"You know, Jesus forgives us for all we have done. It doesn't matter what, he forgives you."

"But don't you have to repent and try to be good in order to receive his forgiveness?" I asked.

"I believe that Camille has repented her past sins and resolved to be good," he said. "Never in my life had I even looked at a tabloid newspaper, but I was drawn to that paper on the newsstand. I believe the Lord directed me to it and wants me to help her." We strolled down the street in front of the courthouse.

"Things aren't always as they seem," he said. "Many people in history have been misunderstood. Christ himself was crucified for crimes he didn't commit."

"But this isn't the first time Sandra has fallen under suspicion," I said. "Many people in her past have felt betrayed and victimized by her."

"She's never been convicted in a court of law," he replied. I pointed out that most of Sandra's past victims weren't as brave as Mrs. Moseley, who considered it her duty to press charges, even though she knew it would result in a lot of trouble for her. I thought it strange that Pastor Younce seemed to have little regard for her—a dedicated Christian who'd worked as a nurse to save for her house.

We arrived at his new white BMW, parked next to the City Cemetery of Raleigh. I glanced through the wrought iron fence at its ornate gravestones, and then at Mr. Younce, who gave me a kindly look.

"These federal boys sure think they're going to get a conviction, don't they?" he said. I thought of the prosecutor who'd just questioned his wife. He'd seemed confident, maybe even a bit cocky.

"I guess they have a strong case."

"Yeah, well, mark my words, there's going to be some big surprises around here before this goes to trial. Big surprises."

"What kind of surprises?"

"You'll just have to wait and see," he said with a grin.

What kind of surprises? I'd recently spent a day at Sue Moseley's home and found her story perfectly credible. She had welcomed Sandra's offer of companionship and help around the house, and she had no conceivable reason to make false accusations against her. I admired Sue's character and courage, and I couldn't imagine how any reasonable juror would doubt her story that was supported by documentary evidence. Or would they? In my interview with Sue, she told me something that bothered me—namely, Sandra's frequent references to her forgetfulness.

"I occasionally have my senior moments, but I'm not *that* forgetful," she said. "By the way Sandra talked, you'd think I have advanced dementia." In fact, Sue was in an early stage of dementia, which made especially her vulnerable to a malevolent form of manipulation called gaslighting. In the popular imagination, gaslighting is often confused with general lying and deception, but in fact the term refers to tricking the victim into believing he is losing his mental competence so that he will doubt his perceptions of reality. The term originated in the 1944 film *Gaslight*, starring Ingrid Bergman and Charles Boyer, in which a woman is manipulated by her sinister husband into believing she is losing her sanity. In his initial gambit, he rigs their home's gaslights to flicker periodically.

When she asks him, "Why do the lights keep flickering?" he says he doesn't know what she's talking about—that the lights are *not* flickering. In another notable scene, he gives her a valuable brooch—a family heirloom that he claims had belonged to his mother—while warning that she must be very careful not to lose it. "You know how you tend to lose things," he says. Later, when the brooch goes missing from her purse, it seems (in her mind) to confirm his concern, as it doesn't occur to her that he removed it.

I was reminded of this scene when I learned that, at the time of her arrest, Sandra had in her purse a foreclosure notice for Sue's house. I wondered if her plan had been to pretend to find it upon her return to Sue's house, thereby tricking Sue into believing that she'd received the notice but then forgotten about it.

"I guess Sandra wanted you to believe that you were too forgetful to manage your affairs so that you would turn them over to her," I remarked to Sue.

"Yes, I'm pretty sure that's what was doing. May I ask you something else?"

"Of course."

"Why do you suppose that Lee Younce wants to get her out of jail?"

"I've been asking myself the same question, and I must say I have no idea."

"I think the devil told him to do it."

CHAPTER 41
KATHRYN

Now that Sandra had been arrested and seemed likely to spend the rest of her life in prison, I thought that at least one of her kids might be willing to talk about what they had seen and heard at the time of Alan Rehrig's murder. By numerous accounts, Alan had been an exceptionally sweet stepfather, so I thought I might be able to appeal to their consciences.

The oldest, Britt, lived in Marin County, California. Coincidentally, I was scheduled to be in Carmel, California at the beginning of October for my younger brother's wedding, and I contemplated heading up to Marin after the ceremony to try to talk to him. On the flight from Dallas to Monterey, I reread the *D Magazine* article "The Black Widow" from May 1987. Though twenty years had elapsed since then, I still vividly recalled the first time I'd seen it in my high school cafeteria.

Beautiful, sunny weather blessed my brother's wedding in Carmel. The ceremony was held on the Carmel River Beach. He looked young and handsome in his tailored suit, and his bride was positively glowing, her blond hair and huge blue eyes catching the golden glow of the late afternoon sun over the deep blue Pacific. She was a native of Tyler, Texas. Located in the middle of the East Texas oil field, the town was famous for producing wealthy men and beautiful women. Sandra had briefly attended Tyler Junior College, perhaps in search of one the town's oil heirs. She didn't land one then, but she did a decade later when she met her second husband, Bobby Bridewell, at his thirty-seventh birthday party in Dallas. Bobby was born into a Tyler oil family, and then got into the hotel business.

The day after my brother's wedding, I decided against attempting to visit Britt in Marin. The last time I'd seen him, he'd beaten the hell out of me, and I reckoned his reaction to my unannounced visit to talk about his mother would be no less hostile, even if it weren't violent. So instead of renting a car, I booked a flight from Monterey to Atlanta via Los Angeles. I arrived on the afternoon of October 13, rented a car, and drove east to the small town in Alabama where Kathryn lived.

Driving through the town center, which had apparently changed little in decades, I wondered how she—after her Highland Park and Belvedere youth—had wound up in rural Alabama. At the time I'd known her, she struck me as an intelligent, communicative, and bold girl, and quite popular. I would have expected her to remain, like her brother, in Marin, or perhaps in a place like Portland, Oregon, where she'd lived for a while in the nineties.

Near the golf course, I found her modest wooden frame house. Feeling very nervous, I walked to the entrance and knocked. I heard a stir inside, footsteps, and then Kathryn opened the door. She appeared twenty years older, but still much the same.

"Hello Kathryn, I hope I'm not disturbing you." She looked a little surprised, but not unfriendly, and the beginning of a smile formed on her face.

"Do you remember me?"

"I think so. You're J—. Is it Jeff?"

"No, it's John. I grew up down the street from you on Lorraine. We used to hang out when we were kids.

"Yes, of course! I remember you! Oh my God." She paused, apparently thinking for a second, and then asked. "But what are you doing here?"

"Well, I know this is pretty awkward, but I came here to talk to you about your mom. I guess you heard she was recently arrested in North Carolina, and I thought—." Her smile disappeared and her expression darkened.

"I can't believe that you would show up here after all these years to talk about my mother. It's just unbelievable." She stepped back into her house and slammed the door. I stood there, shocked, embarrassed, immobile. Then the door reopened and pleasant looking man about my age stepped out.

"I'm sorry about this," he said in a gentle southern accent. "I'd love to invite you in for a meal with us, but we just can't talk about this anymore. A lot of journalists and policemen have turned up over the years, and we really want to put this behind us."

His politeness disarmed me, causing me to reel with shame for bothering him and Kathryn—an apparently decent couple trying to lead their lives and raise their two children.

"I understand," I said. "I'm sorry to bother you."

"It's okay," he said. "I wish you well." I turned, went back to my rental car, and drove to a Bed and Breakfast where I'd booked a room for the night. There, on my laptop, I booked a one-way flight to Dallas. The next morning, I got up, knocked down a horrible cup of coffee, drove back to Atlanta, and then flew home to Dallas. It was a long and expensive journey only to be turned away, but I'd already known that such trips came with the territory being a freelance true crime author.

CHAPTER 42
NO BILL

Three weeks later, my first book—about a Viennese author and serial killer named Jack Unterweger—was published. The true story about the charismatic psychopath who seduced much of Viennese society, and then murdered eleven women in three different countries, was stranger than fiction. Jack was an intelligent and organized serial killer who took great pains to avoid being seen by witnesses or leaving any traces of himself at the crime scenes. This made investigating and prosecuting him very difficult. In the end, it wasn't a particular piece of evidence, but a mosaic of indications that he was the culprit—the totality of circumstances—that persuaded the jury to render a guilty verdict. In researching the story, I got to be close friends with the lead investigator, Ernst Geiger, who had, over the course of two hard years, methodically assembled this mosaic of evidence.

It was a complex story whose mostly foreign characters had foreign-sounding names, so I was uncertain of how it would be received in my native Dallas. As it turned out, it was briefly a bestseller in the Dallas market. My parents hosted a lavish book launch for me, and most of their friends attended and dutifully bought copies. I was flattered by the attendance of the distinguished crime reporter, Skip Hollandsworth. We talked about my book, and then I mentioned the subject of his renowned *D Magazine* piece.

"I recently visited her in pretrial detention in North Carolina."

"Really! How was she?"

"Spooky, though she still has a way with men. Her latest admirer is a church pastor, and he's hot to rescue her from the feds."

"Yeah, I've heard about him."

"Have you ever thought about writing a book about her?" I asked.

"No. I thought it was an incredible story for a long magazine piece, but I never saw how it would work as a book. What about you?"

"I'm going to attend her trial in federal court in a couple of months and see how it shakes out."

"Good luck!" he said.

Two weeks after my book launch party, Sandra's youngest daughter Emily testified before the Oklahoma multi-county grand jury. She stated that she did not recall the events surrounding Alan Rehrig's murder. However, she did have a clear memory of visiting her brother Britt in Marin County in 2001, when he told her that in the summer of 1985, while on an excursion to a lake near Dallas, Sandra had asked him to run over Alan Rehrig with a jet ski and make it look like an accident. While Emily's statement augmented the grounds for suspecting Sandra of murdering Alan, the grand jury concluded that it could only be considered evidence if Britt confirmed it.

Britt initially refused to answer the grand jury subpoena. When OCPD officers travelled to his home in Marin County to serve him in person, he refused to open the door. They then tried to approach his house through the back yard and encountered hostile dogs. Finally, Britt appeared in the backyard, and they told him that if he did not accept the summons, they would arrest him for contempt of court. Britt responded by retaining Mack Martin—the same OKC defense attorney his mother had retained in 1985—even though he was not the subject of the grand jury inquiry.

Due to the closed nature of grand jury proceedings, Britt's testimony was not a matter of public record. All Kyle Eastridge wrote in his e-mail to Gloria Rehrig was that "Britt had been skillfully coached by his attorney," and that the result of the final grand jury hearing on January 8, 2008, was a No Bill. Gloria was a little confused by Eastridge's statement because the critical question for Britt was whether Sandra had indeed asked him to run over Alan with a jet ski in the summer of 1985. Denying that he'd told Emily this story was the same as claiming she'd fabricated it, which wasn't credible. Was the story true, or had he (for some reason) fabricated it?

Some wondered if Mr. Martin had coached Britt to plead his Fifth Amendment right to refuse to answer questions to avoid incriminating himself, which resulted in his avoidance of saying anything that could incriminate his mother. If this was indeed the case, it raised the question of why the grand jury didn't grant Britt immunity from prosecution in exchange for providing full testimony. Altogether, Glory found the "No Bill" puzzling, as she'd long heard it was easy for a prosecutor to persuade a grand jury to indict someone.

CHAPTER 43
THE SURPRISE

I too was surprised by the No Bill. After all, as former New York state chief judge, Sol Wachter, had famously remarked, a prosecutor could persuade a grand jury to "indict a ham sandwich." The news of it reminded me of Pastor Younce's promise of "big surprises" to come during the run-up to Sandra's trial (scheduled to begin on January 14, 2008) in North Carolina. Two days before the trial was set to open, I called the court clerk to make sure everything was still on track. I got her voicemail, on which I requested that she call me back to confirm. The next day, as I was getting out of a taxi at the airport to fly to Raleigh, my cell phone rang. It was the court clerk.

"The trial has been cancelled," she said. "Ms. Powers has agreed to plead guilty to identity theft."

"Does that mean that all the other charges have been dropped?" I asked.

"Yes."

"What is her sentence?"

"Sentencing is scheduled for later, but probably two years."

Two years for identity theft didn't seem to me to do justice to Sandra's perfidy against Sue Moseley. I understood that codified justice can't always reflect the moral quality of a crime, but I figured the worst thing that we can do is to feign love and affection to prey on each other. For good reason, Dante reserved the 9th and final circle of hell, "the lowest, blackest, and farthest from heaven," for people guilty of treachery against those in whom they have cultivated a bond of trust.

I wondered about the prudence of this decision (instead of pursuing all the original charges in trial) as I suspected that two years in prison would have little corrective effect on Sandra. I didn't have much time to ponder it, because a few days later my parents announced they were ending their forty-year marriage. My mother confided in me that her relationship with my father had been strained for months and that she could no longer maintain appearances. My perplexity about the prosecutor's deal with Sandra was displaced by grief over the dissolution of my family. My long-term memory verges on the photographic, and the images of my happy childhood—of my parents always being fond and supportive of each other—went through my head like a movie. That they were now adversaries struck me as a mysterious catastrophe. At a meeting with my mom's divorce attorney, she told me (when my mom stepped out to go to the bathroom):

"Be very careful about what you do and say, because, though you may not be fully aware of it, you are very upset by this, and you will be for a while. Divorce can be far more traumatic for adult kids than it is for children, because your entire life you've been accustomed to a happy family, and now it's gone. The experience is like the death of the former you, and now you must grieve."

Shortly after my mother announced the pending divorce, the *Dallas Observer* columnist Glenna Whitley informed me that she was planning to write a book about Sandra. Glenna had done a great job of reporting Sandra's ongoing adventures, and she had performed the invaluable service of keeping the public informed about Sandra's wanderings and depredations. I understood her desire to write a book about the story, so I set the project aside.

Glenna and Gloria Rehrig attended Sandra's plea hearing in February. Gloria sat in the front row, wearing a large button on her blouse displaying Alan's photo. Sandra shuffled into the courtroom wearing red prison garb, her hands cuffed behind her back and her legs chained. As Glenna reported, though shackled, and sandwiched between two felons, she held herself with quiet dignity. This reminded me of her composure in the Edgecombe County Jail. For a fleeting moment she glanced at Gloria, but her face expressed no recognition or emotion.

"I am guilty," Sandra said to the judge when he presented her with the charge of aggravated identity theft. In September of 2008 Sandra was sentenced to 24 months in federal prison followed by one year of supervised release and a $250,000 fine that would be deducted from whatever funds she received in the future.

Two years later, Lee Younce finally got his wish of having Sandra live with him. In the spring of 2010, he and his wife drove to Bolivia, North Carolina to pick up Sandra's possessions from the county jail.

"You best have a priest cleanse the interior with holy water after you transport this stuff," Jayne suggested. Pastor Younce brushed off her remark, but a look of alarm appeared on his wife's face, and later she confided in Jayne that she'd suffered a severe headache on the drive back to Marion.

During Sandra's stay with the Younces, she lived in a guest apartment near the chapel where Pastor Younce held his services. Just before Christmas, she used his credit card to make a large lingerie purchase at Victoria's Secret. Mrs. Younce recounted the story to Jayne, who told her it was imperative that her husband report the incident to Sandra's probation officer so that she would go back to prison. However, for some reason—perhaps out of fear of embarrassment in the eyes of his flock—Pastor Younce chose not to report the incident.

On May 8, 2011, Sandra posted on her Facebook page: "So very happy to be out of NC, many bad memories there. Especially happy to be away from Marion, NC as I found no real life forms in that God-forsaken town!" Though one of the conditions of her plea agreement was that she could never again present herself as a Christian minister or missionary, her Facebook profile states: "Works at missionary, I work for the Lord." Her favorite TV genre is "Murder Mysteries."

CHAPTER 44

MOONLIGHT
IN VERMONT

Paul Kaplan was an entrepreneur who lived in Burlington, Vermont. One of his businesses was alpaca farming, but due to lingering setbacks from the financial crisis of 2008, he decided to sell his herd, so he advertised it on Craig's List. Soon a prospective buyer contacted him, and he invited her to meet him at his friend's farm where he was boarding the animals. She was an elegant lady named Sandra Powers whom Paul took to be around sixty (about ten years older than him). It was a beautiful late summer afternoon in mid August as they met at his friend's farmhouse and walked down the hill to the pasture where the animals were grazing. Sandra said she was a resident of Virginia but was thinking about moving to Vermont and investing in alpacas. Through her husband, who'd died of cancer years earlier, she'd acquired experience raising thoroughbred horses, and she enjoyed being in the country around animals.

In the farmhouse up the hill, the proprietress looked out her kitchen window and saw Paul strolling through the field with a woman. She was slender with pale skin and long auburn hair that was caught and lifted by the light summer breeze. Seemingly out of nowhere, the proprietress had an eerie perception—the likes of which she'd never had before—that the woman was a witch.

After viewing the animals and asking a few questions, Sandra offered to purchase all of them. She explained that the trustee of her deceased husband's trust—a lawyer in Boston—would write the check, so the transaction would take a few days. She then remarked that it was going to be a beautiful evening and she wondered if Paul would like to join her for a glass of wine. He happily accepted her invitation and said he knew just the place to go. First, they went to a wine store, bought a good bottle, and then proceeded to a place on Shelburne Farms overlooking Lake Champlain. There they sat in Adirondack Chairs, sipping wine and talking about every subject under the sun. Paul felt a powerful connection forming with Sandra, and right at that moment she reached over and touched his right elbow.

A proverbial whirlwind romance ensued from their enchanting evening on the lake. Paul felt the promise of a true partnership in every sense of the word. Sandra seemed to understand perfectly and to share his ambitions. Meeting her, a woman with capital, at this moment in his life—trying to get his business career back on track—struck him as a remarkable benefaction. Soon she suggested that they go into business together. Paul owned a 300-acre parcel of land in southern Vermont, but it was carrying significant debt. She proposed buying at 15% interest in his animals. He could use the capital for debt service on the land. They discussed founding an LLC partnership. She also proposed that they purchase a life insurance policy for each owner.

The first glitch in their incipient partnership happened a couple of weeks after they met, when Federal Express misplaced the package containing the check issued by the trustee of her deceased husband's estate. They went to the FedEx office in Burlington, and the clerk was unable to trace the package with the tracking number provided by Sandra. Intuitively Paul sensed there was something odd about the situation— maybe even something that didn't add up. Sandra perceived his questioning frame of mind and acted insulted. They left the office, and as they sat in the car, she became very upset, causing him to become more concerned about mollifying her than getting to the bottom of the missing package. The incident concluded with her saying she would go to Boston to talk with the trustee about issuing a new check.

Sandra claimed to be staying with a friend in a neighboring town, but as her relationship with Paul deepened, she proposed moving to Burlington to be closer to him. At the time he was temporarily staying with his sister, as he'd recently moved back to Burlington, and didn't yet have his own place. And so, he took Sandra to the Sunset House Bed and Breakfast on Main Street. At check-in, he noticed that she didn't have a credit card for the room deposit, though she did have a decent sum of cash in her purse. Paul offered his credit card for the deposit.

A few days later they drove to Lake Placid for a romantic overnight stay. Paul had never visited the place but was inspired to book a room when he saw he could get a great deal at the local Marriott—a hotel chain for which he'd saved up reward points. Over dinner at a lovely restaurant, Sandra reached across the table, grasped his hands, and looked deeply into his eyes. She spoke of their future together as though they would soon be husband and wife. Paul found this jarring, given they'd only just met, and said nothing to affirm her apparent marriage plans. The same dark cloud he'd seen at the FedEx office came over her face, and she became cold and silent. They returned to the room, where she withdrew into the bathroom for an hour. The next morning, she sat in the corner with an open Bible, reading verses in a murmuring voice. Paul found this disturbing, as it seemed that her fervent Bible reading related to the negative emotions that she was feeling towards him.

They drove back to Burlington through a countryside struck by the final blast of Hurricane Irene and littered with fallen trees. Sandra remained silent and sullen, so he pressed her about what was bothering her.

"I thought you really wanted to be with me," she said. "I thought you were going to propose marriage at dinner."

"I do want to be with you, but I've only just met you. I'm not yet ready to get engaged."

A few days later they made a trip to Boston, where she briefly borrowed his car to run errands. When she returned, his valuable camera and laptop were missing from the back seat, where he'd left them. She said she didn't know what had happened to them. Maybe she'd forgotten to lock the car during one of her errands. Increasingly disturbed by her behavior, Paul did a Google search on the name Sandra Powers. The results were shocking. He saw her mug shot from her arrest in North Carolina in 2007 and read about her crimes against Sue Moseley. Then he saw the *D Magazine* article and read that she was suspected of multiple murders in Dallas. His mind raced, trying to think of what to do. He wanted to buy time to come up with a plan for how to get away from her while minimizing the confrontation. She was still staying at the Sunset House, near his sister's house, and he needed to come up with a story fast.

He decided to say he needed to go on an urgent business trip. She'd recently mentioned that she would soon need to return her friend's car. She'd also mentioned that she needed to make a trip to Boston to speak with the estate trustee. He tried to let her down easy by renting a car for her at the same time he announced his hastily booked business trip. He proposed that she take the car to Boston while he was away.

She volunteered to give him a ride to the Burlington airport, which was awkward because he didn't have a plane ticket. He said goodbye and went inside the terminal, where he figured he should stay for a while in case she decided to linger outside. From the terminal, he called his friend Nanette Asimov—a columnist at the *San Francisco Chronicle*, which had published a long feature about Sandra in 1989. Nanette urged him to get away from her. He then called the Brunswick County Sheriff's Department and asked to speak with Jayne Todd, who was mentioned as a media contact in one of the reports he'd seen.

"You need to get away from her immediately," Jayne advised. "Do not be alone with her again, and do not consume any food or drink she offers you."

Sandra left Burlington and didn't return for several days—a welcome respite. The trouble was, she still had the car that Paul had rented for her, and Avis wanted to know where it was. Finally, Sandra called and said she was still in Boston.

"Please return the rental car now," Paul told her. "Avis wants it back and is going to report it stolen if you don't return it." She returned the car in Boston and took the train back to Burlington. He picked her up at the station and gave her a ride to a hotel in Shelburne, just south of Burlington. During their drive she had some alarming news for him.

"I'm pregnant," she said. "I've missed my period, and my belly is already starting to swell." She pointed at her abdomen, which did indeed look bigger. All the same, Paul didn't believe her. First, they had always used condoms. Secondly, he knew from Jayne Todd that Sandra was born in 1944, which made her sixty-seven years old.

"You certainly don't look old, but I still get the impression you are too old to get pregnant," he said.

"It's unusual for a woman my age but it can still happen. I saw many post-menopausal women in India carry babies to term."

"I guess we'll just have to see how it goes," he replied.

They arrived at her hotel, checked her in, and then went to Pauline's restaurant. After they sat down, he confessed that he'd Googled her name and seen media reporting about her. She didn't seem surprised to hear this, and claimed she'd long been the victim of vicious gossip and slander, and that columnists like Glenna Whitley at the *Dallas Observer* had persecuted her for no reason.

"Of course, I want to believe you," Paul said. "But I can't feel comfortable continuing our relationship unless you explain to me what happened with your two husbands and to your friend in Dallas." To Paul's surprise, she spoke without hesitation.

"My first husband was a dentist. When I met him, he seemed like a great guy—very smart and ambitious. But then, a few years after we married, his dental practice declined. He became depressed and started drinking, which made matters worse. After a while I realized he wasn't the man I thought he was when we married. His depression deepened, and one day he committed suicide."

"How did he do it?" Paul asked.

"He went into the closet in our master bedroom and shot himself in the head."

"What about your third husband from Oklahoma?" Paul asked.

"At first, he too seemed like a great guy. He was young and handsome and seemed very ambitious. But then he started hanging around with ne'er do well friends—guys who weren't of the same social class. He'd go out drinking with them and stay out late and not tell me where he'd been. Then he started doing poorly at work. I then realized that marrying him was the biggest mistake of my life, because he turned out to be a really bad guy. At the end of his life, he was hanging around with bad guys like gambling bookies and drug dealers."

"How did he get killed?"

"We were separated at the time it happened, so I don't know. I just know he was found in Oklahoma City."

"What about your best friend Betsy?" Paul asked.

"I was very close with Betsy and her husband. They were my best friends, and I spent a lot of time with them. But then Betsy became jealous of my relationship with her husband and started saying bad things about me to him and trying to turn him against me."

"I read that she was found dead at the airport. Do you understand how that happened?"

"I have no idea."

Paul sensed she wouldn't tell him anymore, but even from this succinct account, he perceived a pattern. In all three cases, she didn't address how the victim had wound up shot. Instead, she focused on how each had disappointed her, as though she was offering a justification for their violent deaths.

After dinner they returned to her hotel. Flouting Jayne's advice, he had a glass of wine with her in her room. He then said he needed to visit his mother at her assisted living home before it got too late. Sandra seemed to accept his excuse and didn't try to persuade him to stay. She was nothing if not perceptive, and she realized that he was afraid of her. Nothing was to be gained by pursuing a relationship with him any further.

CHAPTER 45
GLORIA

At around the time that Paul had his romance with Sandra in Vermont, my wife got a job at Stanford University, so I found myself leaving Vienna, where I'd lived for a decade, and moving to Menlo Park, California. At our new home in Silicon Valley, I finished my second book, about a Canadian Ice Hockey player named Duncan MacPherson who went missing in the mountains near Innsbruck, Austria in the summer of 1989. What happened to him turned out to be far stranger and more twisted than I could have ever imagined, and the difficulty of unraveling the mystery was compounded by the fact that Innsbruck authorities had deliberately concealed the cause of his death.

One day in 2014, I reviewed my old file on Sandra and wondered where she was living. I did a public records search and saw that, among the myriad addresses all over the country at which she'd lived or received mail, her most recent, in the year 2014, was a PO Box at the UPS Store in Palo Alto, where I often went to mail packages. Either she or someone to whom she'd entrusted her key was picking up her mail a ten-minute walk from my condominium.

Right about then, quite suddenly (it seemed to me) my marriage collapsed. As heartbreaking as it was, it enabled me to put my parents' divorce into perspective. They'd stuck together for forty years, while my wife and I had only managed four. A few years later I moved back to my native Dallas, and on a weekend trip to an old friend's country house, I fell into conversation with his mother. The daughter of a Dallas oilman, she and her friends had known Sandra, and all of them had concluded that there was something badly amiss about her.

"We still talk about her, and we still wonder why she was never tried for murder in Dallas. I wish you would investigate it and discover the truth once and for all."

On a business trip to New York two weeks later, I saw an old friend and fellow writer named Johnny Marciano, with whom I'd often discussed stories I was researching. Over coffee and cake at his in-laws' place in Brooklyn Heights, he brought up Sandra, and remarked that her story seemed to lie at the heart of Dallas during its heyday in the seventies and early eighties.

"Why didn't the Dallas police take a closer look at her for the deaths of her first husband and the doctor's wife?" he asked. "Could it be that both really *did* commit suicide and the suspicion of Sandra is unfounded?"

It was the second time in so many weeks I'd been asked about her. To investigate the story properly, I would need the blessing and support of Alan Rehrig's mother. From my earlier research, I knew she was the most dedicated advocate for discovering and telling the truth about her son's murder. I found Gloria Rehrig's number in an old e-mail and called her from my hotel room. I didn't really expect her to be alive, as she was in her late seventies when I'd briefly spoken with her in 2007. Her voicemail answered and I left a message. An hour later she returned my call, and it seemed as though I were speaking with a woman thirty years her junior. She remembered our phone conversation in 2007. At that time, she'd wanted to give the *Dallas Observer* columnist Glenna Whitley a chance to write her planned book. However, as twelve years had elapsed with no book forthcoming, Gloria said she'd be happy to speak with me at greater length.

Three days later I was driving I-35 North from Dallas to Edmond, Oklahoma. Despite being a Dallas native, I'd never entered our neighboring state to the north. As I crossed the Red River, I thought of the old Chisholm Trail and stories I'd read as a boy about the cattle drives. In my mind's eye, I saw Alan Rehrig's Ford Bronco, driving the same road in the early morning darkness of his one-year wedding anniversary, December 8, 1985, with his dead body riding next to the driver.

Arriving at Gloria's house in Edmond, I rang the bell and was amazed by the lady who answered the door. Slender and ramrod straight, her voice clear and strong, her movements swift and decisive, she seemed to bear no infirmities of age. Over coffee, the amateur historian got the better of me, and I asked about her family history. She was of the German stock that had settled Oklahoma in the 19th century, and I thought of John Steinbeck's characters from the Oklahoma Dustbowl.

"Do you remember the Great Depression?" I asked.

"Of course I do!" she said. "I was a little girl during the Depression. I also remember the attack on Pearl Harbor like it was yesterday. I think of it every year all the more because December 7 is also the day Alan was last seen alive."

I felt affection stirring in me for this lady, with her cheerful, age-defying constitution and twinkling blue eyes. We talked for a couple of hours at her breakfast table. Though I was already familiar with much of her story from the *D Magazine* and *Dallas Observer* pieces and from my research in 2007, she provided far more information and answered many questions I'd long wondered about.

Gloria took a break from telling me her story, and we went into her garage to inspect her file cabinet packed with records of her long, uphill battle. I looked at the oak veneer cabinet and estimated it contained approximately a thousand pages of documents. It would take weeks to go through them all.

"Ma'am, I'm going to make a bold request, and please say no if it makes you uncomfortable."

"Go ahead," she said.

"May I take this file cabinet home to Dallas with me? I promise to bring it back in a few weeks." This was a lot to ask, as Gloria had only just met me and knew little about me apart from what I had written on my author's webpage. She looked me in the eyes, apparently trying to catch a glimpse of my character.

"Okay," she said in what sounded like a tone of resignation. Twenty minutes later I was lifting the cabinet into the back of my car. I then turned to face Gloria, standing in the driveway.

"I promise to do my best to tell your son's story," I said.

"Okay," she said, her eyes again searching mine, perhaps wondering if she was making the right decision to trust me. At that moment she seemed intensely vulnerable, and I instinctively embraced her. I drove away, dismayed, and frightened by the malevolence that had so grievously hurt her thirty-four years earlier.

Back in Dallas, I went through Gloria's documents and marveled at their scope. Between Alan's death in 1985 and Sandra's conviction for identity theft in 2008, Gloria had worked tirelessly to seek justice for her son. It was an extraordinary testament of a grieving mother's love. I'd seen the same devotion before, ten years earlier, in Lynda MacPherson. The mother of Duncan MacPherson—the Canadian professional hockey player who'd vanished in the Tyrolean Alps—Lynda had also worked for decades to seek truth and justice for her son, whose violent death had been concealed. In 2009 I visited her and her husband Bob in Saskatoon, on the other side of the Great Plain, 1500 miles northeast of Oklahoma City. The experience had shown me that a mother's love for her child is the strongest and most enduring of emotions.

Just like Lynda MacPherson, Gloria Rehrig had kept a meticulous diary of the events surrounding her son's death. Also, just like Lynda, she had (thank God) very legible handwriting. Between her diary and her correspondence with countless people about her son's murder, I had an extraordinary record of her "Justice Journey" as she called it. Once it became apparent that the OCPD was not going to arrest Sandra, Gloria spoke freely to the press about Alan's murder with the hope of maintaining public awareness of it.

While I had a super-abundance of information about Alan's murder, I had little about the two other suspicious deaths in Sandra's past, before she met him. Both had been ruled suicides by the Dallas County medical examiner. The famous *D Magazine* feature was a great portrait of Sandra, but it contained only a few paragraphs about the shooting deaths of David Stegall in 1975 and Betsy Bagwell in 1982. Moreover, the piece didn't even mention the shooting death of Alan's cousin, Robert Smith, in 1986. My objective was to learn all I could about these deaths, but it soon became evident that this wasn't going to be easy.

CHAPTER 46

"HER HEART WAS TOTALLY FALSE."

I drove a dirt road through piney woods until I arrived at the home of Jayne Todd—the retired Brunswick County Sherriff's Department detective who had the distinction of being the only law officer who'd ever succeeded in getting Sandra prosecuted for a crime. This was no mean feat. Prior to Jayne, multiple state and federal investigators in different jurisdictions and several private investigators had viewed her with grave suspicion, but none had made a case against her.

I knocked on the front door and heard a dog barking inside, but no Jayne appeared. I then turned to survey the property. There was nothing around but woods. I thought of some of Sandra's former friends in Dallas with whom I'd been speaking. All of them were still afraid of her, and they all asked me a version of the same question.

"What if she finds out that I talked to you and comes after me?" These were affluent ladies who lived in one of the most secure neighborhoods on earth. Jayne Todd, on the other hand, lived in a house in the woods a few hundred yards from the nearest neighbor. And as I would soon learn, Jayne was Sandra's nemesis.

Clearly, she wasn't home, so I called her on my cell phone.

"Marty and I are waitin' for you at the Fire Station in Supply," she said.

"Oh no! I thought I was going to pick you up at your house and then meet Marty at the Fire Station."

"No, we're already here. Come on!" At a table in a lunchroom behind the fire engine garage, we sat for three hours, talking about Marty and Jayne's adventures with Camille Bowers, as Sandra had called herself in North Carolina. We then broke for dinner on the deck of a seafood restaurant overlooking the Intracoastal Waterway, where we talked about their experiences working in Brunswick County law enforcement. They told me wild stories of drug runners, two corrupt sheriffs who'd gone to prison, and a few terrifying psychopaths they'd encountered. But none of these offenders had made the same vivid impression on them as Sandra. During this first meeting, I was careful to avoid expressing my own perceptions of her, because I didn't want to lead them. All the same, they revealed that they regarded her as an exceptionally devious criminal. They had none of the modern hesitation about calling her evil. To them, it seemed the most natural way to describe her.

"The male psychopaths I'd run across were straightforward," Jayne said. "Either they'd try to intimidate me or seduce me. With Sandra, she'd just stare at me with those big brown eyes of hers, and it was like she was seeing into my soul, looking for my vulnerabilities. Miss Sue's vulnerabilities were plain to see. She was an old lady, living by herself, who'd recently had some bad health problems. Sandra moved in on her like a predator. All that business about being a good Christian and a missionary, tending to the needy of the world—that was all just a lie. No doubt she was the evilest person I've ever encountered."

"Why did the federal prosecutor go for a plea bargain instead of taking it to trial?" I asked.

"He and Jimmy Moseley started worrying that Sandra's defense attorney would rattle Miss Sue on the stand and make her seem too confused and forgetful to be a reliable witness against Sandra, who could seem very convincing. Also, Miss Sue wanted everyone to know that she wasn't vengeful and that she had forgiven Sandra, because she wanted to be a good Christian. She also insisted that Sandra wasn't all bad—that she had helped to care for her and her home. We understood her, but the prosecutor was afraid that some of the jury members wouldn't."

I thought of my day with Sue in her home twelve years earlier. Completely guileless, she was perplexed by Sandra's behavior, and struggled to reconcile her good qualities—sweet, funny, and sociable—with her deceitfulness. I was touched by her desire to forgive Sandra and to see good in her. It would have been easy for her to have yielded to feelings of contempt and even hatred.

Marty Folding, who'd also retired from the Sheriff's Department, told me his perspective on Sandra.

"What stands out the most for me about Sandra was how convincing she could be. She'd start twisting things around, saying it was all a misunderstanding with Miss Sue, and damn could she say it with conviction. Pretty much everything she told me was a lie, but you'd never know it from the way she said it. Her heart was totally false."

I spent the next three days talking with Jayne and reviewing her documentation of the case. At the end of my visit, we had lunch together at a restaurant in Southport. Afterwards I walked her to her car in the parking lot.

"Take care of yourself," I said, and gave her a hug. "And be sure to lock your doors at night. I'd be a bit nervous living in your place in the woods. You never know when someone you put away might turn up to settle an old score."

"She ain't gonna come around here. She knows I'll shoot her ass if she does."

CHAPTER 47
STRANGE PARALLELS

Again, back home in Dallas, I studied the federal indictment, at the top of which stated the name SANDRA CAMILLE POWERS and the different aliases she'd used over the years, mostly variations of Camille Bridewell and Camille Powers. My copy of Jayne's file also contained samples of Sandra's handwriting, which displayed an array of styles and signatures ranging from elaborate calligraphy to tiny print. A couple of these samples bore some resemblance to Sandra's handwriting in cards she'd given Alan during their courtship and early marriage. Though hardly an unbiased judge of her prose, I found her cards—closing with "Incurably yours,"—insufferably glib. Likewise, her manner of speaking with friends and neighbors (recorded on Sue Moseley's phone) struck me as simpering in the extreme.

In her wedding photos with Alan, her appearance had the power and the glory that had so impressed me as a teenager.

"Sandra was a beautiful bride," my mother remarked while viewing the album with me. "You know who she reminds me of?"

"Who's that?" I asked.

"Johanna," she said, referring to my ex-wife. I studied Sandra's face. There was indeed something in the set of her jaw and high cheekbones,

197

her bright intelligent eyes, and her coquettish smile that reminded me of the "Imp" as I had called my ex-wife.

"That's really weird," I said.

"Yes, it is," my mom replied.

My mother's observation reminded me that Sandra had, by numerous accounts, many attractive qualities. She was voraciously curious and a first-rate researcher of any subject that captured her imagination. Like my ex-wife, she was a marvelously engaging conversationalist. Like me, she seemed to have a restless, wandering spirit and implacable desire for novelty and adventure. After living on the same street in Highland Park, we both lived on Boston's Beacon Hill in 1994. At different times in our lives, we both lived in Palo Alto, California and on the island of Maui. In 2021, I rented an old friend's duplex a block away from the duplex Sandra rented in 1976. The duplexes near Highland Park High School are where the town's less prosperous live. She was, at that time in her life, an unemployed mother of three. I was recovering from a catastrophic investment in a restaurant that opened right before COVID-19 struck. Every day I passed her former place on my afternoon walk and was reminded of her.

I often reflected on these parallels and intersections. Then one day Glenna Whitley shared with me a suitcase that Sandra had, in one of her hasty departures, abandoned in a motel room in California. Among its contents were sleeves of old-fashioned printed photographs. Opening one, I instantly recognized the first image in the stack as that of Point Lobos in Carmel, California. I knew the exact vantage point from which she'd taken the photo because it was my favorite place to stop and contemplate the natural spectacle whenever I walked the Point's nature trail. I had taken photos of the same subject from the same spot. Flipping through the other photos in the stack, I saw a carpet of California poppies growing in front of the Palo Alto Tower Well, just south of San Francisquito Creek. I'd often walked past the tower and stopped to admire and photograph the flowers.

Among Glenna's interview transcripts, I came across a statement from someone who'd mentioned Sandra's love of red-tailed hawks, which are abundant in Texas and California. If she happened to see one, she would stop whatever she was doing to watch it flying or perching. I understood the delight she took in observing these big, fierce, beautiful birds, because I shared her lifelong fascination with them.

When I first met Sandra in 1983, her peak in Dallas society as the wife of Bobby Bridewell was behind her, and she was in a decline that would end with her abrupt and ignominious move to California three years later. As I learned from my research, she had deeply affected countless people in the society in which I'd grown up, but many were reluctant to talk about their experiences with her because they were afraid that she would retaliate. Their fear had an ill-defined quality.

"Do you really believe that at the age of seventy-five, she's going to return to Dallas and murder everyone in her former social circle who is quoted in my book?" I often asked. My question was met with replies such as "You just never know with Sandra," or "I don't know, all I can say is that she scares the hell out of me," or "She just has an aura about her that is frightening."

I wondered if their perceptions arose from an archaic instinct that had a regulative function among our tribal ancestors prior to legal codes and courts. Had Sandra lived in a pre-modern society, she probably would have been cast out and told to stay away. Indeed, one witness of her life in Belvedere, California said half-jokingly that several of the town's female residents wanted to storm her apartment by the yacht club with pitchforks and torches and drive her out of town.

Who was this woman of many names, who'd play the roles of stylish suburban housewife, skilled seductress, and saintly missionary with equal gusto? Four different people, all college-educated, told me that, though they didn't really believe in witches, they couldn't resist thinking that Sandra was one. Other women who'd known her said they thought she was Satanically possessed, a Princess of Darkness, a female incarnation of the devil, and that the violent deaths recounted in the *D Magazine* feature were the tip of the iceberg. I heard a persistent rumor that she'd killed her college boyfriend by pushing him down the stairs of the Tyler Junior College dormitory, but none of my mother's friends who'd grown up in

Tyler had any recollection of this incident. Other women told me they'd heard that Sandra had pushed her grandmother, Camille Williams, down the stairs of her home in San Antonio. Mrs. Williams died on July 2, 1978, six days after Sandra married Bobby Bridewell. Her death certificate states the cause was a perforated ulcer.

While most women talked about Sandra's alleged perfidy, a few pointed out that she had suffered terrible misfortune, with her mother dying in a car accident when she was two, her father dying when she was twenty-six, and her second husband dying of cancer when she was thirty-eight. Was it possible that the deaths of her first and third husbands—as well as Betsy Bagwell—were part of the same run of exceedingly bad luck?

PART III
CINDERELLA AND
THE SUICIDES

CHAPTER 48
ANTECEDENTS

She was born in Sedalia, Missouri in 1944 of unknown parents and adopted by Arthur and Camille Powers. Originally from Dallas, the couple had, in 1941, relocated to the small city in the Ozarks, situated on the rail line between St. Louis and Kansas City. Her father had made the move to seek his fortune with a new Dr. Pepper bottling plant. On the eve of World War II, the Dallas-based company was growing, so it must have seemed like a promising enterprise. For the sum of one dollar, Art Powers and a partner bought a parcel of land in Sedalia where they built a 5000 square foot, state of the art facility. They had gotten a new local franchise for Dr. Pepper, and would also produce Life, a soda that was *lithiated*—meaning, it contained mood-altering lithium. A few months after the plant opened, Art financed a major promotion: a radio show, a half hour comedy called the *Dr Pepper Parade*, featuring vivacious Margaret McRae in the role of 'Pretty Peggy Pepper, and Molasses 'n' January, "radio's top-flight blackfaces team." Unfortunately, 1941 wasn't an auspicious year in which to start a new consumer products business. Still, by the spring of 1944, the Powers had enough money to buy a spacious house on a quiet street and to start a family. They couldn't have a child of their own, so they adopted the baby girl whom they named Sandra.

On November 12th, 1946, a notice appeared in the Tuesday *Sedalia Democrat* that Art was going to Miami for the American Bottlers of Carbonated Beverages convention, and that he'd be gone for at least ten days. In the Sunday issue, there appeared the headline: "Reports Intruder in Her Home."

> Mrs. Arthur Powers...was startled when she was awakened by a man standing over her at her home. ...The man, she declared, asked for the keys to the Dr. Pepper building. Mrs. Powers told him she did not have the keys, so he went through her purse and found only $2 in cash. He said that amount would do him no good. She described the man to the police as being heavily built ...with light brown hair and wearing a soiled brown leather jacket. 'You shouldn't stay in such a large house being by yourself,' he advised her. He then told her that he had hidden in the attic earlier in the day and saw her leave the house and later return alone.

Shortly after this incident, the Powers vacated the house they'd so recently bought for a smaller property on a busy street. Did Camille not feel safe, or was the money getting tight? And why had the intruder wanted keys to the Dr. Pepper plant?

Two months later, at the beginning of 1947, another article appeared, this one from the AP wire. Its dateline read *January 22nd, Dallas*. It reported a horrible traffic accident that occurred on Route 67, just east of the city. Mrs. Camille Powers was in the car with a man identified as her "cousin," C.A. Christenson, who had been a colonel in the Army air force. They had crashed head on into a tractor-trailer hauling gasoline, the impact crushing the car and its occupants. When police got to the scene, both Christenson and Sandra's mom were dead.

The report further stated that Mr. and Mrs. Powers and their daughter had come to Dallas three days earlier to visit the Christensons. On the night of the accident, they'd had dinner together, but Arthur had left for a hotel afterwards, "intending to go back to Sedalia," while his wife and daughter were to stay on in Dallas. Sandra was apparently with her grandparents—Camille's parents, who lived south of Dallas in the town of Ennis, which is where Christenson was allegedly to have been driving Camille. The circumstances presented in the AP report did not sound out of the ordinary, but Camille's death certificate states that the accident occurred at 4:00 a.m.

Ten weeks later, Easter 1947, a story appeared in the Sedalia paper about something happier: Sandra's third birthday party. It was elaborate, with a live mother rabbit and three babies, a big birthday cake with icing in Easter colors, everything in that theme. On the party table there were "little wagons filled with spring flowers…drawn by cardboard ducks and chickens, placed at intervals' before the children." Sandra led an Easter parade, and "Mr. Powers presented each little guest with a paper hat."

The article makes no reference to the recent tragedy, but it does mention someone who "assisted" Mr. Powers "in entertaining:" Miss Doris Fox. Doris had started working for Mr. Powers back when he first opened the bottling plant. Now she became the new Mrs. Powers, and six months after their wedding they had a son. Shortly after that, Art was severely injured in a hunting accident that resulted in multiple hospitalizations and ultimately the amputation of the wounded leg. Badly disabled, he then lost his stake in the bottling plant, with his-partner "announcing" Art's retirement from management.

In what seems unlikely to have been a happy time, the larger and very different Powers family moved back to Art's hometown in 1950. They arrived in a Dallas much changed from the one Sandra's parents had left. It was growing, fast. East Texas oil had helped win the war, with the Big Inch pipeline delivering its fuel to the industrial cities of the North. Flowing back the other way—into the pockets of oilmen and their Dallas banks—was money. Lots of it.

Most of America didn't realize who was making the money. Probably the Rockefellers, or Sun Oil, or one of the other majors. No one thought it was the local Texas folks. Weren't they just all cattle ranchers and hicks?

That perception changed overnight, when, in 1948, *Life* magazine ran a cover photo of H.L. Hunt with the headline, "Is this the Richest Man in America?" And so, the myth of the Texas oilman was born. The American press ran wild with stories of country boy wildcatters striking gushers and becoming instant sultans. *Giant* enshrined the myth, first as a #1 best seller, then as a Liz Taylor-James Dean movie.

Dallas was, in 1950, rapidly expanding in size and wealth, but Art Powers was not to share in its prosperity. Though only forty-four, something seems to have set him irrevocably back, and his move to Big D marked the end of his business career. Instead of finding another managerial position, he got a job selling burial plots at the Laurel Land Memorial Park in south Dallas. For a home he purchased a small house in the lower middle-class neighborhood of South Oak Cliff.

And so, already during Sandra's early childhood, some of the dramatic themes of her adult life emerged. That she was adopted and never knew her natural parents must have impressed upon her (as she developed adult awareness) of the uncertainty of identity, and perhaps the traumatic perception that she'd been unwanted. Then there was the violent death of her mother Camille. This must have impressed upon her the fragility of life and familial attachments, and how an unnatural death could change everything in an instant. Later, in early adulthood, Sandra told a few friends that her first sweetheart had been a West Point graduate who was killed when they were out on a date and got into a car accident. As she told the story, she wasn't badly hurt, but he was mortally injured and died in her arms. Her story, which was apparently a fabrication, seems to have been inspired by her mother's fatal car accident with an army officer in 1947, and perhaps also by the 1961 Wayne Cochran hit "Last Kiss."

In Sandra's father was personified the theme of stalled upward mobility. Arthur Powers never fully recovered from his hunting accident and the failure of his bottling plant venture, and he ended up spending the last twenty years of his life working a sad job in a sad part of Dallas, on the opposite side of the Trinity River from the city's booming center. He died on April 25, 1970 of suppurative bronchopneumonia due to pulmonary emphysema at the age of sixty-three.

Sandra's friends perceived that she loved and respected her father. They got the opposite impression of her relationship with her stepmother. Doris Fox Powers had worked in the office of Art's Dr. Pepper bottling plan from its earliest days, and it seems likely she was disappointed when her husband, who'd seemed like a man of position, lost his stake in the enterprise right after she married him. Their move to a humble and dull part of Dallas may have also caused her to wonder: *Is this really it for the rest of my life?*

Sandra attended Kimball High School in Oak Cliff, the same that legendary guitarist Stevie Ray Vaughan attended ten years later. To her friends, she described Doris as a "wicked stepmother" who beat her with willow branches, locked her into a dark closet, and forced her to clean the house to perfection. With dramatic imperiousness, Doris would (Sandra claimed) then perform the white glove test on various surfaces. If she detected any dust, she would make Sandra redo the entire cleaning. Likewise, Sandra was forced to iron clothes to perfection, and if Doris spotted the slightest wrinkle, she crumpled up the shirt or blouse and commanded Sandra to do it again. To an adult friend and neighbor, Sandra told the story of how, on one of her childhood birthdays, none of her friends came to a party at her family home. Doris told her that no one came because no one wanted to be with her.

"You're unwanted and you have no friends," she proclaimed. Later Sandra learned that Doris hadn't mailed out the invitations. Most disturbing was the way Doris pretended to be an affectionate mother in the presence of others, and then revert to her usual coldness as soon as they left.

It's difficult to evaluate Sandra's tales of her stepmother's cruelty because, as some of her high school friends noted, she was apparently inclined to making things up. Often, she told anecdotes that rang false or were obvious fabrications. To be sure, the wicked stepmother is an archetype because it's common for a man's second wife to snub the offspring from his previous marriage. Thus, there may have been some element of truth to Sandra's assertions about Doris.

After Sandra was arrested in North Carolina in 2007, the *Dallas Observer* reporter Glenna Whitley tried to learn more about Doris, who died in 1999. Some of her neighbors in South Oak Cliff still remembered her. Sometime in the mid to late nineties (none could remember the precise date) someone broke into Doris's house in the middle of the night and beat her to the point of hospitalization. Though she didn't die from the trauma, she never entirely recovered from it, and shortly thereafter was admitted to an assisted living facility. Her neighbors wondered why on earth someone would severely beat an elderly lady in her home, especially as burglary didn't seem to be the motive.

Glenna Whitley and Jayne Todd wondered if the alleged tension between the stepdaughter and "wicked stepmother" had culminated in a conflict about something—perhaps property in the estate of Sandra's father. The neighbors with whom Glenna spoke were confident that the home intrusion and beating had occurred, but Glenna was unable to find a DPD Incident Report to substantiate it. I too ran into a dead end in my investigation of this alleged incident, but I did find a record of Sandra repeatedly visiting a doctor in Plano (just north of Dallas) in the years 1995 and 1996. In 2003, she claimed to be a resident of Dallas County in a civil suit she filed against pharmaceutical companies for harm she claimed to have suffered from Fen-Phen diet pills. An interesting aside from this period was her transferal, on February 13, 2002, of two cemetery plots at Laurel Land to the Potter's House—an evangelical church run by the Bishop T.D. Jakes. The conveyance deed bears the name and signature of Sandra Powers Stegall, which she had not used since she married Robert Bridewell in 1978. On this document, she claimed to be the sole heir of Edward and Camille Williams, who'd owned the plots and were the parents of Sandra's mother, Camille Powers, who was killed in a car accident in 1947.

The story of Cinderella is ancient and universal, and millions of girls over the centuries have probably, at some point, compared themselves to her. However, in reviewing the testimony of Sandra's friends, as well as her own writings, one gets the impression that, well into her adult life, Sandra really believed she was just like Cinderella, and would someday savor the triumph of marrying a prince of a man.

In the perennial debate about nature vs. nurture, one thing has become clear: an individual's natural impulses can either be encouraged or discouraged by prevailing social and cultural norms. In Dallas between the years 1962 (when Sandra graduated from high school) and 1986 (when she abruptly departed for California), the Cinderella fantasy was a social norm. Indeed, as late as 1996, *D Magazine* published a long feature titled "Beautiful Women, Wealthy Men. "The opening paragraphs went to the heart of the matter:

ONCE UPON A TIME...
Every little girl since the Brothers Grimm knows how the story goes. The beautiful but poor young woman, with several strikes of various sorts against her, combats rivals and the system to wind up on the arm of Prince Charming. Handsome, powerful, rich Prince Charming. And while most of us settle for knights with tarnished armor (and sometimes frogs who never got kissed into princes}, there are those others...

Their tales may seem old-fashioned (and perhaps no longer politically correct), but in truth, their stories are part of a never-ending tale. Around the turn of the century, Edith Wharton planned a novel about nouveau riche young American women in search of titled Europeans. "The Buccaneers," she called it, but she died before she could finish the book. Well, rest easy. Miss Edith. A hundred years later, the quest continues right here in Dallas, where we've never run short of buccaneers.

In 1963, Sandra attended Tyler Junior College, where she was a member of the Sans Souci Club. After a year she dropped out and moved back to Dallas. Years later she told friends and associates that she'd attended and graduated from Southern Methodist University, but the registrar's office has no record of her taking courses at SMU. At her tenth high school reunion she claimed she'd attended Texas Christian University, but the TCU registrar has no record of her enrollment.

In 1966 she lived in the Windsor House Apartments on University Avenue—a popular neighborhood for singles fresh out of college. Soon after her return to Dallas she got a job working as a secretary for an independent oil man named Jimmy Kemp in his offices in the Mercantile National Bank Building—a landmark art deco office tower in Downtown Dallas in which many oilmen had offices. An East Texas country boy, Jimmy had left home when he was a boy to work on oilrigs and had learned the business from the ground up. His manners were rural, and his formal education limited, but he had immense charm and amiability. He was also scrupulously honest and never missed a loan payment (my grandfather John Sears was his banker).

Sandra told her friends that working for Mr. Kemp was excruciatingly boring and that her biggest task of the day was picking up the toothpicks that he dropped from his desk onto the floor. The most exciting thing that happened to her in this job was the time she got mugged. As she told some of her friends, the incident happened when she was walking to Mr. Kemp's bank to make a $3,000 cash deposit. Somehow the mugger seemed to know that she was carrying this large sum and threatened her with violence if she didn't hand it over. Years later, some of her friends wondered if the tale was true. The Neiman-Marcus department store was (and still is) located next door to the Mercantile. Could it be that with such a large sum in her purse, Sandra couldn't resist the temptation to pop in for a bit of shopping?

Her dull work as a secretary strengthened her perception that the professional world contained few if any opportunities for women. It seemed that, apart from being a secretary, a pretty girl could become a stewardess or a saleswoman at a clothing boutique, but obtaining a true career in an interesting field struck her as unrealistic. During this time, her friends noticed her dedication to learning about high culture and the realm of beautiful things. A subscriber to *Southern Living* and a skilled researcher, she assiduously studied the art of living with style. Her diligence paid off. In the coming years, many were charmed by her feminine grace. Men found her "terribly attractive" (as one of her admirers put it). The daughter of a burial plot salesman, mistreated by her wicked stepmother, was fashioning herself to win the affection of a Prince Charming.

In the year 1966, she went on dates with three exceedingly handsome young men. Two were graduates of Highland Park High School named Al Tatum and Jack Sides. As both men would relate decades later, they found Sandra beautiful and exciting, but neither was susceptible to the sort of total enthrallment she sought. And so, she focused her attention on a studious young man who'd had little experience with girls.

CHAPTER 49

THE FATHER OF
HER CHILDREN

The first thing you noticed about David Stegall was his Hollywood good looks. The twenty-six-year-old native of Fort Worth had a finely chiseled face with high cheekbones, widely set brown eyes, and a strong jaw. Living at the Spanish Trace Apartments, just east of Southern Methodist University, there was no end of the attention he got from pretty girls in the neighborhood. In those days the Spanish Trace (which no longer exists) had a reputation for being *the* singles apartment in Dallas for the smart and beautiful. Its owners were pals with Eddy Acker, who ran Braniff Airways, and by some favorable arrangement, several pretty Braniff stewardesses lived in the complex. The owners also hosted an annual Thanksgiving bash in Acapulco with free Braniff flights and hotel accommodations for all tenants who signed a lease that year. The Trace was legendary for its parties. In 1966, its atmosphere of carefree, sexy youth was only partly shadowed by the escalating Vietnam War.

Somehow, despite the myriad distractions offered by his surroundings, David remained focused and goal oriented. Growing up in Fort Worth, he'd studied horsemanship and calf roping with a famous rodeo cowboy and horse trainer named Lanham Riley. Though he had no intention of being a rodeo professional, he pursued his hobby with great dedication. Often while conversing with friends, he still had a conspicuous habit of practicing the wrist and arm movements of tossing a lariat. He applied the same diligence to practicing golf and studying dentistry.

His close friends knew him as an optimistic, happy-go-lucky guy, self-assured that no matter how difficult the task, he could pull it off. After graduating from Texas Christian University in Fort Worth, he attended the Baylor College of Dentistry to earn his DDS. Most people think of dentistry as the business of combatting tooth decay with cleaning and cavity filling. David was interested in a specialized discipline known as Reconstructive Dentistry—the painstaking work of recording the irregularities of the patient's teeth and then correcting them with crowns. One of the great masters of the discipline was Dr. Peter K. Thomas in Los Angeles, who had a roster of Hollywood clients. David made a pilgrimage to LA for special training with Dr. Thomas. Returning to Dallas, he told his friends that in one of his sessions in the doctor's office, he was introduced to the actor Paul Newman, whom he found surprisingly friendly. David aspired to build a practice in Dallas with a well-heeled clientele analogous to Dr. Thomas's.

With his studious habits, David had never shown much interest in girls. This changed when he met a twenty-two-year-old girl who lived in the Windsor House Apartments, across the street from the Trace. Her name was Sandra Camille Powers, and there was something extraordinary about her. It wasn't just her remarkable beauty—her flawless white skin and contrasting dark brown hair and full breasts—but also her graceful, feminine bearing and her elegant style. An engaging conversationalist with a great sense of humor, she was also a marvelous listener. Whenever David spoke, she had a way of fixing him with her big brown eyes as though he were the most fascinating man she'd ever met.

To be sure, he didn't know much about Sandra because she'd grown up in South Oak Cliff, which lies on the opposite (southwest) side of the Trinity River from Dallas's commercial and residential core. In 1966, most of David's friends were either old pals from Fort Worth or new friends from the Park Cities (Highland and University Park). None of them had grown up with Sandra, and she had apparently lost contact with the South

Oak Cliff milieu in which she'd grown up.

Whatever David knew or thought he knew about Sandra's antecedents had no bearing on his interest in her. She was a beautiful and talented girl, and as he told a friend, sex with her was like a religious experience. Instantly he was smitten. Just six weeks after he met her, he proposed marriage. His cousin, Nancy Stegall, who also lived in Dallas, suspected that the hasty engagement may have been prompted by Sandra claiming to be pregnant. Nancy later came to doubt her suspicion, because the couple's first child—a boy named Britton— was born nine months after their May 26, 1967, wedding. Almost twenty years later, when Nancy heard that Sandra had told Alan Rehrig she was pregnant and then shortly thereafter feigned a miscarriage, she wondered if Sandra had done the same double deception to David during the period between their early romance and their wedding.

Initially it seemed that David's professional aspirations perfectly complemented Sandra's social ability and ambition. He wanted to assemble a wealthy clientele; she wanted to live in the best part of Dallas and to entertain in the grand style. With enormous energy, David threw himself into building his dental practice in the Park Cities. He succeeded, and within a few years, his office in Preston Center (in University Park) had a rapidly growing client base.

Their second child, a girl named Kathryn, was born in 1970. Two years later, they bought a home in Greenway Parks—a neighborhood to the immediate west of the Park Cities. Though Greenway Parks doesn't lie in the Highland Park Independent School District, some of its streets and green spaces are more beautiful than many sections of the Park Cities. In the same year David and Sandra bought their new home, OPEC announced an oil embargo against the countries supporting Israel during the Yom Kippur War. Almost overnight, the price of oil—which had been declining since 1957—spiked and doubled in early 1974. Suddenly Dallas-based oil companies were booming and injecting new wealth into the city.

This was the era in which the Dallas Cowboys began their ascent to becoming "America's Team." In 1971 they won their first Super Bowl, which cast the spotlight on its marvelous coach, Tom Landry, and its mediagenic players. The Cowboys' success also generated public interest its owner, Clint Murchison, Jr., son of the legendary oilman, Clint Murchison, Sr. The image of the Texas oilman as a freewheeling, larger than life character originated in the personalities of the elder Murchison and H.L. Hunt. Their children and grandchildren were some of the most prominent members of Dallas society.

And so, the early seventies were the beginning of a new era of confidence, opulence, and optimism in Dallas, when the city overcame the stain of the Kennedy assassination a decade earlier. During this period, the need to "Keep up with the Joneses" became even more imperative. Young and ambitious men craved to make money and display it with big homes, cars, and country club memberships. The ultimate expression of success was having an elegant, well-dressed, and be-jeweled wife. For the city's moneyed class, a Neiman-Marcus charge account was a standard arrangement.

Such was the environment into which Sandra launched herself. Ensconced in her new Greenway Parks neighborhood, she set about making a splash. David was polite and hardworking, but she was the driving force behind their social advance. Stylish and fun, she had a flair for cooking and entertaining. She also joined Saint Michael and All Angels Episcopal—the most patrician church in Dallas—and became the co-editor of its cookbook. She worked hard to get it beautifully illustrated and printed, turning what was originally conceived as a simple pamphlet into a fine book for which she wrote the forward in notably florid prose. Decades later, many ladies still retained and referenced their copies of it.

Quickly Sandra befriended many women in her new, exclusive society. To those who'd grown up in established Dallas families, she seemed to have come out of nowhere. With her soft-spoken, feminine style, she had the distinct aura of a Southern belle, and she told at least one person that she was born in Belleville, Alabama. In the year 1973, she seemed destined to become a Dallas society lady. David shared his wife's optimism and enthusiasm. Nineteen seventy-three was a banner year for his dental practice in which he doubled his income. His growing patient roster included Dallas luminaries such as the pioneering female entrepreneur Ebby Halliday. However, as David had apparently failed to grasp, buying a home was one thing, decorating and furnishing it quite another.

CHAPTER 50

A BLACK BELT IN
HOME DECORATING

In the early seventies in Dallas, the free-spending wife of a rich man was a stock character. As Clint Murchison Jr. once famously quipped about his first wife, "Jane has a black belt in shopping." For him this was more or less a laughing matter, but for David Stegall, his wife's out of control spending was a disaster. The trouble with dentistry is that it's not scalable. Even if a dentist is doing costly reconstructive work, he can still only charge for each job he performs, and there are only so many hours in a day. When Sandra married David in 1967, he was a young man on the make, and his Hollywood training with Dr. Thomas gave a touch of glamour to an occupation that was otherwise lacking it. But no dentist, no matter how industrious, could compete with Dallas's oil, real estate, and banking crowd.

An obvious and unfavorable comparison for David was his friend Bill Hardy, whom he'd met at the Spanish Trace. Bill was married to a beautiful Braniff stewardess he'd met in the apartment complex named Linda Sue McCrary, and he'd made a fortune in real estate. He and Linda lived in a grand house on a beautiful North Dallas property, surrounded by a wrought iron fence with two driveways entering through matching, splendid gates. The centerpiece for summer entertaining was a big swimming pool surrounded by gardens with multiple decks and patios. In the evening the pool area was illuminated by gas torches. It was a true pleasure palace in which the Dom Perignon steadily flowed. Sandra hit it off with Bill and Linda, and they invited her to be the godmother of their second son, Damon.

Sandra frequently visited the Hardy residence, and the experience fueled her ambition to make her own home as beautiful as possible. Shortly after they moved in, she embarked on a major remodeling. For the interior she hired the prestigious designer, John Astin Perkins, whose client roster included Clint Murchison and Ross Perot. Flamboyant and charming, Perkins had a knack for entertaining clients and encouraging them to realize their dreams of having beautiful houses. He is still fondly remembered for his quip to an IRS auditor who refused to believe that he could spend such a vast sum of tax write-off money on client lunches.

"I'd take you to lunch if you weren't so tacky," he said.

He liked to whet the appetite of a promising client by showing up at her house with a pretty painting or piece of furniture.

"I think this would look magnificent in your living room," he would remark. "Why don't you keep it for a while and see if you agree with me?" A month later, after the lady had grown attached to the object, she would receive an extravagant flower arrangement from Perkins, and shortly thereafter her husband would receive a bill for the furniture.

Sandra also bought art and antiques from the Dallas connoisseurs Lloyd Taylor and Paxton Germillion. Like their colleague Perkins, Loyd and Paxton were known for decorating and furnishing the houses of Big D's wealthiest. Sandra told her friends that she aspired to get her home featured in *Architectural Digest*. They were impressed by her style, and everyone loved her dinner parties. Just one year after David and Sandra moved to Greenway Parks, they were in deep financial trouble, with bank debt, credit card bills, and an IRS lien on their new home.

In the fall of 1974, shortly after the birth of their third child—a girl named Emily—David borrowed $100,000 from his father. This got the IRS off his back, but it wasn't enough to cover their still mounting debts. David made a foray into real estate by putting another house under contract with the intent of flipping it for a quick profit. As a fellow dentist's wife observed, he worked increasingly long hours to pay the bills. He seemed strung out, and the quality of his work began to suffer. His marriage to Sandra faltered as they bickered about money. David's friends perceived that she shamed him and made him feel inadequate for his inability to maintain the lifestyle to which she felt entitled. *I guess you're not the man I thought you were*, she seemed to signal. Sandra told one of her friends she suspected that David was having an affair. To other friends she said he'd grown volatile, was drinking heavily, and that she was afraid of him.

One evening around the beginning of February 1975, Sandra called David's estate planning attorney, Jack Sides—the same man with whom Sandra had gone out on a few dates before she married David. She told Jack that David was drunk and that she was afraid of what he might do. Jack rushed to their house and saw what appeared to be a standoff. Sandra and two of her kids were in the master bedroom, seated on the edge of the bed facing an open closet. David sat on the closet floor with his back against the wall, holding a pistol.

"David, just what in hell do you think you're doing?" said Jack.

"I can't take it anymore; I'm gonna kill myself."

"No, you're not," Jack said. "You're just going through a rough patch and you're going pull out of it and be just fine. Now I'm coming in there to get that pistol." Jack slowly approached David and took the gun away without a struggle.

A few days later, David invited Jack to join him for dinner and apologized for the drama.

"It's been a rough time, but I can assure you I'd never kill myself. I love my kids and I'll get through this." Jack believed David's assurance. Sure, he had money troubles, but he was still a young, strong, and handsome man with a valuable dental practice.

CHAPTER 51
"SOMETHING TERRIBLE HAS HAPPENED TO DAVID."

Dr. George Edwards was one of David's oldest friends. They'd grown up in Fort Worth together and were classmates at the Baylor College of Dentistry. After graduation, George married and settled in his native city, while David and Sandra settled in Dallas. In the early days of their marriages, the two couples occasionally socialized, but after David and Sandra bought their house in Greenway Park, George saw less and less of his old friend.

"Why do you live in that cow town?" Sandra once told George in a supercilious tone. "All you have to do is look at all the Cadillacs and Mercedes in our neighborhood to know that Dallas is the place to be." It was a vapid remark and it fell flat with George and his wife.

During the first week of February 1975, George was pleasantly surprised to receive a call from David. He suggested they play golf together in Fort Worth on the coming Saturday. The weather was unseasonably warm, and they shot a pleasant round, over which David spoke candidly about his failed marriage.

"Sandra has spent me to the poor house," he said. "I can't even afford new tires for my car." It was a depressing situation, but to George, David didn't seem so much despondent as resolved to get out of the marriage and start over.

"Maybe I'll move to LA, buy a Porsche convertible, and find a cute blond," he remarked, perhaps only half joking. At the conclusion of their game, David proposed they shoot another round the following Saturday, which they did. They planned to play yet another round the following Saturday, February 22. The day before this scheduled meeting, David spoke with his brother Gene, and mentioned he'd be in Fort Worth the following day to play golf. To Gene he seemed in good spirits, looking forward to his Saturday game.

Sometime around 6:30 the next morning, Saturday, February 22, 1975, Sandra called the house of Dr. Paul Radman and his wife Elizabeth. Paul was one of David's dental colleagues, but Sandra's real connection to the couple was with Elizabeth. The two women had met at a social hosted by the Dallas County Dental Association and really hit it off. Elizabeth answered the phone. Sandra was distraught and said that something terrible had happened to David. The Radmans dressed and rushed to the Stegall residence, about a seven-minute drive away. Approaching the house, Paul noted that no police cars were parked in front. They entered the house and saw two or three other couples in the living room. The women were comforting Sandra; the men were standing around like they weren't sure of what to do. Paul peered into the master bedroom and saw David lying in bed. Even from several feet away, he could see the gunshot to his head and the obvious fact that he was dead. Paul did not attempt to inspect David, but returned to the living room, at which point one of the guests suggested that Sandra call 911. Paul left before the police arrived.

At 7:07 am, Sandra called 911 and reported that her husband had committed suicide. When Dallas police officers arrived, she told them that she had, that night, slept in one of her children's rooms on the other side of the house. At around 7:00 a.m. she'd gone into the master bedroom to find David lying in bed in a pool of blood. She must have told the investigating officers that she had *not* been awakened by the pistol shot, because the DPD Incident Report stated that it occurred between "2:00

am—7:00 am." What else Sandra told the investigating officers was *not* recorded in the DPD Incident Report.

A field agent from the Dallas County Medical Examiner's Office arrived to examine the death scene, and he told the investigating DPD Officer that the death was a "probable suicide." Color photographs were taken of the scene. A few features of the death scene might have given pause to wonder if the deceased had in fact killed himself. However, first impressions are often the strongest, and the initial suspicion of suicide was bolstered by the well-known fact that suicide is far more common than homicide. The beautiful, grieving, thirty-year-old widow in her elegant home also seemed like a credible witness.

At 9:10 a.m., the investigators concluded their work and David's body was taken to the Medical Examiner's Office. At 10:30 a.m., the Chief Medical Examiner performed an external examination of David's body, but not an autopsy. Like the medical examiner field investigator, the Chief Medical Examiner suspected suicide, though he apparently waited for more information from the DPD before he made his final determination. After their initial death scene examination, the DPD traced the weapon found with David to his friend Bill Hardy. A DPD officer visited Mr. Hardy, who explained that he'd kept the pistol in a dresser in his backhouse apartment, over the garage. The investigating officer concluded that David had stolen the weapon from his old friend instead of buying a pistol from a gun or pawnshop. Four days after David died, the DPD closed the case with a file note that stated: "Report from the Institute of Forensic Sciences indicates complainant's cause of death as gunshot wound of head, the manner is listed as suicide. No further inv. required." David Lawrence Stegall was 32 years old.

About an hour after David's body was taken to the medical examiner's office, Jack Sides and his wife Nancy got a call from Sandra, who broke the news that David had killed himself. They too went to the Stegall house to comfort her. By the time they arrived, several friends and neighbors were already there. Jack was surprised by the atmosphere, which seemed more like that of a cocktail party than a gathering to comfort a grieving widow. Sandra looked beautiful in a cute yellow dress, and to Jack, she seemed to be basking in the attention.

Sandra was David Stegall's sole heir and the beneficiary of his life insurance policy. With his death benefit of $160,000 and the proceeds from the sale of their house for $147,500, she was able to pay off their debts and live comfortably with her three children, at least for a while. She also found a buyer for her deceased husband's dental practice. David had worked hard to build his business—four years of dental school, then special training in reconstructive dentistry, and then over six years of diligent practice. Sandra sold it to Dale Rabinowitz, one of the few female dentists in Dallas, for $15,000. The first thing Dr. Rabinowitz noticed when she walked into the office were three beautiful portraits of David's children by the studio photographer, Paul Gittings. Dale told the attorney who handled the sale that Sandra was free to pass by any time to pick up the portraits. She never did.

CHAPTER 52
THE RESTAURATEUR

David Stegall's friends blamed Sandra for his death. As they saw it, her refusal to rein in her spending had driven him to ruin and despair. His troubles with the IRS had been particularly distressing. Nowadays the agency is more inclined to negotiate with individuals who are behind on their taxes. In 1975 its personnel were far more intimidating. Within the dental profession, there were widely known stories of dentists getting into trouble with the IRS and committing suicide because they saw no way out. In David's case, his father helped him to pay off the IRS, which solved his most pressing problem. However, as most of David's friends and colleagues understood it, he was still under tremendous stress. And so, they turned against Sandra.

Thirty years old, with three children aged one, four, and seven, she had to move on with little support from her dead husband's circle. To be sure, she wasn't bereft of *all* support. During her marriage she had cultivated numerous friendships with people who found her delightful and knew little about her relationship with David. They saw her as the victim of a tragedy—a young widow and mother in need. St. Michael Episcopal Church was especially helpful. Because Sandra's oldest child, Britt, was a student in the church's elementary school, she received an outpouring of support from his classmates' mothers. Shortly after David's death, a deaconess contacted Mrs. Nancy Pearcy—the wife of the banker John Pearcy. The deaconess requested that Nancy host Sandra's children for a while to give the widow some quiet time to grieve and gather strength. Nancy, who'd lost a child in 1969, was sympathetic and gladly accepted the responsibility. And so, for a few weeks, Sandra's three kids moved into the Pearcy's big, beautiful home on Beverly Drive, next to the Dallas Country Club.

During this same period, the antique dealers Lloyd and Paxton contacted one of their best customers—an insurance executive named John Ridings Lee. They explained that Sandra Stegall was a great lady in dire need because of her husband's death. Would he be so kind to introduce her to one of his single friends? John agreed, and a few nights later, he and his wife Carole invited Sandra to join them and a bachelor friend for dining and dancing at the Cipango Club. Their concern that the grieving widow might not be much fun was dispelled after a few drinks, when she hit the dance floor with their bachelor friend. A big smile appeared on her face, and boy could she cut a rug!

"Sandra was always so much fun," her former friend, Delia Mullins (now Crossley) said of her during this period. "She just made you want to be with her and do things for her. She had a great sense of humor and was up for anything. She was always immaculately dressed and a pleasure to look at with her lustrous brown hair and big, dancing brown eyes. She had this infectious smile that would turn up in a mischievous way. We used to stay up all night talking and laughing. My God we used to laugh! There was never a time when I didn't want to be with her. And it was always funny and endearing how excited she'd get about a new man. I remember the time she came over the morning after a big date and was just glowing with happiness and singing the Engelbert Humperdinck song 'After the Lovin.'

The trouble with Sandra, as Delia discovered, is that she lived wildly beyond her means, had no intention of getting a job, and was struggling to form a permanent relationship with a wealthy man. All men found her alluring, but after a year of dating, she still hadn't converted the initial excitement into a lasting bond. But then, in late summer of 1976, she almost landed a big fish.

Two months after David Stegall's death, a feature appeared in *D Magazine* about "The Ten Sexiest Women in Dallas." Number seven on the list was Magrit Brinker.

> The wife of Steak and Ale's founder Norman Brinker, Magrit Liselotte Fendt Brinker is probably one of the most widely liked and admired women on the beauty and social circuit... Their intimates cite Norman and Magrit Brinker as one of the most ideally happy couples in the realm of possibility; there is money, travel, an athletic regimen, a quite open affection, and the class to cope with it. Norman, as the saying goes, can pick em. His first wife, the late international tennis star Maureen Connolly Brinker, would have been on this list, too. Magrit Brinker's ebullient appeal has the courtliness and reserved verve of European style. ... Her favorite writer is Dostoyevsky, especially *Crime and Punishment.*

The "intimates" cited in this account of Magrit's marriage didn't know the couple as well as they thought they did. Other witnesses had observed Norm's frank expressions of weariness with his wife. Women who admired him snickered at her heavy German accent and her habit of calling him "my little *Sachertorte*"—an exceptionally sweet chocolate cake with apricot jam named after the Hotel Sacher in Vienna. Three months after this feature appeared, Norm filed for divorce from Magrit. Six months later, a full-page report appeared in the *Dallas Morning News* about Brinker's sale of Steak and Ale—a pioneering casual dining chain of 109 restaurants—to Pillsbury. Though much of his winnings were in Pillsbury stock, the deal was a huge score for Norm.

Norman Eugene Brinker was a man in full. The former Naval officer and 1952 Olympic Equestrian was athletic, good-looking, brilliant, and rich. At this moment in his career, he was on his way to becoming one of the biggest restaurateurs in history, with Brinker International ultimately booking over four billion per year in sales. In the summer of 1976, his eligibility as a bachelor was impaired because he was still married and embroiled in a drawn-out divorce, but this didn't deter Sandra. At that time, she was living in a duplex on University Boulevard, just south of the Highland Park High School, and a one-minute drive from the Preston Road Car Wash, where everyone in the Park Cities got their cars cleaned. Norm lived in North Dallas, near the Willow Bend Polo and Equestrian Club, which he'd founded. He went to a car wash close to his home.

Even at the time, Delia Mullins and Nancy Pearcy wondered if it was just a coincidence that Sandra was at this car wash, far north of her residence, at the same time Norman Brinker was. Could it be that Sandra had followed him and gotten lucky when he pulled into the place? Whether the encounter was fortuitous or intentional, soon he was taking her out on dates.

To Delia, Sandra spoke of Norm in the most idealistic terms. She expressed confidence that she would soon be the next Mrs. Norman Brinker, thereby uniting their two families into what Sandra called "The Brinker Bunch," just like the popular television show *The Brady Bunch*. The only thing standing in her way was his wife, whom she claimed was stalking and harassing her. Sandra told a few of her friends that Magrit had thrown a knife at her. Once, when Nancy Sides was visiting her, Sandra pointed to a broken window in the building's stairwell, facing the street, and said that Magrit had shot it with a gun. One evening, over dinner at the Pearcy residence, Sandra showed them photographs of her bathroom mirror on which was scrawled in lipstick the words SLUT and WHORE. Margrit had (Sandra claimed) broken into her duplex to commit this vile act. There was no telling what the unhinged woman would do. Sandra felt scared for her life and for the lives of her children, and beseeched Nancy Pearcy to give her refuge in their home. For the second time, how could Nancy say no?

The three Stegall kids lived in the backhouse, behind the swimming pool, while Sandra lived in a spare bedroom in the main house. For a while it was fun having them around. And it just so happened that both Pearcy girls were equestrians who rode at Willow Bend. They admired the great Olympian Norman Brinker. The older girl, Camille, had a crush on him. That Sandra was dating him gave her a mystique and fascination.

One balmy evening in the autumn of 1976, Sandra announced that Norm was coming over to pick her up for a date. She wanted to create an enchanting atmosphere for his arrival.

"I'd like to crack the window next to the grand piano to let in the breeze. As he approaches the house, I'm going to start playing. When he rings the doorbell, I'd like you to let him in and direct him here while I continue to play, and the evening breeze catches my hair."

Nancy agreed to play her assigned role. As Norman approached the entrance, Sandra struck up a romantic piece. He rang the doorbell. Nancy greeted him and directed him to the main salon, where Sandra was playing intently, apparently not noticing his entrance. Then, as the breeze caught her pretty brown hair, she turned towards him and acted perfectly surprised and delighted.

"Oh, Norman darling, what a nice surprise! How happy I am to see you!" Nancy Pearcy thought this was the most extraordinary and ridiculous bit of theater she'd ever seen. Decades later the memory still made her laugh out loud. And yet Norm did seem to find it enchanting. All the same, the liaison was not to last. About a month later he broke it off, dashing her dream of the Brinker Bunch. Not long after their rupture, Sandra appeared at John Pearcy's office and asked him for a loan.

"I'm a commercial banker," he replied. "I don't make personal loans." To this she responded by unbuttoning her blouse to reveal her breasts— a catastrophic misjudgment of John Pearcy, who had no interest in her. He threw her out of his office and told his wife, who in turn sent Sandra and her kids packing back to her duplex. Though Sandra's gambit didn't work with Mr. Pearcy, it didn't deter her from trying it again with the independent oilman and banker Searcy Ferguson. One day she unexpectedly appeared at his office wearing a full-length mink coat, shut the door behind her, and asked for a personal loan. When he told her he couldn't help her, she cast off the mink to reveal her completely naked body. He too threw her out of his office.

Around this same time, Linda Sue Hardy—the thirty-six-year-old wife of David Stegall's friend, Bill Hardy—developed an excruciating migraine headache. After a few days of agony, she was, on December 3, 1976, rushed to the Presbyterian Hospital, where she died a few hours later. The Dallas County medical examiner performed a post-mortem examination of her brain and concluded she'd died of a massive hemorrhagic stroke. Shortly after Linda's death, Sandra appeared at the Hardy residence bearing gifts for the children. Something about her demeanor gave Bill Hardy the impression that she wasn't so much grieving her friend Linda's death as hoping to replace her in the Hardy household. He found this spooky, and after the incident, he avoided Sandra and ceased inviting her over, even though she was the godmother of his second son. Shortly after Linda died, a few of Sandra's friends noticed that she frequently wore a full-length mink coat that looked a lot like Linda Hardy's. They wondered if she'd stolen it from Linda's closet or if Bill had given it to her.

Though Sandra's love affair with Norm Brinker ended, it wasn't a clean break. She became embroiled in his divorce, which dragged on for another year. She was deposed on December 27, 1976, and then again on June 2, 1977—a few days after Magrit was deposed and on the same day as Norm's deposition. What Sandra said in her depositions was concealed from the public because Brinker's divorce file subsequently disappeared from the Dallas County Civil Courts archive. Sandra had already complicated his divorce, and it seems likely her depositions contained statements that he didn't want to be available to the public. The lesson was clear: a high-status man—especially if he's married—will take pains to avoid bad publicity.

CHAPTER 53

AN UNFORGETTABLE
SIGHT

One icy morning in the winter of 1977, Sandra broke some bad news to Delia. She was, she claimed, pregnant with a married man's child. And not just any married man, but one of the most prominent bankers in Dallas and a deacon at the Highland Park Presbyterian Church. He wanted to hear nothing about the child and had cut off contact with Sandra, thereby leaving her with no choice but to get an abortion. A few days later, Delia's husband Clark gave Sandra a ride to the hospital for the procedure. Only later did it occur to Delia that the abortion may have been a fabrication, and that her hospital visit was for something else. Maybe Sandra told her the melodramatic story about her pregnancy from a heartless banker to rejuvenate Delia's waning sympathy. A while later, Delia heard from another lady in the neighborhood that Sandra had, in fact, gotten a hysterectomy during this period.

It was around this time that Delia began to grow weary of Sandra. The more Delia and Clark helped her, the more favors she asked. Already they'd loaned her their spare car and paid several of her bills, but her needs never seemed to end. They encouraged her to get a job. With her social ability and interest in homes, furniture, and art, she could be a great residential real estate agent, or she could work in an antique shop or art gallery. But no, Sandra had no desire for employment. She wanted a rich man to take care of her.

In early 1977, Sandra moved from her duplex to an apartment at the Terrace House on Maple Avenue. She asked Delia's husband Clark if he would help her to transport some special objects that she didn't want handled by the movers. Clark arrived at her apartment and was irritated when she started flirting with him. She wasn't wearing a bra under her blouse, and she repeatedly bent over to reveal her breasts. He didn't take the bait. Then, when he handled a porcelain vase in a way that displeased her, her flirty manner abruptly shifted to anger, and she barked at him to be careful. To Clark, it seemed her mask had suddenly fallen away, revealing something aggressive and ugly, and he recoiled from it. She noticed his response and checked herself, reverting to the sweet girl, but it was too late.

"That girl would screw a snake," Clark told Delia when he returned home.

Delia's son Wendell, who was still close friends with Sandra's son Britt, occasionally spent the night at Sandra's new place at the Maple Terrace. Her apartment was on the fourth or fifth floor, and one day Britt and Wendell got into trouble with Sandra for taking light bulbs from her vanity and tossing them off the balcony onto the pavement below. Though Wendell was only nine, he perceived that Sandra was not like other mothers. She was beautiful, with flawless white skin that gave her the appearance of a porcelain doll, and she had an engaging manner that (decades later) Wendell described as "incredibly flirtatious."

One night, Wendell slept on a day bed in a little study adjoining the dining room. For ventilation, he left the door open, and in the middle of the night he was awakened by a sound in the adjoining dining room, whose walls were lined with large mirrors. He opened his eyes and saw Sandra standing in his field of view, in front of the large dining room window. Brightly illuminated by the full moon, her naked body was visible under her sheer negligee. She seemed to be admiring herself in the dining room mirrors that surrounded her. He too was transfixed by her beauty in the moonlight, but what was especially notable about her was the fact that she was holding a large chef's knife.

She held it at hip level, pointed forward and cocked slightly downwards, causing the large stainless blade to catch and reflect the moonlight, which in turn flashed in the surrounding mirrors. Wendell didn't move or make a peep, but just lay there watching her, fascinated and frightened. She stood there for a while, and then quietly left the dining room. It was the strangest thing Wendell had ever seen, truly an unforgettable sight.

Around the same time that Wendell witnessed this spectacle, Sandra called his father, Clark, and asked for a personal loan, hastening to add that he shouldn't tell Delia about her request. As was the case with John Pearcy, this was a terrible error of judgment. Clark told Delia about the request, and she didn't flinch from telling Sandra that she'd had enough of her sponging ways and didn't want to see her anymore.

Two years after the death of David Stegall, the money Sandra had inherited from his estate was running out. The unemployed, thirty-three-year-old mother of three children was in a precarious position. To be sure, she was at the height of her seductive powers. To one of the men whom she dated at the time, she jokingly compared herself to Loretta Young, and in fact she did resemble the film noir screen idol. Nevertheless, she had alienated the sympathy and affection of her closest female friends and spooked the rich men who'd initially been charmed by her.

CHAPTER 54
"THE HEAVIES WANT YOU."

Two years had passed since David Stegall's death, but Dr. Paul Radman still occasionally thought about the mild-mannered, hard-working young man who had taken his own life. David's office had been in the same building in Preston Center, and his wife, Sandra Stegall, still occasionally socialized with Dr. Radman's wife Elizabeth. On the morning of March 9, 1977, he pulled into the building's underground parking garage. As he got out of his car and walked toward the building entrance, a man in his mid-thirties wearing a business suit and sport shirt got out of a parked car, and said, "Are you Dr. Paul Radman?"

"Yes," he replied, at which point the man drew a semi-automatic pistol and said, "The heavies want you." With the pistol he gestured to Dr. Radman to get into the trunk of a beige-colored Plymouth. He complied at first, but then thought better of it as the car ascended the ramp to street level, so he started kicking the trunk lid like mad. The car stopped and the assailant opened the trunk, struck him in the face, and commanded him to hold still. Somehow Dr. Radman managed to scramble out of the trunk, and saw he was in the parking lot across the street from the Sanger-Harris department store. He made a run for it and the man fired a shot that lightly grazed his face. He fell to the ground and pretended to be dead. The assailant walked up, stood over him, and shot him in the back. Some men delivering clothing to Sanger-Harris saw the incident and yelled at the assailant, who got into his car and sped away. They couldn't get the license number because no plate was mounted on the front of the car.

The gunshot did not strike any vital organs and Dr. Radman was soon released from hospital. As he told the police, he was a dentist, knew of no enemies, and had received no threats. Thus, he had no idea who tried to abduct him. That the man had shot him in the back while standing directly over him indicated that the gunman's contractor wanted him dead, but why on earth would someone want to kill him? What could possibly be gained from his death?

CHAPTER 55
PRINCE CHARMING

Around the time that Sandra gave her second deposition in the divorce of Norman Brinker from Magrit Fendt Brinker, Bobby Bridewell discovered that his wife was having an affair with her horse trainer at their ranch in Celina. Their ranch happened to be located near the Cloyce Box Ranch, where shooting was scheduled in a few months for the first season of DALLAS—a soap opera in which marital infidelity, divorce, intrigue, blackmail, and attempted murder played a prominent role. Although the show's writers weren't from Texas—and although the show was originally inspired by Ingmar Bergman's 1973 miniseries *Scenes from a Marriage*—DALLAS captured the melodramatic Zeitgeist of the late seventies, when the city was the divorce capital of the world.

It is no exaggeration that Bobby Bridewell was, at the time, the most popular man in Dallas society. Word quickly spread when his marriage landed on the rocks, and Sandra realized this disaster provided an opportunity for her. As she'd done with Norm Brinker, she researched his background, social network, and hobbies. Just as Norm was pleasantly surprised by her unexpected appearance at the carwash, Bobby was delighted by the spectacle of her jumping out of his birthday cake in a slinky dress.

The latter half of 1979 was the highpoint of Sandra's life in Dallas, with Bobby back in business with the Mansion. Just three years later, he would be dead, and Sandra would be ostracized by Highland Park society following the death of Betsy Bagwell. By the time she had her fortuitous encounter with Alan Rehrig on June 2, 1984, she was socially isolated and running out of money and options.

A notable feature of Alan's story was the strange fact that he remained entirely ignorant of the reality of Sandra's past until the last month of his life. He had no idea that many people in his tight-knit community were mortally afraid of her and afraid for him. Apart from the lady he encountered on Lorraine Avenue right after he met Sandra, no one told him his wife was widely perceived to be dangerous. It would have been easy enough for someone to send an anonymous note to his office or to speak with one of his friends about her. Even though Cissy Alsabrook was Sandra's bridesmaid, she still found it disconcerting how completely unaware Alan was of his bride's reputation. Sandra often complained that she was a victim of gossip in the Park Cities, especially among housewives who were jealous of her. It's a remarkable fact that none of it reached her third husband.

After Alan was murdered, his friends and especially his mother Gloria wondered about Highland Park society. Because its respectable residents seemed to place such a high value on privacy, discretion, and appearances, no individual or institutional leader ever spoken out against Sandra. Ultimately Gloria concluded that the rotten core of the Sandra Bridewell story was the failure to investigate her for the death of Betsy Bagwell. How had this failure come about?

PART IV
MY INVESTIGATION

CHAPTER 56

THE MYSTERIOUS DEATH OF MARY ELIZABETH BAGWELL

After the *D Magazine* feature appeared in 1987, many in the Park Cities figured the Dallas Police Department and Dallas County Medical Examiner must have gotten it wrong with their conclusions that David Stegall and Betsy Bagwell had committed suicide. After Alan Rehrig was murdered, many suspected that Sandra had killed all three. But if this was indeed the case, why had the DPD and Medical Examiner quickly concluded that the previous two deaths were suicides?

"How on earth did Sandra get away with it?" was a question I often heard from her former friends.

Already in the summer of 2007, after Sandra was arrested in North Carolina, I attempted to reexamine the purported suicides of David Stegall and Betsy Bagwell. I submitted requests to the DPD for its reports on both cases, and to the Medical Examiner's Office for its autopsy reports. Both the DPD and the medical examiner replied they had *no* reports on David Stegall.

For Mary Elizabeth Bagwell, I received an Incident Report, a Trace Evidence Report, and an Autopsy Report. These documents revealed that the Medical Examiner had based his suicide ruling on three elements:

1). The contact gunshot wound to Betsy's right temple.

2). The pistol found in her right hand.

3). The gunshot residue found on her right hand.

Based on published statistical analyses of hundreds of suicides, the medical examiner concluded that these three features of Betsy's death were evidence of suicide. The medical examiner, Dr. Charles Petty, was regarded as an eminent authority and greatly respected by the DPD and DA's Office. Thus, in the matter of Mary Elizabeth Bagwell, the DPD had taken its lead from Dr. Petty. As Sergeant Tom Sherman said to the *Dallas Times Herald* less than three days after Betsy's body was found, "Everything is consistent with suicide, and the medical examiner says for all practical purposes, it will be a suicide."

I wondered if Dr. Petty and his trace evidence colleague, Dr. I.C. Stone, had ascribed too much significance to the contact nature of the gunshot wound. Though it's true that most suicidal gunshot wounds are contact wounds, it struck me as a fallacy to conclude therefore that *all* contact wounds are self-inflicted. Ten years after Betsy's death, Dr. Stone reviewed 119 homicides in Dallas County involving a single gunshot wound to the head. Eleven of the homicidal headwounds, or 9.24 %, were contact discharge—the minority of cases, but hardly a negligible number. Thus, it seemed to me that Dr. Petty's conclusion (based on statistical analysis of suicides in general) did not take into consideration the particular circumstances of Betsy's death. As for the revolver found in her hand—obviously her killer could have placed it in her hand after she died. What about the gunshot residue found on her right hand? To evaluate this, I contacted the Boa.

Lynne Herold was a senior criminalist at the Los Angeles County Sheriff's Department Crime Lab. Unbeknownst to her until I told her, LA homicide detectives had, among themselves, called her "the Boa," apparently because she kept a pet python named Penelope that they'd mistaken for a boa constrictor. I'd gotten to know her two years earlier while researching my first book about the Austrian serial killer Jack Unterweger, who murdered three prostitutes in Los Angeles in the summer of 1991. Lynne analyzed the ligatures found around the necks of the murdered women and testified at Jack's trial in 1994. According to Jack's defense attorney, she was the most persuasive witness to take the stand.

At the time I sent her the reports on Betsy's case, she was working on the Phil Spector murder trial, for which she performed a bloodstain pattern analysis and provided expert testimony that challenged Mr. Spector's assertion that the victim, Lana Clarkson, had committed suicide in his home. To argue his claim, Spector hired the forensic pathologist and gunshot expert Vincent Di Maio. According to Lynne and other observers, Di Maio (and Spector's other experts, Werner Spitz and Michael Baden) made assertions with no scientific basis. One forensic science blogger described their work on the case as the "Trifecta of Piffle." Not only did they fail to persuade the jury; they also raised questions about their own integrity, as well as concern that a wealthy defendant could corrupt a murder trial with hired gun scientists. Though the Appeal to Authority has long been recognized as a fallacy, it happens frequently in jury trials when eminent scientists testify about complex phenomena.

Fortunately for Lana Clarkson and her family, Lynne's testimony was more persuasive than Dr. Di Maio's. I wasn't surprised by the guilty verdict because Lynne is the most rigorous professional I've ever encountered in any field. She is ruthless at eliminating biases, and she refuses to state her opinion unless she has obtained all possible data and analyzed it in accordance with the most up to date scientific research. A few days after I sent her the trace evidence report on the gunshot residue found on Betsy's right hand, she called me.

"Gunshot residue on the victim's hand in an unreliable indicator of suicide," she said. "It could indicate that the victim fired the gun herself, but it doesn't prove it. When the gun was discharged in the car, primer residue would have been deposited on every surrounding surface. And if the victim's hand came into contact with the gun after it was fired, residue could have transferred from the discharged gun to her hand."

I wrote all of this down and asked a few questions. And then Lynne raised another subject.

"Was Vincent Di Maio the Dallas County Medical Examiner in this case?"

"No, it was a guy named Charles Petty. Why do you ask?"

"Di Maio was the Dallas Medical Examiner back in the seventies or early eighties before he went to Bexar County. Some of his suicide rulings have been controversial."

After speaking with Lynne, I reckoned there was no proof that Betsy Bagwell had shot herself. The gun found in her hand, the contact wound to her head, and the residue found on her right hand indicated that she *could* have killed herself, but they didn't prove it. Thus, it seemed to me the DPD should have taken a much closer look at Betsy's last known contact, Sandra Bridewell.

CHAPTER 57

WALL OF SILENCE

When I resumed my investigation in the summer of 2019, thirty-seven years had passed since Betsy's death, and still a great contradiction remained at the heart of it. Within the tight-knit society of Highland Park, Sandra was widely suspected of having murdered Betsy. At the same time, the Dallas County Medical Examiner's suicide ruling had apparently never been challenged, even after Sandra fell under suspicion for murdering Alan Rehrig—also found in his car, shot in the head—three years after Betsy's death. Why not?

Normally I would have started my inquiry with the victim's next of kin, as I had with Alan Rehrig. However, I'd heard from multiple persons close to Dr. Bagwell and his two children that they were opposed to speaking with reporters about her death. While investigating Sandra in 2007, Detective Jayne Todd contacted Dr. Bagwell, who—in a tone she interpreted as hostile—refused to speak with her. His children also refused to talk with Jayne. In their responses to Jayne's query, they had starkly contrasted with Gloria Rehrig, who'd welcomed the opportunity to help Jayne to make her case against Sandra.

Such was also my experience with Betsy's friends. While Alan Rehrig's friends were happy to speak with me, Betsy's refused. Some ladies who hadn't been part of her inner circle, but who'd known her, were happy to chat about her story with my mother over lunch or at their book club (of which Betsy had been a member) so long as they were under the impression it was just a private conversation. However, as soon as my mother revealed that I was researching Betsy's death for a book about Sandra Bridewell, they too clammed up. A few agreed to talk to me, but they made me swear I wouldn't reveal their names or identifying characteristics. They were evidently afraid of getting into trouble for divulging information to me, but they didn't explain why. The only logical inference I could make was they believed that an important person didn't want them talking about it.

Who were they afraid of angering? Again, reviewing the *D Magazine* piece, I noticed that it contained no direct quotes from Dr. Bagwell. One of the report's few paragraphs on "The Death of Betsy Bagwell" recounts how, on the morning of Betsy's death, Sandra called her and said she'd found an upsetting letter.

> According to a private investigator hired to look into Betsy's death, Sandra was upset about a letter she had found written from another woman to Bobby. Sandra said the letter, discovered inside a frame behind a photograph, intimated that Bobby was having an affair. For Betsy, something didn't seem right about the story. She told her husband about it that morning and brought it up again with two female friends over lunch at the Dallas Country Club.

Why did a private investigator, and not the Dallas police, determine that Betsy had, on the day of her death, spoken with her husband and "two female friends" about Sandra's disturbing behavior? Did that mean that the DPD investigator hadn't spoken with Dr. Bagwell and these two women about what they'd seen and heard during this critical time? The authors didn't mention the names of these women, indicating the women wished to remain anonymous. Why? Same with the P.I.'s name and the name of the person who'd hired him, again suggesting they preferred to remain anonymous five years after the death occurred. Carefully analyzing each sentence on "The Death of Betsy Bagwell," I noticed that the reporting in this section redacted almost as much as it revealed.

It seemed to me that the "two female friends" mentioned in the section were key witnesses, because Betsy had told them of Sandra's perplexing behavior on that very day. They'd also witnessed Betsy's state of mind shortly before she gave Sandra a ride to Love Field. Who were they, and what exactly had they seen and heard?

Scouring Gloria Rehrig's file cabinet, I found a folder of press clippings from the years 1982 to 1987. The first that caught my eye was the *Park Cities People* article dated June 19, 1986, by the reporter Susan Albrecht under the headline "Murder of Park Cities man still baffles the police." The report was mostly about the murder of Alan Rehrig, but the latter section contained a brief account of Betsy's final day and death, provided by Betsy's friend Janie McKay, whom I'd known during my boyhood. Her daughter Cristin was my classmate and friend. According to the report, "McKay said Betsy spent the morning with Bridewell, and had lunch with friends Dabby Graham and Anne Blakeney at the Dallas Country Club."

I didn't know Dabby Graham, but I knew that Anne Blakeney and her husband Bobby were old friends of my mother. Bobby's brother Tucker (named after my grandfather's best friend, Fred Tucker) had been one of my mother's best childhood friends, and they had once run away from home together. This was a huge lead. Anne, a talented artist and pianist, was known for being exceptionally sharp, and it seemed that she could tell me exactly what Betsy had, shortly before her death, said about her interactions with Sandra.

I told my mother about the lead, which prodded her memory.

"Yes," my mom said. "Now I remember. Right after Betsy's death, Anne was one of the girls who said there was no way she killed herself."

Two hours later I was on the phone with Bobby Blakeney. I prefaced by telling him that I was working with Gloria Rehrig, the mother of Sandra's murdered husband, and the retired Brunswick County North Carolina Sheriff's detective, Jayne Todd, who was instrumental in bringing

Sandra to justice for aggravated identity theft in 2007. Our objective was, I explained, to persuade either the Dallas or Oklahoma City Police to renew their investigation of Sandra for at least one of the three shooting deaths with which she was apparently linked.

"Anne still remembers the events perfectly," Bobby said. "I remember them as well. Andrew Bagwell was babysitting for us on the night of Betsy's death, and John broke the news to us when he came to pick Andrew up. I also helped with the legal review of the *D Magazine* piece. But you should speak with Anne, because she's the one who met Betsy for lunch that day. I'll see her later today and call you tomorrow with a time to get together."

The next day came and went, and I didn't hear back from Bobby. Then, the following morning around 10:30, he called with bad news.

"I spoke with John, and he said he doesn't want us to talk with you about this. In fact, he doesn't want anyone talking to you about it."

"Did he say why?" I asked.

"He said this has been a huge trauma for him and his kids, and he doesn't want it all dredged up again."

"Did you tell him I am going to try to get the investigation of Betsy's death reopened?" I asked.

"Yes, I did, but he said he doesn't want us to talk to you, and he's a good friend of ours, so we will have to respect his wish."

"Do you think he would prefer that the culprit not be found and prosecuted?"

"Oh, I doubt that."

"Okay," I said, not sure how to proceed. And then I thought of something.

"One last thing. Did Anne ever speak with the police about her lunch conversation with Betsy that day?"

"No," he replied.

CHAPTER 58

DREDGING

I contacted the retired *Park Cities People* reporter, Susan Albrecht to ask about her 1986 piece in which Janie McKay had made a statement about Betsy's death.

"Somebody gave Mrs. McKay a hard time about her interview, because she called me after the report was published and said she hadn't given me her permission to quote her. I told her that I'd made it clear before the interview that I don't use anonymous sources."

After I spoke with Susan, I tried calling Dabby Graham and left two messages on her voicemail over a two-week period, but she never called me back. A while later a mutual friend contacted her on my behalf. Dabby told her she didn't want to speak with me about it because it would be "a betrayal." *Betrayal of whom?* A while later I bumped into Dabby's daughter at a Fourth of July party. She was a few years my junior and I hadn't known her growing up, but she was married to a man I'd known since childhood, and she was pals with the party's host. When the host mentioned to her that I was researching a book about Sandra Bridewell, she eagerly engaged me in an intense conversation about the death of Betsy Bagwell.

"My mom and her friends always believed that Sandra murdered her," she said.

"Any idea why your mom never talked to the police about it?" I asked.

"I'm not sure, but I can ask her," she replied. We agreed to have a follow-up conversation in a few days, but then she too fell silent and never replied to my texts. Later I asked the party's host if he understood why she'd ghosted me despite her initial enthusiasm for discussing the subject.

"Because she's scared," he said with a cryptic smile.

Finally, after a long search, I tracked down one of Betsy's old friends who was willing to talk, but only on the condition of anonymity.

"A group of Betsy's friends gathered at the Bagwell house before the funeral, and we were all shocked when Sandra showed up. She didn't stay though, because one of the men asked her to leave. Anne and Dabby were there, and they talked about their meeting with Betsy at the club, and how she was having trouble with Sandra. That morning, Sandra told Betsy that her car wouldn't start, and she needed a ride to Love Field to pick up a package arriving on a Muse Air flight from Houston. Betsy gave her a ride and waited in the parking lot, and then Sandra came out and said the package was put on a later flight. Betsy agreed to give her another ride that afternoon, but I believe she told Sandra that while they were at it, she should rent a car at Love Field until she got her own fixed. That evening about fifteen of us sat around for hours, discussing different scenarios for how Sandra had committed the murder and staged it to look like a suicide."

"Did Anne and Dabby understand why Betsy didn't just tell Sandra to get her car fixed or to take a cab to Love Field?" I asked.

"Betsy felt terrible about Bobby dying and leaving Sandra to raise her kids on her own, so she was very torn about Sandra. She wanted to get away from her, but she wanted to be tactful about it. I know this firsthand, because I spoke with Betsy on the phone about it just a few days before she died."

"Why haven't Anne and Dabby ever spoken with the police about what they saw and heard that day?"

"I don't know."

"Do you think they assumed that Dr. Bagwell would convey an account of their conversation with Betsy to the police?"

"I don't know. I do know that both were terrified of Sandra. They believed that if she could get away with murdering Betsy, she could get away with anything."

"Do you understand why Dr. Bagwell doesn't want Anne and Dabby to speak with me?"

"Everyone is two thousand percent convinced that Sandra murdered Betsy, but no one sees any reason to dredge this up anymore. I'm pretty sure that if John doesn't want them to talk to you, they never will, because they are still very close with him."

A lady named Sue McClain was reputed to have been one of Betsy's closest friends. Upon receiving my call and introduction, her tone became very emotional and defensive.

"I went through this twice—first when Betsy was murdered, and then when that fellow from Oklahoma was murdered and the FBI came in. Everyone knows Betsy was murdered and many witnesses who knew what she was going through with Sandra told the police what they'd seen."

"Did you speak with the police?" I asked.

"No."

"Betsy's friends whom she met at Dallas Country Club shortly before her death also didn't speak with the police. How are the police supposed to know about suspicious circumstances if no one informs them?"

"You don't know what Betsy was going through when she died or what the family went through unless you've been talking with one of her friends who we don't know about. What are you going to accomplish by dredging this up?" This was about the fifth time I heard one of Betsy's friends say "dredge up," as though they'd all used this metaphor in conversation with each other. To dredge means to excavate mud and detritus from a harbor or ship channel. The implication was that I wasn't only trying to obtain facts and forensic evidence about a young woman's murder, but also digging into something that was better left undisturbed.

"This isn't just a private matter affecting the Bagwell family. Murder is not a civil matter, but a crime against all of society—and in this case, the suspect is also suspected of murdering her third husband just three years after Betsy's death."

"So, you're a lawyer too, are you?" she said sarcastically.

"No, but I'm familiar with basic principles of the law."

"So, what do you think you're going to accomplish?"

"Justice for Betsy Bagwell," I replied.

"Sandra has already gone to prison."

"She served two years for identity theft against a lady in North Carolina, not for the murder of Betsy Bagwell or Alan Rehrig and possibly others."

"I'm not going to talk about it with you. You should talk with the family." She hung up. Later a mutual friend told me that Mrs. McClain had expressed deep consternation about my inquiry and had even talked with her attorney about it. What, I wondered, was she so upset about? Her hostile tone, and the fact that she contacted her attorney, were expressive of fear that I was going to discover something that would, if revealed, be damaging to people she cared about, and perhaps even to her.

CHAPTER 59

BETSY'S BROTHER

I called Betsy's brother, Frank Monroe, Jr., who told me what he'd seen and heard at the time of Betsy's death. It was a remarkable coincidence that he was at Camp Longhorn, picking up his son, when he got the news that Betsy had been killed. I too was a Longhorn second term camper, and was there on that same day, less than a hundred yards from him when he called his parents in Dallas from the visitor center.

"Are you sure that no one mentioned anything to you about Sandra Bridewell during the time you were Dallas in the days following Betsy's death?" I asked.

"Positive," he replied.

"Are you sure that John Bagwell said nothing about Sandra when you talked to him?"

"I'm certain of it."

This was notable and strange. Though Betsy's friends were passionately talking about Sandra around the time of the funeral, none of them mentioned her to Betsy's brother.

"When did you finally hear about Sandra?" I asked Frank.

"Sometime later I heard about her from my parents."

"How did they learn about her?"

"Not long before Betsy was shot, my parents were having dinner with her and John at the Mansion. Sandra happened to be there, and she walked up to their table to say hello. Her manner seemed strange, especially the way she addressed John. I guess my mother's female intuition picked up on it. I don't remember exactly how and when my parents learned of Betsy's troubles with Sandra."

"Did your parents remember anything about John's first reaction to the news that Betsy had been killed?"

"Yes, that really struck my dad. He told me that on the evening of Betsy's death, he got a call from John saying that something had happened to her and that he and my mother needed to come over. They arrived before a Dallas police officer arrived. All John said was that 'Something has happened to Betsy.' He didn't say what it was or how he knew, but my father got the strong impression from his demeanor that Betsy was dead and that, somehow, John already knew it."

"Did he say he'd already received a call from the Dallas police?" I asked.

"No, he didn't say that, and a little while later, a police officer arrived and notified him that Betsy had been found shot at Love Field."

CHAPTER 60
DETECTIVE COUGHLIN

That police officer was J.J. Coughlin, who was tasked with notifying Betsy's next of kin. He graciously met me for an interview at the public library in Rockwall, twenty-five miles northeast of Dallas. At sixty-eight, he was still a fit and handsome man, and very easy to talk to. And even though my interview questioned his investigation with respect to Sandra, he never showed the slightest defensiveness. To refresh his memory, I brought along my copies of the DPD incident report and the medical examiner's autopsy and trace evidence reports—the only investigative records I'd obtained thus far.

"Betsy was found in her car with that RG 14 .22 revolver in her right hand and a perfect contact wound to the right side of her head, which is synonymous with suicide. Also, evidence of powder on her hand. Once Dr. Petty ruled suicide, and after what I'd seen at the crime scene itself, you know, it's pretty hard to overcome that without a lot of evidence to disprove it. In fact, in my ten years of working homicide for the Dallas PD, not one time do I ever remember—I remember some suicides being overruled with evidence, but not one contact wound suicide. So, this is pretty hard evidence that it was a self-inflicted wound. Even if Betsy's friend caused her to go crazy and do this to herself, that's not against the law.

Based on the autopsy and the information given by Dr. Petty, and based on what I saw at this scene, this stuff would be very difficult to overcome."

"You don't think it's possible that someone surprised Betsy—maybe drew the pistol while she was looking to her left—and got muzzle contact to her head for long enough to pull the trigger?" I asked.

"If someone holds a pistol to your head, your reflex is to pull away and the gunman would have to grab your head with his other hand and hold it stationary to get firm contact."

"When you notified Dr. Bagwell on the evening of Betsy's death, did he mention any suspicions or concerns about Sandra Bridewell?"

"He told me that Betsy had run errands with Sandra that afternoon. As I recall, we didn't go deeply into Sandra at that time. Later he or one of his family members told me that they were concerned about Sandra because she'd recently been bothersome and needy, calling all the time and showing up uninvited. I noted their concern, but as an investigator, I needed the medical examiner to rule the manner of death a homicide or at least undetermined to pursue a homicide investigation. Dr. Petty told me it was a textbook case of suicide."

"Did you interview the two ladies whom Betsy met at the Dallas Country Club shortly before her death—Anne Blakeney and Dabby Graham?"

"I don't remember talking to them."

"Do you recall your interview with Sandra?"

"Yes, she came down to the station for an interview. She was with a lawyer, though I don't remember which one. He wasn't one of the big criminal defense attorneys I'd seen in court. She was very well put together and attractive, and also very friendly, and cooperative—maybe even a bit too sweet—but she answered my questions in a straightforward way."

"Do you think the interview transcript might still exist?"

"I doubt it, though some of my notes may still be in the file. I'll see if I can get a copy of my investigative supplements for you as well."

"Was there anything about this case that struck you as noteworthy?"

"The one thing in this case that stands out as not fitting is the type of gun that was used. The RG .22 is your proverbial Saturday night special from back in the day in the seventies. It was a cheap gun; you could probably buy a new one for twenty or thirty bucks. It's just a six-shooter, short-barreled .22, really has no use as a target pistol or any kind of sporting type of thing. When I worked the streets a lot of criminals carried RGs. It's really only good for shooting someone in the stomach at close range. It's not a gun that I would expect to see at this crime scene because of the people who were involved."

"Anything else?" I asked Mr. Coughlin.

"One thing struck me as strange at the time. When I went to the Bagwell house to notify Betsy's husband, a little group of people was already there, and it was sort of like walking into a funeral parlor. It was as though they already knew that Betsy was dead. Dr. Bagwell didn't seem surprised."

"You don't think someone from the Dallas police had already called before you got there?"

"That wasn't the procedure. Notification of next of kin is an important part of an investigation because it enables us to see the relative's reaction, so we always did it in person."

"It is possible that someone from your department called ahead to make sure he was at home."

"I guess it's possible, but even then, I doubt that any details would have been provided, because that was my job."

"But if someone from the police did call ahead, couldn't Dr. Bagwell have reasonably assumed that Betsy had been found dead?"

"Yes, but she could have had a heart attack or been in a car accident. He didn't seem surprised when I told him she'd been found shot, and nor did he ask many questions about it. I can't say for sure, but I definitely got the feeling that he somehow already knew."

CHAPTER 61
"FRIEND OF THE DECEDENT"

Detective Coughlin mentioned in my interview that he would try to track down his investigative supplements, which could potentially shed light on what he knew at the time he closed the case. A few weeks later I followed up with him, and he said he'd been unable to find these reports.

And so, I went back to the DPD records division and submitted another request, this time specifying J.J. Coughlin's Investigative Supplement Report. Several weeks later I received a copy of it. The first thing I noticed was that it was dated July 22, 1982—less than one week after Betsy was found. The report read as follows:

Complainant was found to have a gunshot wound to her right temple and was holding a .22 caliber pistol in her hand. Further investigation showed that the complainant was last seen at approximately 5:00 P.M., on July 16, 1982, at the Highland Park Presbyterian Church by a Sandra Bridewell, white female, 4318 Lorraine, University Park, Texas. Mrs. Bridewell related that she and the complainant had been together most of the day and had talked about many subjects, including the suicide of

BRIDEWELL'S first husband. Investigator found a Love Field parking ticket in the complainant's car with entry time into lot at 6:05. Dr. Charles Petty of the Dallas County Medical Examiner's Office performed an autopsy on the complainant's body. Dr. Petty found the wound to the right temple to be a contact type wound. Handwashings from the deceased were positive. Analysis revealed that lead and barium were present on the right palm and right back of complainant's hand. Dr. Petty has ruled complainant's death as a Suicide. The offense will be reclassified to a Suicide [from Unexplained] and will be closed.

This statement contains a conspicuous falsehood and a conspicuous omission. Mrs. Bridewell and the complainant had *not* been together most of the day, but for a couple of hours that morning, during which they discussed Sandra's emotional trauma over her discovery of a letter to her late husband from another woman intimating an affair. That afternoon (the critical period for the investigation) Sandra stated that Betsy had given her a ride to Love Field around 4:15 p.m. and then back to the Highland Park Presbyterian Church around 5:00 p.m. Coughlin omitted this latter detail from his final report, though he *did* relate it the medical examiner field agent, E. Gray, on July 16. As Gray noted in his Investigative Report:

DPD feels note was found at house & destroyed by Next of Kin. FRIEND of decedent (DPD did not identify) advised she & decedent drove to Love Field earlier this (7/16) afternoon & discussed Next of Kin & Next of Kin's nurse, & friend's husband's death which was Gunshot Wound-head suicide. Friend advised decedent asked a lot of questions re details of death ... Blood spatters in back seat. ... Parking sticker found in vehicle has time 6:05 P.M. No receipt for weapon found at scene.

Detective Coughlin's final report indicates that he remained attached to the suicide theory, not only because Betsy was found with the revolver in her hand, but also because Dr. Bagwell had not seemed surprised by the news of Betsy's apparent suicide.

Field Agent Gray, on the other hand, noted that the "friend of the decedent advised she & decedent drove to Love Field earlier this (7/16) afternoon." Gray also noted, "Blood spatters in back seat." Though he didn't state the significance of this fact, it's clear that he understood it was inconsistent with the proposition that Betsy shot herself in the right side of the head while sitting in the driver's seat.

Sandra told Detective Coughlin that she and Betsy drove to Love Field that afternoon but were unable to rent a car because she forgot her driver's license. Betsy therefore gave her a ride back to the Highland Park Presbyterian Church around 5:00 p.m. However, instead of simply grabbing her driver's license, Sandra tried starting her car again, and this time it started. She then drove her (self-fixing) car to go shopping and never saw Betsy again. This could only mean that, after parting company from Sandra around 5:00 p.m., Betsy drove *back* to Love Field an hour later and shot herself in the parking lot near the Hertz car rental agency.

It's hard to imagine that Detective Coughlin didn't find Sandra's story strange at best. Nevertheless, nothing in his final report indicates that she was a person of interest, but merely the last person known to have seen Betsy. Instead of remaining silent about the extraordinary fact that her first husband had committed suicide—also with a .22 caliber gunshot to the head—Sandra emphasized it and claimed that this suicide was the topic Betsy had most wanted to discuss.

At the time Detective Coughlin wrote his report, he seemed to know nothing about Sandra's suspicious conduct. He was apparently operating under the assumption that Sandra really was Betsy's friend. He interpreted Dr. Bagwell's lack of surprise at Betsy's death to mean he already knew (by means of a suicide note) that she was dead. It apparently didn't occur to the detective that Dr. Bagwell had another means of knowing she was already dead.

Betsy was found on Friday evening; Dr. Petty performed the autopsy on Saturday morning, and the following Monday afternoon, DPD spokesman Sergeant Tom Sherman told the *Dallas Morning News*: "Everything is consistent with suicide, and the medical examiner says for all practical purposes, it will be a suicide." In other words, there was no investigation of Betsy's death beyond noting the pistol in her hand, the gunshot residue on her hand, and the contact gunshot wound to her head. Her last known contact, Sandra Bridewell, made statements to Detective Coughlin, and he took these at face value.

CHAPTER 62
A PRIVATE INVESTIGATION

The "private investigators" repeatedly mentioned in the *D Magazine* piece gave readers the impression that someone who cared about Betsy had been unsatisfied with the DPD investigation and had therefore hired PIs to reexamine her death. The only PI mentioned by name was Bill Murphy at Dale Simpson & Associates. In her June 1986 diary, Gloria noted that he'd worked for Betsy's parents. In Gloria's ongoing correspondence with Frank Monroe Sr. and his wife Percye, they mentioned they'd also spoken with the private investigator Al Teel.

Teel wasn't mentioned in the 1987 *D Magazine* piece. However, seventeen years later, in a follow-up report about Sandra in the *Dallas Observer* titled "Return of the Black Widow," Glenna Whitley wrote: "Dr. Bagwell hired Al Teel." If this was indeed the case, I figured that Teel must have assembled a timeline of Betsy's final hours and checked out Sandra's story. He was reputed to be a competent investigator. What information had he discovered, and to whom had he given it? These questions led me into one of the strangest phases of my investigation.

In the fall of 2019, I did a Google search for Al Teel's contact information and learned that he had just died on September 9, 2019. A few months later I contacted Glenna Whitley to inquire about her statement that "Dr. Bagwell hired Al Teel," but she was busy with other projects and still contemplating writing her own book about the story. A year later, I again requested an interview to inquire about her reporting. This time she agreed, and over lunch she reiterated that Dr. Bagwell had hired Al Teel to investigate Betsy's death.

"Did Dr. Bagwell tell you that?" I asked her.

"No, Dr. Bagwell declined my request for an interview. Al told me." Not only had Teel told Glenna about his assignment, he'd also—several years after his work for Dr. Bagwell concluded—given her a copy of his investigative file. Glenna wasn't exactly sure *why* Teel had given her a copy of the file because he hadn't explicitly stated his motive. As best as she could remember, he'd simply thought it would be pertinent to her reporting on Sandra. As Glenna understood it, Teel had also shared this information with the Dallas police and medical examiner, but it had not persuaded them to revise their conclusion that Betsy had committed suicide.

Another thing that emerged from my conversations with Glenna was that the medical examiner's records division had not divulged to me the full contents of its file on Mary Elizabeth Bagwell. This was the case even though I had explicitly asked a ranking member of the agency if the file contained any documents apart from the autopsy and trace evidence reports.

"No, the file only contains Dr. Petty's autopsy report and Dr. Stone's trace evidence report," she replied. In fact, as I learned from my conversation with Glenna, Betsy's file also contained a field agent's report and an investigative memo authored by Dr. Petty. And so, I went back to the medical examiner's office and submitted a request for these two documents.

Dr. Petty's memo revealed that on August 16, 1982—three weeks after the DPD closed Betsy's case—Dr. Bagwell and his sister Judy visited Dr. Petty at his office and told him they were concerned about the wife of one of Dr. Bagwell's deceased patients. Dr. Bagwell said he was contemplating hiring a private investigator to examine this woman and her past. Dr. Petty endorsed hiring a PI to investigate the deceased patient's wife. As he put it in his memo:

I also told him that I could not rule out the possibility of homicide any more than he could as a clinician rule out the possibility of a misdiagnosis in a patient whom he had been treating.

The significance of this assertion cannot be overstated, and it raises a critically important question: why didn't Dr. Petty revise the manner of death to "unexplained" and tell the DPD to consider "the wife of one of Dr. Bagwell's deceased patients" as a person of interest?

Judging by Dr. Petty's memo, his meeting with Dr. Bagwell had an air of collegial discretion. The Chief Medical Examiner seemed to understand that Dr. Bagwell's inquiry about the wife of one of his deceased patients should be handled in a confidential, behind the scenes way that wouldn't alert the subject of the investigation. Finally, though his memo makes it clear that he was open to considering the results of a private investigation, his subsequent narrative contains no memos of conversations with Al Teel or any reports from Teel and his associates.

CHAPTER 63

THE GUNSHOT RESIDUE REPORT

One of Teel's most important actions was to commission Dr. John Thornton to evaluate the Dallas County medical examiner's trace evidence report on the gunshot residue found on Betsy's right hand. Dr. Thornton concluded that the proximity of Betsy's right hand to the discharging weapon could have deposited the residue that was found on it. This second opinion was highly significant because it challenged one of the medical examiner's main reasons for ruling Betsy's death a suicide.

Because the DPD had deferred to the medical examiner's ruling, persuading the medical examiner to reconsider his opinion was the key to getting Betsy's case reopened. Dr. Thornton was an eminent criminalist who'd studied with Dr. Paul Kirk, who was widely regarded as the founder of modern forensic science. I wondered why his analysis wasn't mentioned in the 1987 *D Magazine* feature. The lead author, Skip Hollandsworth, was known for being a thorough reporter, so it seemed likely he would have included this critically important detail. I contacted him to seek clarification. He replied that he'd forgotten the particulars of the research he'd conducted so long ago, and that I should contact Glenna

Whitley, to whom he'd given his file. After I finally met Glenna, I asked her. She figured the only plausible explanation for Skip's omission was that he hadn't been aware of Dr. Thorton's report.

I contacted Dr. Thornton and told him that I was researching the shooting death of Mary Elizabeth Bagwell in Dallas on July 16, 1982—a case for which he had written an independent analysis of the gunshot residue detected on her right hand.

"You concluded that the residue could have been deposited on her hand as a result of its proximity to the discharging weapon in the car, and not necessarily because she fired the weapon herself."

"I don't remember that specific case, and many of my old records were recently destroyed by a wildfire here in Napa. However, I can tell you it's now the consensus that when a handgun is discharged, a plume of residue about the size of a beach ball expands around it. This is especially conspicuous when a shot is fired from a revolver, and there are good photographs of this phenomenon. The particles of lead, barium, and antimony are deposited on the surfaces around it, and because they don't evaporate, they remain on surfaces and can be transferred to other objects. Thus, any object in proximity to the gun when it discharges can be covered with these particles."

After this conversation I reviewed Dr. Thornton's publishing resume in the *Journal of Forensic Sciences*. An article from the year 1986 titled "Close Proximity Gun Shot Residues" seemed pertinent, so I purchased it. My attention was piqued on the first page when I read the following:

A case was recently submitted to the author's laboratory... in which the issue was whether a hand held in close proximity but not in contact with a firearm would intercept enough gunshot residue to confuse the interpretation of whether the subject had actually handled or fired a weapon. Stated in more concrete terms, the issue was whether a deceased subject had handled or fired the weapon (the interpretation indicating suicide) or had defensively and reflexively thrown up a hand at the moment of discharge of the firearm by another person and consequently intercepted a portion of the gunshot residues (the interpretation indicating homicide). ... The present study attempted to develop a data set of the set needed to apply toward the resolution of the suicide vs. homicide issue.

What really caught my eye in this paper was Thornton's statement of the weapon and ammunition used: "An RG 14 .22 caliber revolver" and "Remington-Peters .22 Long Rifle." This was the same kind of pistol found in Betsy's right hand, and the ammunition was identical to that which Dr. Thornton stated using in in his analysis IN THE MATTER OF MARY ELIZABETH BAGWELL. Most of the wording of the Bagwell report was identical to that of his 1986 CASE REPORT on "Close Proximity Gun Shot Residues," as was his conclusion in both documents:

...a hand held in close proximity to the firearm in question at the time of discharge will intercept a level of antimony consistent with having fired or handled the weapon, even though the hand was not the instrument of firing. . .

The death of Betsy Bagwell was the case study for a paper published in the official journal of the *American Academy of Forensic Sciences*. Both Dr. Thorton's analysis IN THE MATTER OF BETSY BAGWELL and his analysis in his 1986 paper called into question the Dallas County Medical Examiner's suicide ruling. And yet, Dr. Thornton's conclusions apparently did not persuade the medical examiner to reconsider his suicide ruling in the case of Betsy Bagwell. Why not?

Dr. Irving Charles Stone—the medical examiner's trace evidence specialist who'd detected gunshot residue on Betsy's right hand—was retired but still living in Dallas. I called him and a strong voice answered on the first ring. I told him the same story I'd told Dr. Thornton about my research on the strange case of Mary Elizabeth Bagwell, who was found shot in her car at Love Field on July 16, 1982. I jogged his memory by sending him a link to the *D Magazine* story. He reiterated his conviction that the gunshot residue on Betsy's right hand and the contact nature of the gunshot wound to her head were strong evidence of "a suicidal discharge of the firearm by Betsy Bagwell." However, he did not recall receiving Dr. Thornton's report. I gave him an account of Thornton's analysis, to which he replied, "Yes, certainly that could have happened. I would agree with that."

"If your institute received Dr. Thornton's report, is it likely it would have gone into Betsy Bagwell's file?" I asked.

"If we received any outside reports on one of our cases, we would add it to the file. We wouldn't destroy it," he replied.

To double check, I posed the question again in a follow-up e-mail, to which he replied: "I feel certain that I would remember a John Thornton report ... he was respected, and I would have considered his view." Dr. Stone's recollection is consistent with Dr. Petty's Investigative Narrative, which contains no documents from either Al Teel or Dr. Thornton.

Al Teel's investigative file reveals it was his idea to commission the analysis from Dr. Thornton. The totality of circumstances indicates that he gave Dr. Thornton's report (dated August 23, 1983) to Dr. Bagwell with the understanding that he—the victim's next of kin—would present it to the medical examiner. The fact that the medical examiner never received the report indicates that Dr. Bagwell did not give it to him.

CHAPTER 64

THE PISTOL

Detective Coughlin's initial Investigative Report and his Investigative Supplement Report do not mention the origin of the RG-14 revolver found in Betsy's right hand. However, Al Teel's report documents his exhaustive attempt to trace the weapon, which was initially purchased by Lonnie Virgil Edwards, a resident of Oak Cliff, in 1970. Mr. Edwards died in 1975. His wife told the DPD that the weapon had been stolen from her deceased husband's glove box in his truck sometime in the early seventies, though he hadn't reported it stolen. Teel's file indicates that he checked every pawn and gun shop in Dallas but could find no record of the weapon. How on earth had Betsy acquired an RG-14 revolver that had been stolen around ten years earlier? She could have purchased a gun at one of several legitimate dealers. Oshman's sporting goods store in the Highland Park Village, a few blocks from her house, had a huge gun selection. The idea of Betsy going to a grungy pawn shop in a dodgy part of town seemed extremely unlikely.

Equally mysterious was the person of Lonnie Virgil Edwards, purportedly a resident of Oak Cliff. My great, great, great grandfather, William Ambrose Edwards, was an early settler of Oak Cliff. After serving in the Confederate Army and surviving the hottest action at Little Round

Top in the Battle of Gettysburg, he became a Methodist minister. The history of the Edwards family of Oak Cliff had been well documented by my father, an avid genealogy buff who is adept at researching anyone in history whose existence is documented by any vital records. Nevertheless, my father could find nothing about Lonnie Virgil Edwards of Oak Cliff.

Al Teel's notes indicate he'd heard gossip that Mr. Edwards had been a lawn maintenance man with clients in Highland Park. One could imagine him parking his truck on a street in Sandra's neighborhood and leaving the windows down on a hot summer day with the assumption that no one in the affluent town would look in his old truck's glove box. While he was doing yard work in the back yard, someone walking past his truck on the sidewalk could have searched the vehicle. If anyone reading this book has information about Lonnie Virgil Edwards, please contact me through my website (authorjohnleake.com).

CHAPTER 65
THE ALIBI
THAT WASN'T

Reviewing Detective Coughlin's final report, I focused on the following two sentences:

> Further investigation showed that the complainant was last seen at approximately 5:00 P.M., on July 16, 1982 at the Highland Park Presbyterian Church by a Sandra Bridewell. ... Investigator found a Love Field parking ticket in the complainant's car with entry time into lot at 6:05.

Five years after Coughlin wrote his report, the authors of the *D Magazine* story wrote:

> According to police and private investigators, Betsy got another call that afternoon from Sandra. Again, her car had stalled, this time at a church, and she needed help. Betsy couldn't say no. She drove Sandra to Love Field at about 4:30 to pick up a rental car, but because Sandra had forgotten her driver's license, so she couldn't get a car. According to police, Sandra said Betsy then took her back to her car at the church. Again, the car started.

The police say that Sandra told them she then left Betsy and went shopping at Preston Center.

The name of "the church"—the prestigious Highland Park Presbyterian—was yet another detail conspicuously omitted from the *D Magazine* story. As I later discovered, the part about Betsy getting "another call from Sandra" wasn't relevant to the events that followed. Already that morning, Betsy had agreed to pick up Sandra at her house just after 4:00 p.m. to go back to Love Field, which indicates that the package was, according to Sandra, on a flight arriving around 4:30. Sandra told the police that her car had functioned at midday, enabling her to give her daughter Kathryn a ride to Vacation Bible Study at the HPPC. However (as she told the police) the car had stalled at the church, and because there was no one available to give her a ride, she had walked home to her house on Lorraine Avenue (1.6 miles away).

The different iterations of Sandra's repeatedly stalling and self-resolving car trouble created a great deal of confusion, but in the final analysis, she acknowledged that:

1). She was Betsy's last known contact.
2). Betsy gave her a ride to Love Field at around 4:30 p.m.
3). Betsy was found shortly thereafter, shot to death in her car at Love Field.

Sandra does not have an officially documented alibi because she was never the subject of a homicide investigation. Her statement to Coughlin that she last saw Betsy at the Highland Park Presbyterian Church at 5:00 is merely noted in his final report, with no reference to confirming witnesses or records. From this assertion, and from the Love Field parking lot ticket bearing the 6:05 p.m. time stamp, Detective Coughlin concluded that Betsy was shot in the parking lot after 6:05, over an hour after she parted company from Sandra.

Upon reviewing the *D Magazine* piece, I suspected that Sandra probably did go shopping in Preston Center shortly after 5:00 p.m. to be seen by a salesclerk and to obtain a sales receipt. The purpose of this trip was to document her claim that she was no longer with Betsy after 5:00 p.m., while Betsy (according to the parking ticket) entered the Love Field parking lot at 6:05.

CHAPTER 66

BETSY'S LAST DAY

Ultimately Glenna Whitley shared with me a copy of Al Teel's file. Dr. Bagwell hired him in September 1982. I was thunderstruck as I flipped through Teel's notes and memos about Sandra's conduct with the Bagwell family just before and on the day of Betsy's death. Of greatest significance was the timeline of Betsy's last day. This is what I'd painstakingly tried, and to a large degree succeeded, in piecing together over two years of toil. It had been a grueling process of researching and identifying witnesses, finding them, and trying to persuade them to talk. How strange it was for me to see that Teel had already done this same work just a few weeks after Betsy's death. I wondered why Dr. Bagwell had hired a private investigator to gather this information, given that he already knew most of it on the night of Betsy's death and could have simply given it to the DPD at that time.

Teel's timeline of Betsy's last day is as follows:

10:00 am: Betsy meets Sandra to discuss the letter, and then gives her a ride to Love Field to pick up a package arriving on a Muse Air flight. The package does not arrive.

12:00 noon: Betsy's daughter, Wendy, takes the Bridewell girls to lunch at

Los Vaqueros restaurant in the Highland Park Village, and then back to the Bagwell residence.

1:00 p.m.: Betsy calls Dr. Bagwell at his office and tells him about her morning's adventures with Sandra and her melodramatic letter story. Around this same time, she pulls pasta and sauce from the freezer for dinner and puts them in the sink to thaw.

2:00 p.m.: Betsy meets Anne Blakeney and Dabby Graham at the Dallas Country Club and discusses with them "the Sandra predicament."

4:00 p.m.: Betsy drives to Sandra's house to give her a ride to Love Field to pick up the package and rent a car.

4:15 p.m.: Betsy and Sandra drop off Betsy's daughter Wendy at the Bagwell house, and then drive off together.

5:00 p.m.: Dr. Bagwell calls home from his office and learns from his daughter Wendy that Betsy left about thirty minutes earlier to run an errand with Sandra.

5:30 p.m.: Dr. Bagwell calls home again; Betsy still hasn't returned from errand.

6:15 p.m.: Sandra calls the Bagwell house and tells whoever answers the phone (name not noted in Teel's file) that Betsy is running another errand and will be home soon.

6:30 p.m.: Dr. Bagwell calls Bridewell house and speaks to Sandra, who says she last saw Betsy at the Highland Park Presbyterian Church around 5:30 p.m.

Most remarkable in Teel's timeline was Sandra's 6:15 p.m. call to the Bagwell residence to say that Betsy was running another errand and would be home soon. If Sandra had, as she told Detective Coughlin, parted company from Betsy at 5:00, why did she call the Bagwell house at 6:15? What exactly did Sandra ask or say during this call? Did she begin by asking to speak with Betsy, or did she indicate that she (somehow) already knew that Betsy hadn't yet made it home? This should have been carefully examined. The 6:15 call was ten minutes after 6:05, when the parking ticket time stamp indicated Betsy's car entered the Love Field parking lot. Three years later, after Alan Rehrig was seen alive for the last time, Sandra made a similar call to the Askew residence at 6:15 p.m. to assert that Alan hadn't made it to the storage warehouse.

CHAPTER 67

"THEY KNOW ABOUT THIS STUFF?"

The Oklahoma City Police Department steadfastly refused to give me any of its casefile on the murder of Normal Alan Rehrig. However, after three years of seeking, I was finally able to obtain a critically important document from the file—that is, the transcript of a February 10, 1986, interview with Dr. Bagwell, conducted by OCPD Detectives Shupe and Fairchild. The detectives were in Dallas to investigate the murder of Alan Rehrig, and they perceived it was connected to Betsy's shooting death three and a half years earlier. Just as Betsy Bagwell was last seen alive as she ran out to meet Sandra Bridewell, Alan was last seen alive as he ran out to meet her. Both Betsy and Alan were later found in their cars parked at or near airports, killed by gunshots fired from the right.

Dr. Bagwell explained that he and Betsy had gotten to know Sandra while he was treating her late husband, Robert Bridewell, for cancer that turned out to be fatal. After Bobby died, Sandra became increasingly needy and constantly asked for favors. Ultimately, around the beginning of July 1982, the situation became intolerable. Betsy found it especially onerous when Sandra showed up, uninvited, at their vacation home in

Santa Fe. At that point, Betsy insisted it was time for them to "disentangle" from Sandra. This set-in motion the endgame that culminated on the fateful day, Friday, July 16, 1982, when Betsy was last seen leaving her house to run an errand with Sandra, who said that her car had (once again) stalled.

As Dr. Bagwell described it in his long interview, Sandra's conduct was way outside of social norms. Had she not been a "grieving widow," suddenly bereft of her beloved husband and left to raise three kids on her own, it's likely that no one would have tolerated her behavior at all. Reading the interview transcript, I wondered why he had found it so difficult to "disentangle" from Sandra, as Betsy had insisted. Was it purely out of sympathy for her, perhaps admixed with guilt that he hadn't been able to save her husband's life? For whatever reasons, he found it impossible to free himself from what can only be described as an extremely aggressive stalker. Detective Shupe noticed that Sandra's conduct strongly suggested she'd had sexual intimacy with Dr. Bagwell.

"Did you, at any time, ever sleep with Sandra?" he asked.

"No, I did not. I did not. I know that Sandra has alleged that," Dr. Bagwell replied.

"You know that sounds a little unreasonable, don't you?" said Detective Shupe.

"What?"

"From an outsider looking in," Detective Shupe continued.

"That I would have."

"Right. We know how Sandra was."

"Yeah."

"The way she would come on to men and things of that nature."

"No, I did not," Dr. Bagwell repeated. "After Betsy was found at the airport, I know the rumor has been there ever since. Sandra told her attorney that. I don't think her attorney told me that, but he told Bobby Blakeney that."

"That you and she had a relationship?" Shupe asked.

"That we had an affair. Sandra and I did not have an affair. Now, there are two things that happened," he continued.

Sometime after Bob died, Sandra went to California to visit somebody, and she came back and called me from the airport. I was in the office, and she said, "I'm at the airport and I don't have any money for a cab." And I said, "Sandra, I can't leave here and come get you." You know, Betsy was in New Mexico. And I said, "I don't have any money and I can't come and get you. I mean, I have some money, but I can't come get you." And she said, "Well, I have called so and so and so and so and so and so, and nobody is there, and I don't have any way to get home from the airport." I said, "Okay, I tell you what let's do. I'll go downstairs and I'll put some money in my car, parked in the doctors' parking lot. I'll put it in the front seat and leave the car unlocked. You just have the cab come here, and the money will pay for the cab, and you can go on home." Well, I came downstairs at 6:30 or 7:00 at night, and there was Sandra. The money was gone. She had just come there and paid the cab driver. And there she was with her bags and everything. And I said, "You know, what are we doing?" And she said, "Well, I just can't go home. I just can't go home and be by myself. I'm just too distraught." I really didn't think too much of it, and I said, "Okay, I'll take you home." So, I took her home and left her there, and then went out to Presbyterian Hospital. I came back home at nine or ten that night. We were adding a room at the back of the house, and she was in that room. The room wasn't finished, and the windows weren't yet in, and she was in this structure. She was there and scared the hell out of me, and I said, "What are you doing?" and she said, "I just can't stay there by myself." You may think I'm really dumb and naïve, but I didn't think very much about it. She came in the house, and we talked for about thirty minutes, and then she went home.

On the second occasion, I was coming back from New Mexico. I had been out in New Mexico with my wife, and I was coming back. And I don't know—I must've told Sandra I was coming back. She knew I was coming back, and she met me at the airport. I know that may sound really strange to you, but she met me at the airport. She was in her yellow car, and she said, "You know, I can't stay at home tonight because they're doing air-conditioning duct work in my house. ... So, I said, "Okay, you can stay in a hotel," and she said, "Well, I haven't eaten," so I said fine, and we went to a Mexican restaurant and then checked into the hotel. I went upstairs with her. I then took her car and went home. Then I got up the next morning and went and got her there. You know, she came back to her house, and I went to work.

Those are these two incidents. I didn't spend the night with Sandra. You know that second episode bothered me, but Sandra and I did not spend the night together. We did not have intercourse. That may sound funny to you. I've told people that story you know, and it sounds kind of fishy, but that was not the kind of relationship we had. I may have been dumb about it, but that was not what was going on.

Two days before Betsy's death, on Wednesday, July 14, Sandra called the Bagwell house at dinner time and said that her car had broken down and she needed John's help. As he recounted this incident:

I went [to help her] and she was up on the corner of Central Expressway and Yale, and her car was in the street. I started to help her push it aside, you know, out of the middle of the street, and a policeman came by and said, "Can I help you?" and I said, "No, I think we're all right." And then I tried to start it, and it started right up, so I pulled over to the side of the road, and I said, "Now look, you know you gotta stop calling. I can't do these kinds of things for you." There had been other times when she'd done things like that. But I, we, were nice to her, and I really liked her. And she said, "Well, I can't go on home; I'm afraid it'll break down again. I want you to follow me home." And I said, "I can't follow you home; I gotta go to the

Presbyterian Hospital." So, I said, "Why don't you just ride with me to Presbyterian, and I'll do my business, and then I'll come back and, you know, we'll see about your car. I was a little irritated with her, but not bad, so I took her out there to Presbyterian. She stayed in the car. I went inside and saw a patient, and then we came back and her car started up.

Regarding Betsy's last day, he recounted her phone call to his office sometime around 9:30 to 10:00 a.m. in which she told him she'd just received a call from Sandra, who was hysterical because "she's found some sort of letter and she says she just has to talk to somebody about it." Betsy then called him back around 12:45 p.m. and related how she'd gone to visit Sandra, who'd made the greatest conceivable drama about a letter from a married woman to her late husband Bobby, referencing an affair and the child he'd secretly fathered. Dr. Bagwell told the detectives he did not believe the letter was authentic. It was, he suspected, a hoax perpetrated by Sandra. He said he'd pointed out to Betsy that the timing of Bobby's alleged paternity was impossible because his chemotherapy at that time rendered him unable to father a child.

Dr. Bagwell perceived this letter to be of great forensic significance. Sometime after 6:00 p.m. that evening—after he called home and was informed that Betsy never returned from her errand with Sandra—he called Sandra's house and asked to speak with her. She was taking a bath, but her daughter summoned her to the phone. As he related this incident to the detectives:

Sandra came to the phone and seemed to be normal on the phone. And the first thing I said to Sandra was—I didn't ask her whereabouts—but said, "I'm really sorry about the letter. Betsy told me about the letter and I'm really sorry about it. Sometime this weekend we'll see if we can talk to you about it—see if there's any way we can help." Sandra said, "What letter? I don't know anything about a letter." And at that moment I knew something God awful was going on because Betsy doesn't make up things. I know you didn't know my wife, but she wouldn't have made that up. I said, "Wait a minute, Betsy told me about the letter you found. And she said, "I don't know what you're talking about. There's no letter." I just hung up and I knew something bad was happening. I had a terrible feeling about it. I knew something was going on. I then tried to make rounds. I ran into one of my partners and I said, "Listen, I've got to quit making rounds. You'll have to take it. I'm going home." I got home at about seven o'clock, and by that time the kids were panicked. They didn't know where she was.

He then drove to the Highland Park Presbyterian Church to look for Betsy, but she wasn't there. An intriguing detail that he omitted from his interview is that, though Betsy never returned home from the excursion, Sandra apparently did later return to the Bagwell house (in her suddenly working car) to pick up her daughters, Emily and Kathryn. The girls had stayed at the Bagwell house while their mother ran the errand with Betsy. Though this detail was never mentioned to the police or press, Kathryn Bridewell retained a vivid memory of it and related it to the private investigator, Carrie Huskinson during a 1994 interview in Portland, Oregon. According to Kathryn, Sandra returned from the errand, alone and in her own car, and said that Betsy had gone shopping and would be home soon. She collected Kathryn and Emily and drove them home, whereupon she bathed and dressed for dinner.

After Dr. Bagwell drove to the church to look for Betsy, he went home and called Sandra's house again. A babysitter answered and said Sandra had gone to dinner at La Tosca restaurant. He called the restaurant around 7:30 and asked the maître to summon her to the phone. She came to the phone and said that she and Betsy had gone to Love Field around 4:30 to rent a car but hadn't rented a car because she'd forgotten her license. They'd then returned to the church around 5:00 or 5:30, where Betsy had dropped her off. From this phone conversation with Sandra at the restaurant, Dr. Bagwell deduced that Betsy was dead. About forty minutes later, Detective Coughlin arrived to inform him that she had indeed been found dead in her car at Love Field.

A while later in the interview, Detective Shupe questioned Dr. Bagwell further about his phone conversation with Sandra while she was at the restaurant.

Detective Shupe: Let's get back to that conversation ... Al [Teel] indicated there were some more things said by Sandra.

Dr. Bagwell: Okay ... The main thing I asked about was the letter again.

Detective Shupe: Right.

Dr. Bagwell: She said she didn't know anything about the letter. I said, "Well, what did you do?" And she said, "Well, we had a girl talk." And I said, "What do you mean girl talk?" And she said, "Well, Betsy asked me if I thought you were having an affair." Betsy wouldn't have asked Sandra that. I mean, that's totally foreign to us. I mean, if she thought I was having an affair, she would simply ask if I was having an affair. She wouldn't have asked Sandra that. And then Sandra said she [Betsy] asked her about the suicide of her first husband—you know the dentist. She [Betsy] wanted to know how he killed himself, and so they discussed that. This doesn't make sense. I don't believe that. And then I asked her again, "What have y'all been doing? If there wasn't any letter, what in the hell is this? What is this all about?"

Detective Shupe: Okay. So, Al [Teel] was telling me that at one point she makes a statement—something to the effect of, "Well, you sound very accusatory," or something like that. How did that come about?"

Dr. Bagwell: It was about the letter. I mean, I just said, "I know that's not right. I know that she talked to you about some letter. I can't tell you how important that letter was. So, she makes the statement in reference to the letter. I kept on her about it in the conversation at the restaurant. I said, "I know that's not right." I knew the conversation about the letter had taken place.

Another conspicuous fact that emerges from the interview is that Sandra and Stanley Crooks went to the Bagwell residence after they finished dinner at La Tosca. Though Dr. Bagwell's reference to this is fleeting, it is nevertheless clear.

> **Dr. Bagwell:** Sandra came to our house about 9:30 or 10:00 at night, after the police [arrived] while the police were there and was with some guy she'd been having dinner with. I didn't talk to her then.

This is consistent with medical examiner Field Agent E. Gray's note in the Investigation Report he wrote on the evening of July 16, 1982.

> FRIEND of decedent (DPD did not identify) advised she & decedent drove to Love Field earlier this (7/16) afternoon . . .

This confirms that Sandra had her initial conversation with Detective Coughlin on the evening of July 16 after she arrived at the Bagwell residence with her attorney friend, Stanley Crooks. It was a brazen move. Under those circumstances, it's understandable that the young detective found it hard to imagine that she—a beautiful, elegantly dressed woman—should be regarded as the prime suspect.

Her arrival at the Bagwell residence provided Dr. Bagwell with an opportunity to confront her about the letter and other suspicious elements of her conduct with Betsy. One wonders why he remained silent instead of telling Detective Coughlin something like: *Ms. Bridewell was not my wife's friend. She has been stalking me for weeks and driving me and my wife crazy. She is also lying about her last conversation with my wife in which they discussed a letter whose existence she now denies.*

The evening of July 16, 1982, and the few days following it presented a critical window for Dr. Bagwell to persuade the Dallas police and medical examiner that their initial assessment of the crime scene was erroneous—that Betsy had in fact been murdered and that her last known contact and apparent friend, Sandra Bridewell, should be regarded as the prime suspect. It's notable that, during this window, Sandra continued to stalk him. As he told the OKC detectives, during the three weeks following Betsy's death, Sandra had her children deliver notes to his house, proposing that he take them and their mom away to Santa Fe. He also stated the following:

> **Dr. Bagwell:** I knew Sandra had been instrumental in her death. I didn't how she had done it, but I wouldn't talk to her. At one point Sandra cornered me in the doctors' parking lot when I came out to get in my car outside the hospital. I just kind of kept trying to walk away, and she was yelling and screaming. And I just left.
> **Detective Shupe:** Why did she corner you?
> **Dr. Bagwell:** She wanted to talk.
> **Detective Shupe:** In regards to?
> **Dr. Bagwell:** Betsy's death. She also stopped in front of my house one time when I was watering the flowers.

Detective Shupe seemed to recognize the significance of the statement that he *knew* that Sandra had murdered Betsy—not deduced but *knew*. What exactly did Sandra say to him when she ambushed him in the doctors' parking lot? He repeatedly emphasized that he *knew* Sandra was culpable because of her denial of the letter. As he put it, "I think Sandra knew when I talked to her—when she got out of the bathtub and said there was no letter—that the only person who said there was a letter was dead."

Reading the transcript of Dr. Bagwell's 1986 interview with the OKC detectives, I wondered if he had emphatically related this same information to DPD Detective Coughlin in 1982. This struck me as a critically important question, and I was disappointed that Detective Shupe didn't ask it. I also wondered if Dr. Bagwell had additional means of *knowing* (not merely deducing) that Sandra had murdered Betsy and chose to keep his knowledge to himself, just as he'd kept Dr. Thornton's gunshot residue report to himself. He emphasized his conviction that Sandra's denial of the melodramatic letter proved she knew of Betsy's death before Betsy was found. And yet, for some reason, he falsely stated to Detective Shupe that the letter's purported author was unaware that

Sandra had told Betsy about the letter.

"Susan Nowlin, who is the subject of the letter and who does not know about the letter, has been hounded by Sandra for some reason," he said.

This prompted a lengthy exchange in which he insisted there was nothing to be gained by discussing the letter with Susan. In fact, Susan was aware that Sandra had told Betsy about the purported letter. She considered Sandra's fabrication of the letter story to be evidence of her malicious intent with Betsy. She also regarded Sandra's denial of the letter story (after Betsy's death) to be evidence of her culpability, which amplified her fear of Sandra. The two women had once been friends but had a dramatic falling out just before Bobby died, while he was staying in a hotel because Sandra did not welcome him back into their home. Susan had felt terribly sorry for Bobby and frequently visited him at the hotel, during which she noticed that Sandra was never there. During one exceptional occasion when Sandra *did* show up and saw Susan visiting Bobby, she threw a fit, as though Susan was out of line and trying to ingratiate herself with the dying man. A dramatic scene erupted, which led Susan to conclude that Sandra was insane.

After Betsy was murdered, Susan was informed about Sandra's letter story. To reiterate: she knew the letter was a fabrication. Indeed, she suspected that the basis of the fabrication was a polite condolence letter she'd written to Sandra shortly after Bobby's death. Like many women, Susan believed that if Sandra got away with murdering Betsy, she could get away with murdering anyone. From this perception, Susan has remained mortally afraid of Sandra, and she declined my interview request. However, in the spring of 2023, she bumped into my mother at the pharmacy and inquired about my forthcoming book. When my mother told her it was scheduled to be published soon, Susan replied, "Aren't you afraid that Sandra will kill you when the book comes out?"

"Not really," my mother said.

Why did Dr. Bagwell falsely claim that Susan wasn't aware of Sandra's story about the letter? This raises another, more critical question—namely, was Detective Coughlin aware of Susan Nowlin and her potentially valuable witness testimony in July of 1982, *before* he closed the case? His reports do not refer to Susan, just as they do not refer to Anne Blakeney and Dabby Graham.

Dr. Bagwell told Detective Shupe in the same interview that he'd learned about the murder of Alan Rehrig from Anne Blakeney, who'd called him around December 12, 1985, to break the news. He told the detective he hadn't known at the time "that Sandra was still in Dallas." I found this hard to believe. After Betsy was murdered, Dr. Bagwell sold their house on Maplewood and purchased a house on the 4300 block of Versailles Avenue, two blocks from Sandra's home on the 4300 block of Lorraine Avenue. In the fall of 1984, she moved 1.5 miles to a duplex in University Park, but her children remained at Highland Park High School with Dr. Bagwell's kids, and she continued attending Sunday services at the Highland Park Presbyterian Church. Everyone in our tight-knit community knew she was still in town when Alan was murdered.

A poignant moment in Dr. Bagwell's interview was his lament that no one had warned him about Sandra. As he put it, "The thing that has been so devastating to me was that a lot of people I know well knew some things [about Sandra] and never said anything to me."

His terrible feeling of being left in the dark by people who could have warned him may explain why he became upset when he learned from Detective Shupe that Alan Rehrig's family was aware of Betsy's death. "You mean, they know about this stuff? I mean, they know, I mean they know there's another, that there's something else in her past?"

"Their suspicions are like yours are now," Detective Shupe replied.

"See, I almost called them, and I said, God, you know, I have no way to win by doing that."

CHAPTER 68

A DRAMATIC
CONFESSION

In Janie McKay's June 1986 interview with reporter Susan Albrecht at the *Park Cities People,* she made the following notable statement:

> Also, Betsy, on Tuesday before she was found dead on Friday, had called Dabby to ask about Sandra and said, 'What is the deal with this woman?' She said, 'I feel like a mother and I can't get away from her?' And she said, 'Who could tell me about her?' And Dabby said, 'Well I want you to talk to Candy Hill.' Well, Candy was teaching Bible study and they had just not made contact before Betsy was found.

This was intriguing. Candy Hill was the wife of Bill Hill, a prominent criminal defense attorney who had, a few years before Betsy's death, been one of Dallas County District Attorney Henry Wade's prosecutors. Later, in the years 1999 to 2007, Mr. Hill was himself the Dallas County District Attorney. By the time I called Candy, I'd grown so accustomed to unreturned calls, evasions, expressions of fear, and guilt trips for "dredging up" this painful old story that I figured she too would refuse to talk.

"I'd be happy to talk to you about it," she said on the phone. A few days later we had a long conversation about truth, religion, marriage, crime, and punishment. She had a wonderful frankness, and unlike Betsy's friends who felt compelled to remain silent, she believed there was nothing wrong with stating the facts of what she had seen and heard.

Candy and Bill had gotten to know Sandra after she married Bobby Bridewell, and their experience with her was mostly from couples' dinners and other group occasions. From Bill's experience as a prosecutor and defender, he'd become very perceptive, and to him, there was something very strange about Sandra. Initially she struck Candy as an exceptionally curious woman with a rare dedication to learning. It was amazing how she'd learned everything about thoroughbred racehorses and could discuss the subject with Bobby as though she'd long been a horse aficionada. She had an extraordinary ability to acquire and retain information.

Like others who'd loved Bobby, Candy had been disturbed by Sandra's behavior during the final months of his life. In the spring of 1982, when Sandra had acted overwhelmed with it all, Candy had been happy to lodge and look after her son Britt. However, as weeks passed with no sign from Sandra that Britt could come home, Candy wondered what on earth she was doing. When Bobby died, she seemed chiefly concerned about what she and her children were going to wear to the funeral. The red dress she finally chose was beautiful but wildly inappropriate for the somber occasion.

Shortly after the funeral, Sandra announced that she was taking her kids and their best friends on a vacation to Maui. After living in the Hill residence for two months, Britt had come to regard Candy's son Trey as his best friend, and Sandra wanted him to join the fun. By then, however, Candy didn't want to leave her son in Sandra's care, so she made a polite excuse for why Trey couldn't go on the trip. Upon Sandra's return from Maui, Candy treated her and her kids to lunch by the pool at Royal Oaks Country Club. Afterwards, while the kids went swimming, Sandra made a dramatic confession.

"I'm having a torrid affair with John Bagwell," she said. She then declared that while she was remodeling her house, she stayed at the Mansion, where John visited her nightly to give her updates on Bobby's condition. They were, she claimed, madly in love, in contrast to John's loveless marriage to Betsy. She and John didn't know what to do because of their five children. She got teary while speaking about the kids and how hard it was going to be to tell them.

"How did this happen?" Candy asked.

"He's just enthralled with me and he's this brilliant doctor, so it just happened."

Candy didn't know what to make of Sandra's confession, which sounded like something out of a romance novel. There was also the fact that Dr. Bagwell was well known and could have easily been recognized at the Mansion. Fervid admiration for doctors was common among women of their generation. Doctors possessed knowledge of how to heal the sick, which gave them special status, perhaps even putting them closer to God than other mortals. And in addition to his medical mystique, Dr. Bagwell held an esteemed position in Highland Park society. He also owned a beautiful house and a vacation home in Santa Fe. Candy wondered if Sandra was just fantasizing about having a great love affair with the great doctor.

On the morning of July 16, 1982—about a month after Sandra made her confession by the swimming pool—Candy saw her friend Dabby Graham at the Highland Park Presbyterian Church, where they were teaching Vacation Bible Study. During a break, Dabby told her that Sandra Bridewell was driving the Bagwells crazy, and that Betsy was trying to find a tactful way to get Sandra out of their lives. Betsy was mystified by Sandra's behavior. It was puzzling because everyone had thought the world of Bobby, and he had loved Sandra. And yet, her life seemed to be in constant turmoil that she kept thrusting onto Betsy. Dabby hoped that, because Candy had experienced Sandra's strange behavior while Bobby was dying, she could explain to Betsy what she was dealing with.

"I'd be happy to talk with her," Candy said.

"Anne Blakeney and I are meeting her this afternoon at the Dallas Country Club," Dabby said. "I'll give her your number and tell her to call you."

That Friday turned out to be a busy one for Candy, so she didn't notice that Betsy Bagwell didn't call her that afternoon. The next morning the phone rang, and she answered.

"Hello Candy, it's Sandra," came her breathy voice over the receiver.

"Hello Sandra," Candy said, a little surprised, as it had been some time since they'd spoken.

"Betsy Bagwell is dead," Sandra said. With these shocking words, Candy's mind raced back to her poolside confession.

"May I attend the funeral with you and Bill?" she asked. Candy made a polite excuse for getting off the phone, and then sat on the edge of her bed in shock.

The next day, Dabby Graham asked Candy Hill if she would speak to Dr. Bagwell in person. Candy visited him at his house, and they sat upstairs in a study near one of the children's rooms.

"Sandra said you're her best friend, and there are some things that I need to know about her," he said.

"I'm not her best friend," Candy replied. "Bill and I were close with Bobby. We knew her through him, but I've never been close with her." This distressed him.

"This is how she gains credibility—by falsely claiming to have friends like you. Did she ever say to you that she was having an affair with me?" he asked.

"Yes," Candy replied. "She said y'all were in love."

"Did you believe her?"

"No, because I know that you and Betsy had a solid marriage. I know Sandra has been encroaching on your lives, and I know she's a very beguiling woman, but I don't believe her."

Shortly after this meeting, Sandra showed up at Candy's house and said she wanted to talk. Candy's habitual politeness got the better of her, and she invited Sandra into the living room, but didn't offer her a seat. Sandra commenced asking questions.

"I want to talk about why you're avoiding me," she said. "I don't understand why you're not being my friend. Why don't you allow Trey to visit us anymore? Why have you pulled away from me?" Candy didn't know how to respond, and in the awkward silence, Sandra approached to embrace her. Candy stepped back to dodge it. Darkness seemed to fill the room, and she was so terrified it seemed the breath was being sucked out of her. Her perception of darkness was mirrored outside by a summer thunderstorm moving in, obscuring the sun in seconds. Right as Sandra extended her arms to hug Candy, an enormous thunderclap exploded outside. Candy remembered seeing Sandra arrive in her Mercedes convertible with the top down.

"Oh Sandra, you've got to put your car's top up or the interior will get soaked!" Candy exclaimed. Sandra rushed out to her car. Candy then locked the door and went back to the living room couch, where she sat down and was overcome with the shakes.

I recorded my conversation with Candy and listened to it several times. Sandra's pronouncement that she and John Bagwell were "in love" and "having a torrid affair" contradicted her profession to multiple women that "Betsy is my new best friend." Her teary-eyed expression of concern for how her love affair with John was going to affect their children was also indicative of a greater design than occasional trysts. Candy thought it possible that Sandra was in the grip of a romance novel fantasy. Even if this was the case, Sandra's confession revealed a desire to supplant Betsy. Her statement to Candy was reminiscent of her statement to Delia Mullins in 1976 that she and Norman Brinker had fallen madly in love. As soon as Brinker's wife (whom Sandra claimed to be an unhinged stalker) was out of the picture, Sandra and Norm would unite their families into the "Brinker Bunch." The letter that Emily Bridewell delivered to the Bagwell house after Betsy's death, expressing a desire for the two families to unite, was further evidence of this design.

I also found it notable that, after Betsy's death, Dr. Bagwell sought a meeting with Candy in which he asked if Sandra had ever said that she'd had an affair with him. Candy answered in the affirmative, which equipped Dr. Bagwell with certainty of Sandra's representations, even if they were based on fantasy. Whether Sandra's conduct had arisen from an actual affair or a fantasy, Candy assumed he would tell the Dallas police about it.

If Sandra was a stalker in the grip of psychotic wishful thinking—as has been documented in cases of women stalking movie stars—he could have explained this to Detective Coughlin in the immediate aftermath of Betsy's death. Four years later, in his interview with OKC detectives, he *did* describe Sandra as a stalker who ambushed him in his office parking lot after Betsy's death. And yet, neither Detective Coughlin's investigative report nor Medical Examiner Petty's report indicate that Dr. Bagwell told them about this incident. Did OKC Detective Shupe share his interview transcript with DPD Detective Coughlin in 1986? I don't know because Detective Shupe never returned my calls and Detective Coughlin had no recollection of it.

Sandra made her dramatic confession to Candy Hill, then called her with the news that Betsy was dead, then asked if she could attend the funeral with Candy and her husband Bill. Sandra knew that Bill Hill had been one of Henry Wade's skilled prosecutors. He had also been one of Bobby Bridewell's best friends and a member of his Bible study. How would Bill feel about Sandra's confession of having an affair with Bobby's cancer doctor? How would he—a man who possessed keen understanding of criminal behavior—react to the news that Betsy had been found shot in her car at Love Field?

"Do you recall if Bill ever spoke with any of his contacts at the Dallas police or DA's office about Betsy death?" I asked Candy.

"Maybe he did," she replied. "I'm not sure."

Candy and Bill had been divorced for some time, so I called him separately, and he told me it was a story he no longer wished to discuss.

Betsy's friends were shocked that Sandra was so brazen in pursuit of Dr. Bagwell right after Betsy's death. In the year 2007, shortly after Sandra's arrest in North Carolina, one of Betsy's best friends wrote the following in an e-mail to Detective Jayne Todd:

> At the time of Betsy's death, we were all SURE what had really happened. To endure her at Betsy's home following the death and prior to the funeral—and to see her attempts afterward to "get" John Bagwell was terrible on top of losing a best friend.

She even forged a long note from her daughter (1st or 2nd grader) begging him to start over with her mom since they had both experienced great losses. Her teachers at school said she could not possibly have written the note.

Aggressively pursuing a widower even before his wife's funeral struck everyone as outrageous, and multiple witnesses saw her escorted out of the Bagwell house when she showed up before the service. And yet, none of Betsy's friends seemed to have grappled with the question of *why* the DPD didn't investigate Sandra. Some seem to have assumed that Dr. Bagwell provided the police with a full account of Sandra's suspicious conduct, but that the police didn't consider it sufficient grounds for investigating her.

CHAPTER 69

BLACKMAIL

During Gloria's trip to Dallas in the spring of 1986, she spoke with a lady who mentioned that Sandra's attorney in the wake of Betsy's death was one "Mr. Marshall." A bit of research led me to a distinguished civil attorney named Roger Marshall, who'd represented Bobby Bridewell in various matters. I figured it was unlikely he would talk to me about Sandra, and I was therefore surprised by his frankness. He told me how he'd represented Sandra in her contest with "Mr. Big" in 1978, and how she'd been happy to speak on public record, with a court reporter typing away, about her affair with him.

Four years later, after Betsy's death, she appeared at his office and announced that she'd had an affair with Dr. Bagwell and saw no reason to conceal it from her friends. In fact, she had saved room receipts from the Hotel Anatole to document their trysts. She further explained that he was trying to silence her and even implying that she may have had something to do with his wife's death, which had been ruled a suicide by the Dallas police and medical examiner. She therefore wanted Mr. Marshall to represent her if Dr. Bagwell threatened her with legal action.

He agreed, and a few days later, Dr. Bagwell's attorney (whose name Mr. Marshall had forgotten) called and demanded that his client cease telling people she'd been having an affair with Dr. Bagwell, and cease showing up at his office and waiting for him in the parking lot. Mr. Marshall replied that Sandra had spoken the truth about her relationship with him and had documented their extra-marital affair with hotel room receipts. Upon hearing this, the attorney backed off and Mr. Marshall never heard from him again.

I asked Mr. Marshall if he understood how exactly Sandra had obtained receipts bearing Dr. Bagwell's signature.

"Yeah, I asked her that. She said he paid for the rooms at check in and she just grabbed the receipts in the room when he wasn't looking," he replied.

"Did she tell you why she kept a record of these encounters? I mean, it sounds like blackmail."

"It was a form of blackmail. She never said why, but it was obvious why she wanted to document them being together illicitly in a hotel room. It was just like the other married guys she got involved with and got money from without paying them back. She put them in a hard position to sue her."

"Is it possible she fabricated the hotel receipts?" I asked.

"Like I said, when I told Dr. Bagwell's attorney about them, he backed off and I never heard from him again."

"I wonder why he didn't insist the receipts were fabrications."

"I guess he thought it wasn't the best strategy for his client. It was an open secret in Highland Park that Sandra had seduced Dr. Bagwell, but the police, who have all their investigative tools, were unaware that this romantic relationship was going on, which would give Sandra every reason to be pleased with Mrs. Bagwell not living. As far as I can see, no journalist has ever investigated this aspect of the story. You're the first person who has ever called to ask about Sandra."

"But how in hell did Sandra think that Dr. Bagwell would react to her killing his wife?"

"I think she assumed that with Betsy's apparent suicide, Dr. Bagwell would need her as his new partner and mother for his kids. When Sandra wanted something, she pursued it aggressively without thinking about social norms or consequences."

Throughout Dr. Bagwell's interview with OKC Detective Shupe, he made statements indicating he felt helpless against Sandra. When Detective Shupe asked him why he discontinued Al Teel's investigation of Sandra, he replied:

> Sandra had threatened to sue me, you know. We had a medical examiner who said it was suicide, so what were we going to do. I did not want Teel getting so close to Sandra that Sandra knew that it was me doing it. She may have known anyway, but I just didn't want that. I have two children. … I'm really frightened of her. I think she's frightening.

His expression of helplessness reminded me of the 1991 film *Cape Fear* in which society and law enforcement are helpless against the implacable villain, Max Cady, who in one scene proclaims that he cannot be beaten.

> I can outlearn you, I can out-read you, I can outthink you, and I can out-philosophize you. And I'm gonna outlast you. You think a couple of whacks to my good-ole-boy gut is gonna get me down? It's gonna take a hell of a lot more than that, counselor, to prove you're better than me. I am like God and God like me. I am as large as God, he is as small as I. He cannot above me nor I below him be!

Everyone marvels at Cady's preternatural strength and wonders where it comes from. Likewise, Dr. Bagwell seemed awed by Sandra's mysterious power. He mentioned a man in California whom she visited shortly before Betsy's death who believed Sandra was an incarnation of the devil. After Betsy's death, others suggested the same.

I thought a lot about fear while researching this story, and it reminded me of a conversation I'd once had with a prominent plastic surgeon. I asked him what his occupation had taught him about the human condition.

"That people are governed mostly by fear—fear of loss of wealth and status, fear of growing old and ugly, and fear of death." In an affluent society like Highland Park, fear of loss is a major motivating force.

Dr. Bagwell and his father, Dr. John S. Bagwell, were physicians of some of the most powerful people in Dallas. Their position contrasted with that of Sandra—an ostracized single mom whom many regarded with fear and loathing. He told the OKC detectives he was intimidated by her threat to sue him, even though Al Teel and Dr. John Thornton had armed him with information to go on the offensive, and Dr. Petty had stated his openness to reconsidering his suicide ruling. As Dr. Bagwell told the detectives, he *knew* Sandra had been instrumental in Betsy's death.

And yet, even after Alan Rehrig was murdered three years later in an almost identical way—an incident that was widely perceived as confirming everyone's worst suspicions of Sandra—Dr. Bagwell *still* did not ask the medical examiner and police to reevaluate Betsy's case and to consider the evidence that she had been murdered by Sandra. On June 15, 1986, he wrote a letter to Gloria Rehrig in which he stated:

> I believe Betsy's death and Alan's are linked to Sandra, but I can give you nothing of substance to confirm this. ... Somehow, with enormous difficulty, I came to accept the uncertainty of Betsy's death, putting aside the tremendous need to reach a final conclusion. In the end, I suspect you and your family may need to do the same, realizing that all of us will learn everything eventually.

Dr. Bagwell's resignation contrasted with the hope expressed by Betsy's parents, who encouraged Gloria to continue publicizing Alan's murder and seeking justice for it.

"We hope the news will speak far & wide and that eventually 'truth will out,'" they wrote to her in a letter in July 1986.

Dr. Bagwell's decision to end Al Teel's investigation and make no attempt to overturn the suicide ruling indicates that Sandra succeeded in blackmailing him. Her claim that she had hotel receipts to document the affair revealed that she prepared to blackmail him before their relationship became conflicted. The totality of circumstances indicates that Dr. Bagwell did *not* give the Dallas police a full and candid account of what was going on with Sandra. She let him know that if he tried to make the case that she had murdered Betsy, she would testify that Betsy had fallen into a suicidal depression upon discovering their affair. This was a cunning defense, apparently supported by police and medical examiner assessments of the crime scene. Indeed, OKC Detective Shupe stated during their interview,

"We've seen the photographs. We've seen the evidence, and I mean there's not a detective [who wouldn't conclude the same] based strictly on what we've seen, you know, crime scene, photographs, and so on."

"So, you think she killed herself?" Dr. Bagwell asked.

"No, we're not saying that at all. I'm just saying that it appears that she killed herself."

Al Teel took the first step in overturning this perception by hiring Dr. John Thornton to render a second opinion on the gunshot residue found on Betsy's right hand, but as already noted, Dr. Bagwell did not forward Dr. Thornton's report to Dr. Petty. I wondered how an expert criminalist—trained in the most up-to-date methods of crime scene analysis—would interpret photographs of the crime scene.

CHAPTER 70
"A BIG CLUE THAT SCREAMS HOMICIDE"

Obtaining copies of the DPD death scene photos of Betsy wasn't easy. I made my initial request in August of 2019 and received digital copies of the images three months later. However, these images were redacted with whiteout to obscure areas that displayed blood. To perform a full forensic analysis, I needed un-redacted images. After consulting with an Open Records Act attorney, I modified the language of my request and finally succeeded in obtaining un-redacted copies of the images.

Dr. Lynne Herold was skeptical the photos would reveal anything sufficient to overturn Dr. Petty's suicide ruling. Over the years, she had corrected me on several occasions about jumping to conclusions in my true crime research. She frequently scolded me for allowing my reflections on psychological and sociological factors to influence my interpretation of evidence. She herself was very disciplined about limiting her interpretations to the physical reality presented at actual crime scenes or displayed in crime scene photos. She also frequently emphasized that crime scene photos must be taken in accordance with exacting technical standards.

At the time I forwarded the images to her via e-mail, she seemed weary of me and my frequent queries, so I didn't expect to hear back from her for a while. Thus, to my surprise, she replied about an hour later.

Well, I will continue to contemplate this for a while before opening my mouth officially, but I think you may have a big clue here that screams homicide.

One of the first things that Lynne noticed was Betsy's body position. Though her feet are still on the driver's side floorboard, her midsection is lying across the center console, her upper body is resting on the passenger seat, and the top of her head is resting on the far-right edge of the passenger seat. Her hips and thighs are on the right side of the large steering wheel. A photograph of her body, taken through the open driver's side door, shows her hips and thighs relative to the narrow gap between the bottom of the steering wheel and the driver's seat. If she had simply slumped to her right after the shot was fired into her right temple, her left thigh would have certainly hung on the bottom of the steering wheel.

Both of her arms are stretched back towards the console, and her right, upturned palm, cradling a .22 caliber revolver, is braced between her right thigh and the driver's side of the gearshift. This body position is conspicuously inconsistent with the proposition that she shot herself in the head and then slumped to her right.

The "clue that screams homicide" is the blood on Betsy's right thigh. Blood from either the gunshot wound on Betsy's right temple or running from her nose has fallen onto her right thigh and run down the skin before drying. The direction of the flow is clearly visible. It shows that her thigh was rolled in the opposite direction when the blood dropped onto it, ran down the skin, and dried. In other words, when she bled onto her right thigh, she was seated upright, and possibly slumped slightly to her left.

After the blood dried while her leg was in this position, someone moved her body all the way to the right and placed it on the passenger seat, as it was found by Lloyd Durrett and noted in the Incident Report.

Lynne told me about these two observations, which was the beginning of a long and painstaking analysis of the crime scene photographs that I present in **Appendix I**. The images show that Betsy Bagwell was murdered, and the crime scene was staged to look like a suicide. Vernon J. Geberth, a retired Lieutenant-Commander of the New York City Police Department, has written about how homicides are sometimes erroneously perceived to be suicides by responding officers. The initial perception of suicide may result in a lack of careful analysis. So it was with Betsy's death scene. No suicide note was found in the car, but at first glance, the responding officers perceived that she'd shot herself in the head and then slumped to her right. However, upon closer inspection, it's clear that someone moved her upper body onto the passenger seat after she was shot and put the revolver into her right hand, bracing it between her right thigh and the gear shifter to hold it in place. The objective of moving her upper body onto the passenger seat was to prevent it from being seen by people passing the car so that the culprit could get away from the crime scene and establish an alibi before the body was discovered.

CHAPTER 71

GETTING AWAY
WITH MURDER

The totality of circumstances convinces me that Sandra is culpable for the murder of Betsy Bagwell. I believe it was for good reason that Dr. Bagwell told OKC detectives in his 1986 interview, "I knew Sandra had been instrumental in her death." Sandra's treatment of Betsy—pretending to be her friend while scheming to supplant her in her marriage and home—was a psychopathic act of deception. The melodramatic letter she claimed to have found was a ruse for luring Betsy to be with her that morning. As Dr. Bagwell correctly perceived, Sandra's denial of the letter's existence while Betsy was still missing revealed she knew Betsy was dead before her body was found. Her story about her intermittent car trouble, and then forgetting to bring her driver's license to the car rental agency, was obvious fraud. By her own account she was Betsy's last known contact, getting a ride to Love Field from Betsy.

In the days just prior to her death, Betsy's chief complaint to her friends was the trouble she was having with Sandra, who was stalking her and her husband. Upon Sandra's return from Santa Fe after the Fourth of July weekend, she realized that Betsy wanted to end the relationship and was urging her husband to do so. Judging by Dr. Bagwell's statement to the OCPD detectives, Sandra became increasingly erratic and demanding and wouldn't leave him alone—a scenario reminiscent of the dramatic situation in the films *Fatal Attraction* and *Crimes and Misdemeanors.*

On Wednesday, July 14, 1982, when Sandra called the Bagwell residence at dinnertime to say her car had broken down, she signaled to Dr. Bagwell that she was going to force a crisis. When Betsy called him at work two days later to say that Sandra was hysterical about the letter, he advised her not to get drawn into the drama. As he told OCPD detectives four years later, he suspected the letter was a ruse. When he called home (a second time) from his office at 5:30 p.m. and one of his kids told him that Betsy still hadn't returned from her errand with Sandra, he sensed danger. When he called Sandra's house around 6:30 p.m. and she said she didn't know where Betsy was and she knew nothing about the letter, he knew Betsy was dead.

Sandra was confident that when Betsy was found dead of an apparent suicide, the police wouldn't closely inspect her death. After all, they hadn't closely inspected Sandra's first husband's death after she found him shot in his bed with his left hand lying on a .22 caliber pistol. Their initial perception of suicide in Betsy's case would also result in a cursory investigation. By masquerading as Betsy's intimate friend, Sandra positioned herself to tell the investigating officer that Betsy was having suicidal ideation just prior to her death. The scheme worked: Detective Coughlin told Medical Examiner Field Agent Gray that Betsy had spent her last day with her "friend" to whom she spoke about suicide. The fact that Betsy did *not* commit suicide proves that Sandra's statement to Detective Coughlin was false and should therefore be regarded as further evidence that she planned Betsy's murder and staged it to look like a suicide.

How exactly Sandra carried out Betsy's murder—between 4:15 p.m., when Betsy was last seen, and 6:30, when Dr. Bagwell spoke to her on the phone at her home—is, to a fair degree, a matter of speculation. As Dr. Bagwell stated to the OKC detectives, it seems likely she had an accomplice. Based on the totality of circumstances, I have formulated a theory of how Sandra committed the murder (see **Appendix II**).

I suspect it is no coincidence that Sandra went out to dinner with Barbara and Stanley Crooks right after she murdered Betsy. A few months earlier, when Bobby Bridewell was dying of cancer, Barbara visited Sandra at her home and the two women were drinking champagne on the couch when Dr. Bagwell arrived for a visit. Barbara found this a bit puzzling, given that Bobby was in hospital. I suspect this was a setup. Sandra told him to pass by her house after work and then pretended that Barbara had unexpectedly dropped in before his arrival. This made Barbara a witness to the extraordinary fact that her dying husband's physician was visiting her in her home. When Dr. Bagwell called her at the restaurant looking for Betsy, she probably told him, "I'm having dinner with Barbara. Remember Barbara?"

Already in the 4th Century BC, Hippocrates recognized the conflict of interest that could arise if a physician had intimate relations with a member of a patient's household. As he wrote in his famous Hippocratic Oath:

Into whatever homes I go I will enter them for the benefit of the sick, avoiding any voluntary act of impropriety or corruption, including the seduction of women or men, whether they are free men or slaves.

In this spirit, the Texas Medical Board and Baylor University Medical Center would have taken a very dim view of a doctor who had, according to his dying patient's wife, had an affair with her. When Sandra made a pass on Dr. Don McKay, she acted as though it cramped her style that her husband was impotent from the chemotherapy (administered to him by Dr. Bagwell). While Bobby languished in hospital with his life and manhood ebbing away, his wife invited his treating physician over for an after-work drink. She did this with the awareness of how deeply he was invested in his medical career, and this gave her leverage over him, as well as an intoxicating feeling of power. The great oncologist, to whom the high and mighty of Highland Park desperately turned in their hours of need, was under her thumb and he wouldn't dare raise a finger against her.

Not only was Dr. Bagwell heavily invested in his medical career and reputation, so was his father—the eminent John Spurgeon Bagwell, former president of staff at Baylor University Medical Center, which was, in those days, an avowedly Baptist institution. In one of my perusals of Gloria's file cabinet, I found her memo of a phone call on Saturday, March 29, 1986.

> Talked to Mr. Frank Monroe (Betsy Bagwell's father)
> …Sandra called Betsy Bagwell (wife of cancer doctor) to take her to Love Field to pick up a package. There was no package. They returned home. Later Sandra called Betsy Bagwell again to take her Love Field to rent a car because her car wasn't dependable. They found Betsy in her own car—shot in the head. The coroner ruled it a suicide—case closed. The elder Dr. Bagwell wanted it kept quiet so as not to ruin his son's reputation.

As things turned out, Dr. Bagwell avoided scrutiny in the press and courts, as well as from the Baylor University Medical Center and Texas Medical Board. Betsy's two closest friends also didn't tell the police about the trouble she was having with Sandra just hours before her death. The *D Magazine* report implied that her "two female friends" had understood the grounds for suspecting Sandra but had been obliged to accept the medical examiner's suicide ruling. In fact, Anne Blakeney and Dabby Graham never told the DPD what they'd seen and heard during the critical period just before and after Betsy's death, even though their witness testimony could have persuaded the police to take a much closer look at Sandra.

Anne's husband, Bobby Blakeney, was also under no illusions about the reality of the situation. As I discovered when I read Dr. Bagwell's interview with the OCPD detectives, Bobby was the attorney who called Sandra's attorney, Roger Marshall, and then backed off when Mr. Marshall told him about the hotel receipts. He was also the attorney who did the legal review of Skip Hollandsworth's *D Magazine* feature whose section on the "Death of Betsy Bagwell" contained so many conspicuous redactions.

CHAPTER 72

DAVID STEGALL

One fine summer day in 2019 I parked my car across the street from the house in which David Stegall had purportedly committed suicide in 1975. The charming English style cottage had a small room in a gable above the garage, but I knew from a real estate database and witnesses that all the bedrooms were on the ground floor. The owner—the sister of an old high school friend—would not allow me to inspect the premises because she "did not want to give murder any energy" in her house.

I glanced at a police photo of the house taken in 1975. A tree flanking the driveway was now much bigger, but everything else was the same. It was a fine house for a young couple full of ambition and hope for a happy future. Strange to think it had been the scene of such a catastrophe. Viewing its relatively small dimensions, I knew that a pistol shot—even a .22 caliber pistol shot—would boom like thunder through its interior space. Sandra told the police she was sleeping in the children's room with her three kids when the shot was fired. What were the odds that neither she nor any of her kids were awakened by it? Later she told her friend, Barbara Crooks, that David had said he wanted to be alone that night and asked her to take the kids and stay somewhere else. In January of 1986, she told Gloria Rehrig that her kids had never known that their father had committed suicide. This raises the suspicion that Sandra did, in fact, lodge the kids—at least the older two—somewhere else on the night David was shot.

Scouring the inventory of online gun dealers, I found the same model of pistol that was found with David's body. The Ruger Standard .22 caliber semi-automatic was what my grandfather would have called a "jim-dandy" pistol. Modeled after the Luger Pistole Parabellum, it was deadly accurate, even at fifty yards. And damn was it loud. One day, at my youngest brother's shop, which backs to the Trinity River flood plain, I performed some shooting experiments on a manikin. A group of guys wanted to observe, and they assumed that, because the pistol was "just a .22" they didn't need ear protection. They were standing a few yards behind me when I (wearing ear protection) fired the first shot—POW.

"Goddamn, son of bitch!" erupted their cries behind me. "Bloody fucking hell that thing is loud!" exclaimed an English friend.

They hadn't understood that even a small .22 long rifle cartridge produces 20,000 psi of pressure in the firing chamber. This explosion blasts out of the muzzle and ejection port, striking the eardrums with a massive percussion. In a 2014 study titled "Auditory Risk Estimates for Youth Target Shooting," published in the *International Journal of Audiology*, a .22 Long Rifle cartridge fired in a Ruger target pistol produces 157.5 decibels. A thunderclap produces 120 decibels. A jet taking off 25 meters away produces 150 decibels. Any pistol shot is *extremely* loud. Additional tests in a closed room—firing the weapon through a cracked window—produced a deafening percussion. I found it very hard to believe that anyone could possibly sleep through this weapon discharging in the Stegall's small, one-story house. Pondering this reminded me of Jack Sides, Jr.'s account of Sandra entering Britt's bedroom down the hall from her master bedroom and telling the boys to pipe down because they were keeping her awake.

According to the DPD Incident Report, the pistol found with David Stegall had no cartridge in the firing chamber and none in the magazine. One spent casing was found on the floor to the right (facing the headboard) of the bed. I wondered if the police had asked Bill Hardy (from whom the pistol had been stolen) if he'd kept the magazine loaded.

Investigating David Stegall's life and death was challenging because few who'd known him were still alive. His parents and his brother Eugene were deceased. Even if his children had been willing to speak to me, they were, I figured, too young (one, four, and seven) at the time of his death to remember him. After their mother married Bobby Bridewell a few years later, she persuaded him to adopt her three children and to give them his surname. On the Texas Birth Register, they were registered under the surname Bridewell, even though they had been born with the surname Stegall. There was, I thought, something very poignant about this. It was as though David Stegall and his paternal legacy had been erased.

I found his Death Notice in the *Dallas Morning News* and noted the names of his pallbearers. A few were still alive, and I contacted them. Then I tracked down a couple of his former dental colleagues, as well as the female dentist who'd purchased his practice—a colorful character named Dale Rabinowitz, who'd been a high school classmate of my mother. Slowly I pieced together a picture of the young man's life.

I was struck by how little David's death had been scrutinized, even after Sandra fell under suspicion for murdering Alan Rehrig. It seemed that the Dallas County Medical Examiner's suicide ruling was final and immutable. And because David's death had been ruled a suicide, it had received no media coverage until the 1987 *D Magazine* feature. The authors did not, in their published account, question the suicide ruling, but flatly asserted that David "succeeded" in committing suicide. I wondered why they'd stated this so unequivocally. Their understanding of David's death seemed to have been shaped by Jack Sides's account of his experience three weeks earlier, which they characterized as David "trying" to commit suicide. However, what Sides described was not a man *trying* to commit suicide, but a man *threatening* to commit suicide. Large studies of suicide have shown that many who make suicide threats do not actually plan to attempt suicide. In contrast, a true suicide attempt involves self-harming actions with the intention of ending one's life. Those who make verbal threats of suicide are often attempting to elicit help or to change the behavior of others with whom they are having intense interpersonal relationships.

I called Sides, who happened to be an old friend of my parents. Over thirty years had passed since he'd told his story to Skip Hollandsworth and Eric Miller, but he told me an almost identical account. A remarkable detail he told me that was not mentioned in the *D Magazine* feature was that Sandra and two of her kids were sitting on the edge of the bed, facing David as he sat in the open closet, brandishing a pistol. To me, this suggested that Sandra knew he was bluffing, otherwise she would have ordered the kids to leave the room.

I was haunted by the image of two small children seeing their father so beside himself and threatening to kill himself. Later I was reminded of this dreadful scene when I finally received a copy of the Medical Examiner Investigation Report, written on the day of David's death (February 22, 1975). The handwritten (in barely legible script) document notes Sandra's statement:

> saw decedent circa 10:30 last night—was watching TV, decedent has been under psychiatric care for several months— [2.5 lines of script redacted with whiteout].
> has been acting very strange recently, had physical fight w/wife ca 1 week ago, [word redacted] had mentioned murder/suicide of Dr. Henninger (shot wife & killed 3 children ca 2 yrs ago) & made recent statement "I'll do it upright—", Henninger's wife loved, stole gun from friend yesterday.

Dr. Waldemar Henninger lived in Dallas with his large family. On the night of May 7, 1973, he shot and killed three of his sleeping children with a pistol, wounded his wife and another child, and then killed himself. I found the phrase **"I'll do it upright"** so puzzling that I wasn't sure I was correctly reading the investigator's chicken scratch. The rest of the statement seems clear. Sandra told the investigator that David had recently mentioned Dr. Henninger's murder of his three children and his suicide in a way that implied he was contemplating doing the same. If this was indeed the case, why didn't she immediately report this extremely alarming statement to the police? She could have also taken the kids and sought refuge at a friend's house instead of remaining in the same house with David.

Another conspicuous feature of Sandra's statement to the investigator—at least as it was recorded in his Investigative Report—is that it contains nothing about the incident that Jack Sides had witnessed three weeks before David's death. It struck me as very odd that Sandra told the investigator the questionable anecdote about Dr. Henninger but mentioned nothing about David's suicide threat. Why not? Did she, for some reason, think it was better to leave Sides out of the official investigation?

CHAPTER 73

THE EXTERNAL
EXAM REPORT

In response to my 2007 request for David's autopsy report, the Medical Examiner records division claimed there wasn't one on file. Twelve years later, I wondered if this was really the case, or if there had been a clerical error. Who, I wondered, had filled out David's death certificate? Thank God for Ancestry.com, on which I obtained a copy a few minutes later. The cause of death noted was "gunshot wound to head" and the manner of death noted was "suicide." The certificate indicated that no autopsy had been performed. At the bottom of the form, I saw it had been signed by Dallas County Medical Examiner, Vincent Di Maio.

Vincent Di Maio—Lynne Herold's opposing expert in the Phil Spector trial. Instantly I remembered her remark during my conversation with her in 2007: *Some of his suicide rulings have been controversial.* In David's case, I found it strange that, according to Di Maio, no autopsy was performed. If Dr. Di Maio didn't perform an autopsy, how did he determine that David had committed suicide? It occurred to me that he must have at least performed an external examination of David's body, so I submitted a request to the Medical Examiner's Office for a copy of its

"External Examination Report" in the matter of David Lawrence Stegall, and it arrived in the mail a few days later.

It was a brief (three-page) document, but it contained a few notable details. The first was Dr. Di Maio's description of "the gunshot wound of entrance."

> Present in the left fronto-temporal region, 1 ¼ inches above and ¾ inch anterior to the left external auditory canal, in the left sideburn, there is a gunshot wound of entrance, consisting of an irregular area of dense hemorrhagic powder tattooing, measuring ¾ x ¾ inch maximally with a perforation at the medial portion of this area of tattooing. The wound of entrance and area of powder tattooing lie at the upper end of an irregular area of powder blackening, measuring 1 ½ vertically x 1 inch horizontally. This area of powder soot deposition extends up to the medial edge of the ear.

The dimensions of the powder tattooing and surrounding area of powder blackening were noteworthy because they indicated that the pistol's muzzle was *not* in contact with David's temple when the shot was fired but positioned a certain distance from the victim's head. Had the muzzle been pressed firmly to David's temple, the area of powder tattooing and blackening in the dimensions noted would *not* have been deposited around the wound. Test firing the weapon could have revealed the distance that would produce these dimensions of tattooing and blackening, but the Examination Report mentioned nothing about test firing. Dr. Di Maio noted only that in David's case, it was a "Close-up wound of entrance," rather than a contact wound.

The next defect noted on David's body was the following:

> Present on the palmar aspect of the left hand, in the skin overlying the metacarpal bone of the thumb, there is a rectangular impression, measuring 7/16 inch x ¼ inch horizontally. This impression consists of five linear imprints. This patterned impression corresponds to that on the bolt of a Ruger .22 automatic pistol.

I wondered why the pistol's bolt had left this impression on this region of David's thumb, as it seemed to me that his thumb's logical position would be grasping the pistol's grip when he fired it, and not in contact with the bolt. The metal ridges that had left the impression on David's left thumb are located on the butt end of the bolt, providing a grasping point for the thumb and index finger to pull back the bolt to chamber a cartridge. Why had the *back* of the weapon left an impression on David's left thumb?

Another strange injury noted in the External Examination Report was the following:

> Present on the flexor surface of the right lower arm, just above the wrist, there are three incised wounds, measuring 2 ¾ X 1/8 inch, 3 x ¾ inch and 2 x 3/16 inch, proceeding proximally. They are all sharp edged and extend down to the fascia overlying the muscle. No major blood vessels are incised.

This struck me as very strange. David's training at the Baylor College of Dentistry had included a year of anatomy, and he certainly knew the point on the wrist at which the radial artery lies close to the skin—the point where you take a patient's pulse. Why, before shooting himself in the head, would he slash himself three times on the forearm, completely missing the radial artery? He certainly knew that this would only cause pain and distress with no lethal outcome.

Judging by what Dr. Di Maio's presented in his "External Examination Report," the only clear finding was that David had died from a gunshot wound to his head. The .22 caliber bullet had entered the left side of his head, travelled through his brain, and exited the right temple, which was resting on a pillow. The bullet was found in a clot of blood adhering to the pillow. But how had Dr. Di Maio determined that David had fired the pistol, as distinct from another person shooting him in the head while he lay fast asleep? Whatever analysis Dr. Di Maio had performed to reach his conclusion was not presented in his report. Thus, I reckoned that *unexplained* would have been a more fitting classification of the Manner of Death than *suicide*.

CHAPTER 74
DR. RADMAN

I needed more information, so I submitted a request to the Dallas Police Department Records Division for all their records on the death of David Lawrence Stegall. Not knowing what, if anything, the DPD had on file, I specified the "Incident Report," the "911 Call Sheet," the "Death Scene Photos," and the "Investigative Reports." A few weeks later, the Records Division responded with a copy of the 911 Call Sheet, indicating the call had been placed from the Stegall home phone on February 25, 1975, at 0707 hours. No other records were forthcoming, so I submitted a second request for the other files. A few weeks later I received a copy of the Incident Report, but no Death Scene Photos or Investigative Reports. And so, I submitted a third request for these other files.

I then pursued a lead supplied by Detective Jayne Todd—namely, that Sandra did *not* initially call 911, but one—and possibly more than one—of David's dentist and doctor friends. Jayne didn't recall exactly who'd told her this; she figured it was probably the *Dallas Observer* columnist, Glenna Whitley. Reviewing Glenna's 2004 piece, "The Return of the Black Widow," I noted the following in her account of David's death:

An emotional Sandra called a doctor friend at 7 a.m. "I think something has happened to David," she said. The doctor and his wife raced to the Stegall home. Sandra explained that she'd been sleeping in a child's bedroom and had heard something ominous; she hadn't looked in the master bedroom. The doctor found David slumped in the king-size bed. He'd slashed his wrists and shot himself in the head with a .22-caliber pistol.

Thus, it seemed that when the police arrived, they encountered not only the distressed widow, but also a doctor. Who was he? The *D Magazine* piece mentioned that one of David's dental colleagues was Dr. Paul Radman. I wondered if he was "the doctor friend" whom Sandra called on the morning of David's death. I found Dr. Radman, who was still alive and remembered the story well.

"David was very collegial, but I can't say that I knew him that well. It was Sandra and my wife—who is now my ex-wife—who really hit it off."

Dr. Radman shared with me his recollections of Sandra, and then told me about the fateful morning on which she called his house and announced that "something terrible has happened to David."

"Did you have any suspicions about Sandra at the time?" I asked him.

"No, not really. Seems like it was later that some of David's dental colleagues started wondering if he'd really killed himself. A couple of years after David's death, I myself had a close shave."

Dr. Radman then told me about his encounter with the gunman who shot him on March 9, 1977. I was thunderstruck. What on earth was an assassin doing lurking in the parking lot of the Preston Center medical building? Since my childhood I'd been in that building dozens of times. It was located in one of the safest, most affluent neighborhoods in the world.

"My God! Who the was the guy?"

"I have no idea."

"Did the police ever catch him?"

"No."

"Why on earth would someone want to kill you?"

"I don't know. I never figured it out, but just now, talking about David

Stegall, I was reminded of it, because I too had a life insurance policy with a large death benefit, and my ex-wife was the beneficiary."

"I see," I said, and thought about this for a bit.

"And you say that Sandra and your ex-wife were friends at the time?"

"Yes," he replied in a matter-of-fact tone.

"Did it ever occur to you that Sandra knew the gunman?" I asked.

"I don't want to speculate about such things," he said.

CHAPTER 75

SPLITTING

I had a few follow-up conversations with Jack Sides during which I developed a fondness for him. He had an old school Texas accent and dry sense of humor that reminded me of my paternal grandfather.

"David was just a great guy, but he was a bit naïve about girls, especially an ambitious girl like Sandra. He was real studious and focused on his work, and I don't think he understood the big dreams that his wife had. I remember when they bought that pretty little English cottage over there in Greenway Parks. It would have worked fine for them, but then she hired that big interior designer—that John Astin fellow—and started buying art and antiques hand over fist, and before you knew it, David was in real trouble."

"What was your impression of Sandra?" I asked.

"Well, I thought she was a real cute girl. I just don't think she had a very good sense of reality where financial affairs were concerned."

"What can you tell me about the pistol you took away from David on that evening he said he was going to kill himself?"

"I believe it was a pistol that Mr. Phipps gave him when they were neighbors on Purdue. You remember Mr. Phipps?"

"No, who was he?"

"He was orphaned in the Great Galveston Hurricane and made his way up north. I think he made his fortune in the lumber business. Anyway, he took a shine to David when they were neighbors and gave him this pistol as a gift. I recall it was a little semi-automatic, maybe .32 caliber, though I can't remember for sure."

"Do you still have it?"

"No, a while after David died, Sandra called me and said she wanted it back." This struck me as odd. Growing up in Texas, I'd known a lot of guys with pistol collections—I myself owned one—but I'd never heard of a woman from Sandra's generation showing any interest in them.

"That's kind of weird, don't you think?"

"Yeah," he said, laughing. "And I'll tell you what else is weird. Not long after David died, I got a call from his life insurance agent. I knew him because I'm the one who recommended him to David for purchasing his policy. Anyway, this guy—Ken Smith was his name—calls me up and says that, not long before David killed himself, Sandra called to inquire if his life insurance policy was still valid in the event of suicide."

"I wonder why she would ask him that," I said.

"It's a hell of a question, isn't it?" Jack said. "I never could decide if David really killed himself. He threatened to do it a few weeks before his death. But then, on the other hand, just before he died, I met him at Gordo's Pizzeria for dinner. Do you remember that place over there off Knox?"

"Yes," I replied, vividly remembering its booths, each equipped with a little jukebox.

"David and I met there for dinner. He said he was sorry he'd married such an ambitious girl and allowed her to get him into such a bind, but that he was determined to get his life back together. I believed him, because for all his troubles, David was still a young guy with a lot going for him."

"Do you remember the day he died?"

"Oh yeah. My wife at the time was close with Sandra, and Sandra called her up all hysterical and said that David had killed himself. We went over there a couple of hours later, and I remember thinking the atmosphere was real strange. The house was full of people, but it wasn't what you'd expect right after a young man shot himself in the master bedroom. It was more like a cocktail party. Sandra was wearing a pretty yellow dress, going around talking to everyone, and to me it seemed like, well, how to put it, like she was—."

"Basking in the attention?" I asked.

"Yes, that's exactly it! You've got a better way with words than I do."

I thought of something that wasn't mentioned in the *D Magazine* piece.

"Do you think that when you saw David at Gordo's, he'd already resolved to divorce Sandra?"

"Yes, he told me he was going to file for divorce."

"Do you think there's a good chance that he told Sandra of his intention?"

"I don't think he was keeping it a secret from her."

After I hung up with Jack, I contemplated the remarkable fact that—of all people whom Sandra could have called when David brandished a pistol and threatened to shoot himself—she called Jack, an ex-boyfriend who also happened to be the executor of David's estate. I suspected that she called him not only to end the standoff, but also to obtain a *witness* that David was threatening to kill himself.

After Jack Sides, the most valuable witness I could find was Dr. George Edwards. A fellow native of Fort Worth, he'd also been David's classmate at Baylor College of Dentistry. Though Dr. Edwards had never been mentioned in any press reporting, his name was among the pallbearers mentioned in David's death notice in the *Dallas Morning News*. He was still practicing dentistry in Fort Worth, and like Jack Sides, he still had a vivid memory of the story. He told me that he and David had played golf two Saturdays in a row before his death. David had expressed unhappiness with his wife's out of control spending and his desire to exit the marriage, but he had not seemed suicidally depressed.

"We were going to play golf again on the Saturday he died, but that morning I got a call from one of Sandra's friends. She said David had killed himself and that I needed to tell his father. I just couldn't believe it."

"Do you think David told Sandra of his intention to divorce her, or was he still keeping it to himself at the time of his death?"

"I'm not sure, but I got the impression he'd discussed it with her."

"Had you known anything about David's troubles before he came out for that first round of golf?"

"I also played golf with his father, and he told me that Sandra was spending David to the poor house and that he'd recently given David a loan to pay an IRS lien. I think it was a hundred grand."

"Did Sandra pay him back after David died?"

"The last time I spoke with Dr. Stegall about it, he said she'd told him she didn't think it was her responsibility and that she needed the money to look after her kids. She insinuated that he might not be able to see his grandkids anymore if he pressed for it."

David's situation just before his death resembled case studies presented in the book *Splitting: Protecting Yourself While Divorcing Someone with Borderline or Narcissistic Personality Disorder*. According to the author, as the marriage falters, there are "Key Times of Risk of Extreme Behavior," and these include saying you wish to separate, or making requests that represent a loss to your partner. Three weeks prior to David's death, he reached the end of his tether in his marriage with Sandra. He *threatened* to kill himself in a final, desperate gambit to force her to change her behavior. The totality of circumstances indicates that she knew he was bluffing. The spectacle of him threatening to commit suicide also made her realize that if he subsequently died of an apparent suicide, most would automatically assume that he succeeded in carrying out his threat. And so, she called Jack Sides, the executor of David's estate, to the scene, not only to defuse the situation, but also to witness David's suicide threat. Jack's wife Nancy, a close friend of Sandra, would also likely mention to her friends what Jack had witnessed. Following this episode, Sandra called their life insurance broker to make sure the death benefit would pay out in the event of suicide.

After his suicide threat was witnessed by Jack Sides, David told Jack that he was going to file for divorce, and it's very likely he told Sandra the same. If they divorced, their assets and debts—including the $100,000 that David owed his father for paying off the IRS lien—would be divided pursuant to Texas family law. If David died prior to the divorce, Sandra would get the house and all its contents, plus his large life insurance death benefit.

CHAPTER 76
STAGING AND MANIPULATION

As in the case of Betsy Bagwell, it wasn't easy to obtain unredacted death scene photos of David Stegall. After multiple requests and months of waiting, I finally received them. The photos show David Stegall wearing pajamas and lying on his right side in a typical sleeping position. The right side of his head is resting on a pillow and his arms are resting on the bed. Generally, he is under the covers as though he were sleeping. In the first three photos in the sequence, his left hand and most of the pistol are concealed by covers. The fourth photo was taken after an investigator drew the covers down to expose the left hand lying on top of the pistol. It was physically impossible for David to have pulled the covers over his left hand, resting on the pistol, *after* he fired the shot through his head with his left hand. Who did? It's hard to imagine the investigators didn't notice this and ask Sandra about it. She could have claimed that she or one of the doctors whom she called after she discovered David that morning had drawn the covers over his left hand, though there was no reason why anyone would do this. This looked like a staging error.

David's left arm and left hand are lying in a natural-looking sleeping position. His left hand, with fingers outstretched, is lying on top of the bolt and frame of the pistol. This position is incongruous with the proposition that he fired the shot. I experimented with lying in this exact position and aiming the muzzle of my Ruger Standard .22 at my head as David must have aimed it if he had fired the shot. To hold the pistol in this position, it is necessary to cock one's shoulder back and exert a fair amount of muscular effort. If David pulled the trigger, firing the bullet through his brain, which created a shock wave in his skull that ruptured his sinuses, it is highly doubtful he had the nerve and muscle coordination to continue gripping the heavy (2.19 pound) target pistol as he extended his left arm back to a comfortable sleeping position, then lay the pistol on the bed, then released his hand from the grip and retracted his index finger from the trigger guard, then lifted and extended his hand and fingers to rest them on the gun.

According to the medical examiner's report, the gunshot entrance wound to David's left temple was NOT a contact wound, but a **"close-up wound of entrance."** This means that David did *not* rest the muzzle on his left temple but held the muzzle at a slight distance from it. This makes no sense. If you lie on your right side and raise the gun with your left hand to fire it into your left temple, the entire weight of the arm and the pistol are bearing down. Trying to hold the pistol in this position without resting the muzzle on the temple is awkward and difficult and it makes it much harder to be sure of one's aim. This is one reason why almost all self-inflicted gunshot wounds to the head are *contact* wounds. In 1992, researchers at the Dallas County Medical Examiner's Office performed an analysis of 199 known suicides by a single gunshot to the head in the years 1991-1992 and found that *all* of them were contact wounds.

In other words, the death scene photos of David Stegall do not display a single feature that contradicts the proposition that he was laying fast asleep when someone else held the pistol muzzle close to his left temple without touching it, fired a single shot through his brain, planted the pistol underneath his outstretched left hand, and slashed his right forearm three times (missing the radial artery) with a razor to enhance the appearance of suicide.

To obtain expert opinions of the photographs, I forwarded them to Drs. Lynne Herold and Jan Garavaglia. **Appendix III** presents a detailed analysis of the crime scene photos. From what is displayed in these images, and the totality of circumstances, I believe that someone else shot David in the head. The culprit then staged the scene to make his death appear to be a suicide. Apart from Sandra (the beneficiary of David's estate and life insurance policy) and possibly their small children, no one else was in their house on the night David was shot.

Why didn't DPD and medical examiner investigators notice the clear elements of staging and conduct a more thorough investigation of the young man's death? To start with, Sandra told the medical examiner's field agent that David had stolen the pistol the day before from his friend Bill Hardy. Neither the police nor the medical examiner report states Sandra's explanation for how she already knew this on the morning of David's death. Whatever she told them should have been scrutinized. A plausible theory is that Sandra occasionally spent the night in the backhouse apartment of the Hardy residence. She stole the pistol and then left something in the apartment—perhaps a piece of jewelry. Because the Hardy house was just a couple of blocks north of David's dental office in Preston Center, she asked him to pass by their house after work to retrieve it. This set him up to appear to have stolen the pistol.

In the final analysis, what seems to have persuaded the police and medical examiner that David had indeed killed himself was the statement of Dr. David G. Hubbard, a psychiatrist who claimed to have been treating the unhappy man for psychiatric disorders since November of the previous year. A medical examiner field agent took Dr. Hubbard's statement over the phone at 9:10 a.m. on the morning of David's death. As noted by the field agent:

> Patient since circa November—patient being heavily in debts, practice falling apart, drinking heavy. Diagnosis Acute Manic Depressive, seen circa 10 times in last 2 weeks [2.5 lines redacted] not surprised at death.

At first glance, Dr. Hubbard's statement strongly favors the suicide interpretation of David's death. However, it's likely that Sandra was Dr.

Hubbard's initial and primary information source about her husband. Ten years later, she told her neighbor, Margaret, that she was urging Alan to join her in counseling with *her* therapist (Harvey Davisson). She told Bill Dear that Davisson had perceived Alan to be gay. I doubt that Dr. Hubbard's evaluation was based solely on his conversations with David. Sandra told multiple friends about David's purportedly dark, drunk, and volatile moods, so it's safe to say she told Dr. Hubbard the same. As was the case with her fourth husband, Dr. Joseph Dandridge in the winter of 2001, she made David's life a living hell, subjected him to heavy gaslighting, and likely pressured him to go to so many therapy sessions to produce a witness and record of intensive psychiatric care.

Dr. Hubbard made national news six years after David's death when he addressed the Dallas Council on World Affairs about terrorist hijackings of commercial flights. As UPI reported the event on May 29, 1981:

> Dr. David G. Hubbard said Thursday the United States must be willing to sacrifice U.S. hostages if it wants to be taken seriously by other countries. 'What other nation could ever take seriously our defense preparations when we are unwilling to lose even a handful of lives to a minor enemy,' he said in an address to the annual meeting of the Dallas Council on World Affairs. Hubbard, one of the first to apply clinical methods to the study of terrorists and their victims, currently is directing a research project in which captured terrorists are interviewed and tested. Referring to the Iranian hostage situation, he said: "We must not dance a crazy 444-day jig to a ragtag terrorist tune sung by a few men. We can't allow the presidential office to be gambled by shooting craps with a hairy old hermit."

I wonder if Dr. Hubbard applied similar, utilitarian reasoning when he told the medical examiner investigator that he "wasn't surprised" at David's death. Performing a thorough investigation to *make sure* it wasn't foul play would have required time, effort, and resources, and it would have subjected the pretty young widow to discomfort.

CHAPTER 77
ALAN REHRIG

Unlike Betsy Bagwell's friends, Alan's Rehrig's friends were happy to speak with me, and were still hopeful that someday justice would be served for Alan. The resistance I encountered was mostly from the Oklahoma City Police and Oklahoma County DA's office, which refused to release *any* of their investigative reports. In the summer of 2019, I helped Gloria to draft a request for the case file, pursuant to the Open Records Act. In her letter, Gloria pointed out that she was almost ninety years old, but still hoped to see her son's murderer brought to justice. Weeks passed with no reply, so on July 23, Gloria visited DA Office Investigator Mike Burke. He told her she was welcome to look at some of the files in his office, but that he wouldn't allow her to copy any of them, and that he refused to speak with me.

A lawyer in Tulsa advised me that that fastest way to obtain records in Oklahoma is for a man of wealth and influence to ask for them to be leaked. This made me think of the legendary oilman T. Boone Pickens—an alumnus and enormous benefactor of Oklahoma State University, where Alan had double lettered in basketball and football. His attorney, Bobby Stillwell, was an old family friend. Right as I was about to ask my mother for Bobby's number, I saw the news on September 11 that T.

Boone had died. A farewell letter was posted on LinkedIn and Twitter shortly after his death. The best part of it was his quotation of the poem "Indispensable Man," by Saxon White:

> Sometime when you fear that your going
> Would leave an unfillable hole,
> Just follow these simple instructions,
> And see how they humble your soul;
> Take a bucket and fill it with water
> Put your hand in it up to the wrist
> Pull it out and the hole that's remaining
> Is a measure of how you'll be missed.

I thought these lines rang true. Our passing really doesn't leave much of a hole, even if we're famous. For those who survive us, the business of living is too pressing to concern themselves with the dead for long. There is, however, a notable exception to this rule—namely, the mothers of children who die young. For them, the death of a child is "an unfillable hole."

After Gloria's request was denied, I retained an attorney to submit a request to the OCPD and the Oklahoma County DA. As I pointed out, most of the OCPD investigation was performed between December 11, 1985, and April 6, 1987, when lead detective Steve Pacheco told *The Oklahoman* newspaper: "The local investigation is open but not active." Thus, on May 6, 2020, when my lawyer sent his letter to the police department and DA's office, the case file was 33 years old.

The OCPD did not reply to our request. On June 10, 2020, Assistant DA Aaron Etherington denied our request. Not one of the records we requested would be granted. She justified her refusal by citing numerous exceptions provided by the Open Records Act. Gloria and I both found it hard to understand why the OKC authorities wished to keep the 33-year-old file confidential. Obviously the OCPD was no longer investigating the case.

In late 2020, I had a long conversation with retired OKC detective Ron Mitchell, who acknowledged that—with my lack of time constraints and my connections in Dallas society—I might well be able to uncover additional evidence. He remarked that I knew a great deal about Sandra—more than he and Steve Pacheco had been able to discover during their brief visits to Dallas. I figured there was a good chance the case file contained information that could augment the evidence that I had discovered.

Another maddening aspect of researching Alan Rehrig's death was reading his probate file. Its 240 pages documented the legal contention over the $102,000 life insurance (roughly the first half of the death benefit) that was paid to Alan's estate at the end of May 1986. Going through this morass of legal wrangling was a depressing slog. I thought of Alan's statement to his friend Kirk Whitman at the Maverick's game two nights before his death: "She says she's afraid I'll get her property in a divorce, but all I want is my stereo equipment and my camping gear." To be sure, Alan also wanted Sandra to pay the $24,743 of debt (equivalent to $69,000 in 2023 buying power) she had racked up on his credit cards and at Neiman-Marcus. This money, and not his camping gear and stereo, was what she didn't want to part with. Alan's death relieved her of the pressure to pay it back, and it conferred to her his life insurance benefit net of this debt and lawyers' fees.

As was the case with David Stegall a decade earlier, after Alan informed Sandra that he wanted a divorce, he entered the "Key Time of Risk of Extreme Behavior" noted by the author of *Splitting*. Alan's demand for repayment of the debt was precisely the sort of trigger of extreme behavior described in the book, as was Alan's request to see a statement of her financial condition. The exposure of her financial condition in a divorce proceeding—including her recent loan and investment in the play *Crime and Punishment*—could subject her to additional liabilities. She apparently also fantasized that her investment in a theater and film production company would yield big gains. She didn't want to share them with Alan, hence her omission of her investment in *Crime and Punishment* from the asset inventory in the probate file. Finally, there was the life insurance policy with the $220,000 death benefit she had asked Alan to purchase the year before.

While the probate file revealed motive, the autopsy report revealed method. The first gunshot entered the right side of chest just beneath his right nipple, traveled through his chest cavity "backward, slightly downward, and to the left across the midline" and exited the left side of his chest. As Gloria learned in one of her early conversations with the investigators, the bullet then lodged in the driver's side door, but was removed by the shooter or an accomplice. The autopsy report does not state the bullet's caliber, but the OCPD told Skip Hollandsworth it was a .38. The second shot was fired into the back right side of his head, just to the left of his right ear.

The path of the bullet through Alan's body and the location of the bullet depression in the door are what enabled a police technician to determine Alan's position in the driver's seat when he was shot. His body had then been moved out of the driver's seat, which had been pulled forward. A logical deduction for this was that—following Alan's murder—a shorter driver had operated the car and pulled the seat forward to reach the pedals.

According to the pathologist, no firearm residue was present on his clothing or around the chest entry wound, indicating the shot was probably fired over two feet away from his body. The shooter could have been sitting in the passenger seat and leaned right while aiming to the left at Alan. Or the shooter could have opened the passenger door wide and fired from a standing position next to the vehicle. If the passenger door window was already rolled down (possible in the unseasonably warm weather that day) or if Alan rolled it down to speak with the shooter (not realizing the person's murderous intent) the shooter could have fired from a standing position next to the car, through the open window.

SANDRA'S ONLY
PRESS INTERVIEW

Why did Sandra propose meeting at the storage warehouse after 5:00 p.m.? The logical time to have done this chore was any time during the day, not on a Saturday evening right before her scheduled meeting with out-of-town friends. She told Margaret that the storage unit was hers and that it was Alan who'd requested the meeting to retrieve his camping gear. In fact, it was Alan's unit on which she had placed her lock. If, when she became estranged from him, she was worried about him taking her valuables from the storage unit, why didn't she remove her valuables and her lock from his unit? If Alan was disagreeable—never mind ruthless and untrustworthy—he would have simply cut the lock with bolt-cutters.

The shooter did not simply flee the scene, as one would expect of a hit man, drug dealer, or robber. Nor did he drag Alan's body out of the vehicle and dump it near the scene, as one would expect of a homicidal carjacker. Instead, the shooter or his accomplice moved the body out of the driver's seat and then drove the car, containing the body, all the way to Oklahoma City. This indicated that the objective of this peculiar and risky criminal scheme was for Alan's body to be found in Oklahoma City.

As Gloria noted in her journal, she first heard about Alan's disappearance from her niece, Cynthia Smith, in Tulsa. Cynthia told her that she'd just gotten a call from her brother Robert in Dallas. That morning, Robert's wife Glady received a call from Sandra, who said that Alan had been missing since Saturday afternoon, and she wondered if he'd driven to Tulsa to visit his cousin Cynthia. Alan had spoken fondly about his cousin, and Sandra thought that maybe he'd felt the desire to be with her during this difficult time. Seeing this note in Gloria's journal reminded me of a conversation I'd recently had with one of Kathryn Bridewell's friends. She had a distinct memory of seeing Kathryn at school on the Monday morning following Alan's disappearance. Kathryn was obviously distraught and said her stepfather had headed up to Oklahoma to visit relatives that weekend but never made it. Kathryn had certainly gotten this notion from Sandra. Two days before Alan was found in Oklahoma, Sandra postulated that instead of attending his appointment at the warehouse, he had spontaneously driven to Oklahoma without telling his host and boss, Phil Askew. This was a wildly implausible theory. That Sandra offered it strongly suggests she had foreknowledge that Alan would be found in Oklahoma.

When a DPD officer called Sandra to inquire about Alan, Sandra interjected with the question, "Is it bad news?" When he replied that it was, she told him to call Alan's friend Ron Barnes in Edmond, Oklahoma. Why did she tell the officer to call one of Alan's friends who lived *in Oklahoma* instead of his friend and host in Dallas, Phil Askew? When Ron Barnes called her to inform her that Alan had been found shot, she didn't ask him any questions about the circumstances or even where Alan was found. Again, this strongly suggests she already knew he would be found in Oklahoma.

At the time the DPD officer called, Alan had not yet been positively identified. Per standard procedure, the officer began by asking Sandra what the subject was wearing at the time he was last seen. He framed the question: "Was your husband wearing shorts and a navy-blue sweater the last time you saw him?" Sandra answered in the affirmative, indicating that she had, in fact, seen him that evening. For some reason this was overlooked at the time. In 2007, when the OCPD cold case investigator

Kyle Eastridge reexamined the case, he noticed the contradiction and mentioned it to a reporter for *The Oklahoman*.

After Alan's murder, Sandra refused to make any statements to the press, with one notable exception. In June of 1986, when Gloria Rehrig visited Dallas in search of witnesses and information, Sandra spoke with Susan Albrecht at the *Park Cities People*. Her interview revealed her attitude towards the police investigation and Gloria's private investigation. Only some of her statements were included in Susan's report, but Susan retained the micro-cassette recording of the interview. Sandra's voice sounds defensive and irritated, as though the investigation of her husband's murder was vexatious. Susan began by asking her about Alan's disappearance on the evening of Saturday, December 7, 1985.

> **Sandra**: He had been living out in North Dallas with friends.
> **Susan**: Right. I also wanted to ask you where you called from to tell Phil that Alan hadn't showed up at the warehouse.
> **Sandra**: All of this information was given to the police at the time. And I called from out on Northwest Highway when he didn't show up.
> **Susan**: From a payphone or from the storage warehouse?
> **Sandra**: No, from a payphone. All of this information was [given] to the police and when the investigation being conducted by them, and I don't really have—this is very upsetting to me. Anything that I knew, I gave that information to the police.
> **Susan**: Okay. I just wanted to check everything. The University Park Police aren't handling this at all, so—
> **Sandra**: No, and I don't know if you realize it or not, but the Oklahoma City police has no jurisdiction or authority in Dallas.
> **Susan**: Right, I understand. But I wanted you to know that everything I have gotten about the case has come from what's been printed in the newspapers, and I know that not all of it is correct.
> **Sandra**: It's been sensationalized, and I don't think that is helping anything.

Susan: I want to make sure that I have the story straight...

Sandra: Well, I just feel like everything has been done that could be done and if anyone had seen the Bronco, I think they would have come forward at the time. Because as far as I know he was never around, other than during the week he'd drop by our house and was waiting out in front and that was it. And that doesn't have any bearing on what happened to him Saturday. He had made arrangements to meet me, and he never showed up. And you know, he had done that in the past, and so that was not, you know. I called Phil, from the pay phone, I came on, and I had plans with my friends from out of town. And we had plans for Sunday, and he, you know, he was missing.

Susan: Are you still a resident of University Park?

Sandra: Yes, I am. I had nothing to do with this. I don't know if that is what is being implied or not, but I don't appreciate it, and anyone who is saying it is setting themselves up for a libel suit.

Susan: There's certainly a lot of hearsay going on and I'm not able to print any hearsay, only—

Sandra: That's all there is. This has been very painful and difficult for me and my children. Alan was my husband and I loved him, and it hurts.

Susan: Were you able to talk with the police when they were in Dallas this last week?

Sandra: No, I wasn't.

Susan: Do you know if they tried to contact you?

Sandra: I don't know. When that happened to Alan and we went up there for his service, I voluntarily went down to the police station. As one of my ministers said at the HP Presbyterian Church, if there was anything I had to hide, I certainly wouldn't have gone there and submitted myself to their interrogation for several hours and volunteered everything I knew. I know nothing about what happened to Alan. If I had I would have revealed it then, and I know nothing. I need to run.

Sandra was put out by Gloria's posters and miffed that the local press was covering the case of her murdered husband, even though he was a resident of the Park Cities, where murder almost never happened. She acted distraught about Gloria's activities in Dallas, and she refused to participate in the search for Alan's murderer. Instead of using the interview as an opportunity to establish a factual record for the public, she used it to threaten a libel suit against anyone who "implied" that she had something to do with it.

Especially notable was her statement: "I just think that everything has been done that could be done"—that is, she believed public awareness of her husband's murder wasn't going to help solve it. Why was she so confident that no additional inquiry could solve Alan's case? How did she know that Gloria's search, combined with press coverage, wouldn't yield a witness who'd seen Alan that night in Dallas? If he didn't drive to the storage warehouse, he must have driven somewhere else, and there was no reason to believe he'd driven from Phil Askew's house straight to the electrical substation on South MacArthur near the Oklahoma City airport. When Phil called her on the Monday after he disappeared to ask her to file a missing person report, she replied that Alan was probably off gallivanting around town or had headed to Oklahoma to visit friends (another indication of foreknowledge). If that were the case, wasn't there a chance that someone had seen him and would recognize his face on one of Gloria's posters or in a press report?

Why did Sandra feel compelled to call Phil Askew from a payphone on Northwest Highway? She told Phil that she wasn't going to wait any longer, and in fact she had already left the storage warehouse, so what was the point of calling him? She didn't express concern that something had happened to Alan, only her irritation that he hadn't shown. Moreover, she didn't follow up with a call the next day to inquire if he'd returned home or to reschedule their appointment. She claimed she'd made plans that evening with friends from out of town and needed to get home, so why did she take the time and trouble to find a payphone on Northwest Highway instead of simply driving home? A plausible inference is that she made the call to be on record at the critical time of Alan's disappearance that she hadn't been in his presence—that is., *to establish her alibi.* It's also likely that she called Phil to ascertain what, if anything, Alan had told him about the errand he was running out to perform. Calling the Askew residence at 6:15 was the same thing she'd done three years earlier when she'd called the Bagwell house at 6:15, two hours after Betsy was last seen alive.

Also notable was Sandra's statement that "the Oklahoma City police have no jurisdiction or authority in Dallas." This assertion, and the tone in which she made it, revealed her animus towards the OKC police for investigating Alan's death in Dallas, even though he was last seen alive in Dallas. Why? She herself proclaimed in the same interview, "Alan was my husband and I loved him, and it hurts." If that were the case, why didn't she welcome the OKC investigation?

In fact, the OKC police had a duty to investigate Alan's murder wherever necessary. Though her statement was erroneous, she apparently believed it to be true. This touches on the question of why Alan's murderer decided to drive his body all the way to Oklahoma City. Did the culprit believe that the Oklahoma City police wouldn't investigate the murder in Dallas because they didn't have the jurisdiction to do so?

CHAPTER 79

DUMP SITE

I made another road trip from Dallas to Oklahoma City and Edmond, this time driving straight to the electrical substation where Alan's Bronco had been found. The drive was entirely on Interstate Highways. A major point of orientation from I-35 North was the Will Rogers Oklahoma City Airport, situated just twelve minutes west of I-35, off I-44, via I-240. Even at night on I-35 North from Dallas, it was impossible to miss the huge signs for the airport. Just past the exit for the Oklahoma City Airport was the exit for South MacArthur Boulevard.

About three hundred yards north of the freeway exit, on the west side of South MacArthur, I turned into the dirt parking lot next to the electrical substation. Behind it was a large field. Across the street was a warehouse district that would have been devoid of humanity after midnight. It was the perfect place to dump a car containing a dead body, and it occurred to me that the murderer had scoped it out in advance. There were no lights to illuminate the dirt parking lot, so the killer or accomplice would not have spontaneously seen it at night and recognized how favorably situated it was. I sat for a while in the parking lot, a light drizzle falling on the windshield, thinking about Alan's Bronco, parked in the same spot thirty-four years earlier. *Yes,* my gut told me, *the killer selected this place in advance.*

I wondered if, in the weeks prior to Alan's death, Sandra had driven from Dallas to Oklahoma City. And then, reviewing Gloria Rehrig's diary, I saw her entries from October 27-30, 1985, in which she noted that Alan and Sandra made an unexpected visit to Edmond, purportedly to sell Alan's Bronco. To me, this looked like a trial run. The mystery car buyer in Edmond (even though Dallas was a much bigger car market) who couldn't be reached raises the suspicion it was Sandra who claimed to have found the buyer. Leaving the car for this unreachable buyer then provided an excuse for flying from Oklahoma City back to Dallas. Then Sandra said she wanted to fly back with Alan to fetch the Bronco so that she could see his old friends Ron and Debbie Barnes. They missed the 6:00 p.m. flight out of Dallas, which necessitated catching a later flight and driving back to Dallas in the middle of the night. All of this looked an awful lot like an orientation and rehearsal tour.

The lead detective, Steve Pacheco, theorized that Sandra had dropped the Bronco that Saturday night and then walked to the airport terminal "to take the first flight back to Dallas." Pacheco reiterated this theory in his *Dateline* interview in 2007. This seemed plausible, but on the other hand, the road between the electrical sub-station to the terminal entrance was 3.5-miles long, with no sidewalks. The longest stretch was on Meridian Avenue, a large, four-lane thoroughfare with bridges crossing highways. A woman walking along the edge of this road would look conspicuously out of place and could have easily drawn the attention of a police patrol.

In addition to the airport being a major point of orientation, I wondered if Sandra was already familiar with the stretch of South MacArthur just north of the airport. I noticed that, just 0.5 miles north of the electrical substation was a horse auction house called Heritage Place, which had been founded by a breeder named Robert Moore in 1978. Moore was a major player in both racing and polo circles. His cofounder of Heritage Place was Robert Gentry of Lubbock, Texas, who was one of Bobby Bridewell's friends, and Bobby occasionally attended horse auctions in OKC. Finally, one of Alan's friends and colleagues at Nowlin Mortgage—a guy named Chuck Shealy—also recalled an occasion of Sandra talking about investing in racehorses. Thus, it seemed likely that

Sandra had, at some point, visited Heritage House, which was located just north of the airport so that purchasers could fly in for auctions.

About a year later I was reminded of the Heritage House when I had a conversation with the man who'd been Sandra's boyfriend in Vermont in the fall of 2011. He'd met her when she answered his Craig's List notice for the sale of his alpaca herd. She mentioned that she'd learned about horse breeding through her deceased husband—an experience she thought she could apply to alpaca husbandry. They discussed founding two businesses together—an alpaca farm and an ice cream shop in Burlington. Sandra proposed the name for the latter: Heritage Ice Cream.

It seems likely that an accomplice drove the Bronco to Oklahoma City with Sandra following in a second car or vice versa. Without a following car, there was the risk of disaster if the Bronco ran out of gas, blew a tire, or broke down on the interstate. With a following car, she could ditch the Bronco and still have a means of getting away. I also found it notable that—according to Sandra's neighbor, Margaret—Sandra was using a rented car on the weekend that Alan disappeared.

Also conspicuous was the fact that on the Monday following Alan's disappearance, Sandra's youngest daughter Emily missed her morning classes and arrived at school during lunch recess. In the cafeteria she told two friends that she was tired because she'd been up late the night before, driving a long distance away from Dallas to pick up a car. After word got out that Alan Rehrig had been murdered in Oklahoma City, one of the girls thought Emily's late-night driving anecdote may have related to her stepfather's death. She told her mother the story, and the anecdote made its way to an FBI investigator who reviewed the case in 1987. He interviewed Emily's friend. Her mother was present during the interview and retained a vivid memory of the story her daughter told.

What, if any, significance the FBI investigator attributed to the girl's statement remains in his confidential case file. I thought it was a valuable lead and attempted to question the two girls (now in their forties) about it. Both had older siblings in my class at Highland Park. I approached them through family members—the mother of one, the brother of the other—but both refused to speak with me about it. Given that Emily apparently missed school on Monday morning, it struck me as likely that the late-night drive had occurred on Sunday night, after Sandra and Emily went to the cinema to watch *Rocky IV* with their neighbor Margaret.

Theoretically, a second vehicle was used to follow the Bronco to Oklahoma City in case it broke down and to give Sandra a ride from the dump site on South MacArthur to the OKC airport to catch the early morning flight back to Love Field. However, for some reason the accomplice chose not to drive this second vehicle all the way back to Dallas, which necessitated Sandra making a subsequent road trip to fetch it. To preserve the appearance of following her normal routine on the Sunday and Monday following Alan's disappearance, she decided to retrieve the car late on Sunday night, and (for some reason) to bring Emily along for the ride.

CHAPTER 80

THE PRESBYTERS
OF HIGHLAND PARK

In Gloria's journal of her trip to Dallas in June of 1986, she noted that the Highland Park Presbyterian Church Pastor, Don Riley, had also spoken with Emily about a late-night drive around the time of Alan's disappearance. I called Gloria to discuss it.

"We visited Pastor Riley at his home. He told us that Sandra had made a couple of romantic overtures. He said he had reminded her that he was a married man and wasn't interested. He told us that to understand her character, we should look to John 8:44. He also told us Emily's story about being up late at night, driving a long distance, to pick up a car. Later he realized the timing of it coincided with Alan's murder. Pastor Riley told me the story, but then he said he wouldn't testify.

"Did he explain why not?" I asked.

"No. He just said he wasn't comfortable doing so."

After we hung up, I Googled John 8:44, and saw it was an account of how Jesus characterized the Pharisees who were trying to lay verbal traps for him:

You belong to your father, the devil, and you want to carry out your father's desires. He was a murderer from the beginning, not holding to the truth, for there is no truth in him. When he lies, he speaks his native language, for he is a liar and the father of lies.

Pastor Riley had, in the interim, left the HPPC and moved to Memphis, Tennessee, where he was ministering at an organization called Discipling Men. I introduced myself, explained that I was writing a book about Sandra Bridewell, and that Gloria Rehrig had recommended that I speak with him. He was very friendly.

"Bobby Bridewell was a tremendous guy, friend, and entrepreneur. I counseled his kids and officiated at his funeral. After Bobby died, Sandra seemed to take an interest in me, and I was warned by some of the women in the congregation to be wary of her. I told them that, as a minister, I wasn't rich and was therefore safe from her. After Alan Rehrig was murdered, the FBI called and said they'd heard I might know something about it. They asked me to come down to their office in Dallas. In fact, I thought that I possibly did know something, but I wasn't sure that it could be substantiated. I had a struggle with my conscience, but I ultimately chose not to get involved. The FBI man acted like I was legally obliged to divulge the information, but I knew he was bluffing. They left me alone in an office to stew for a while, but then they let me go."

"Well, Gloria Rehrig and I sure would be grateful if you would share any information that may be pertinent to my investigation."

"I will seriously consider talking to you about it, but first I'd like to know more about you and your work. Can you e-mail some information about yourself so I can be sure I know who you are?"

"I'd be delighted," I said.

As soon as we hung up, I sent him a brief bio, a link to my author's webpage, and two references—a former Dallas County Assistant DA and a former Dallas Junior League President—both members of the HPPC. Two weeks passed and I didn't hear back from him. I called him again and he told me he hadn't forgotten about me, was occupied with some personal business, but would certainly get back to me. A month passed and I sent him an e-mail reminder. Another two weeks passed, at which point I forwarded him an e-mail from Gloria Rehrig.

> Dear Mr. Riley,
> I know it's been a long time since we have communicated regarding my son's murder in 1985. I wanted to let you know that I fully endorse the writer, John Leake, to research and write a book about Alan and Sandra (Bridewell) Rehrig. If you would be willing to talk to him and tell him what you remember about Sandra, I would appreciate it. Since I am approaching 90 years of age, I still am very interested in seeking justice in Al's murder while I am still alive. In my opinion, Sandra killed him for his insurance. Thank you.
> Gloria Rehrig

We never heard back from him, which made me wonder if Sandra had succeeded with one of her romantic overtures, thereby ensuring his silence. A while later I tried to contact him again through a mutual friend who texted his wife on my behalf. Mrs. Riley texted back that they'd sensed great evil in Sandra at the time of Betsy's death. She wrote that she would remind Don of my interview request, but I still never heard back from him.

My experience with Pastor Riley prompted me to review Sandra's relationship with the Highland Park Presbyterian Church. As a boy I hadn't grasped its social significance in my community, as I had grown up in the Episcopal Church—a place where you could be a part of the Christian tradition without wearing it on your sleeve. During her marriage to David Stegall in the early seventies, Sandra had been an active member of Saint Michael, where I was confirmed, and the editor of a cookbook produced by some of the ladies in the congregation. After she married Bobby Bridewell in 1978, she moved to the HPPC, where he was a member. Many of the wealthiest families in Dallas attended the church, and its congregation was the go-to place for men trying to cultivate connections. Being an active member was widely viewed in the business community as a strong social and moral credential. In short, it enhanced one's public image, and as Sandra understood, a man who take pains to cultivate his public image will also take pains to preserve it. Thus, when some of the women in the HPPC congregation warned Pastor Riley that Sandra was a seductress, they knew whereof they spoke. In 1977, Sandra told Delia Mullins that she'd had an affair and unwanted pregnancy with one of the church's deacons, a well-known banker (and junior colleague of my grandfather).

Starting in 1982, the church appears frequently in this story. Bobby Bridewell's funeral, with Pastor Clayton Bell officiating, was held on May 11, 1982. Two months later, on July 16, Sandra's car purportedly broke down at the church and then magically started again after her excursion to Love Field with Betsy Bagwell. In her interview with Detective Coughlin, she claimed that Betsy had dropped her off at the Highland Park Presbyterian Church at 5:00 p.m., thereby making the institution a key element of her alibi. Betsy's two friends with whom she had lunch on the day of her death were both HPPC members; neither told the police about the trouble Betsy was having with Sandra on that very day. Then the HPPC deacon, Clyde Jackson, called Joy Adam and sternly insisted that Betsy had committed suicide. Betsy's funeral was held at the church on July 19, 1982, with Pastor Don Riley officiating.

When Betsy died, disapproval of Sandra within the congregation turned to fear. Nevertheless, two years later, Pastor Clayton Bell officiated at Sandra's wedding to Alan Rehrig, thereby enhancing her moral and religious credentials in the eyes of Alan's family, even though Bell knew Sandra wasn't suited for holy matrimony. On the Sunday morning following Alan's disappearance, Sandra attended service at the HPPC and later emphasized this in her interview with OCPD detectives. In her sole press interview (with the *Park Cities People*) she mentioned that "one of my ministers at the HP Presbyterian Church" had spoken in her defense. Finally, Pastor Don Riley had, by his own admission, withheld information about Sandra—information of possible forensic value— from an FBI investigator. In his conversation with Gloria, he compared Sandra to Jesus's characterization of the Pharisees as "sons of the devil," who was "a murderer" and "the father of lies."

One wonders why Pastor Riley was unable or unwilling to oppose Sandra. He said he'd chosen not to "get involved" in the FBI's investigation of Sandra. Why not? His statement expressed a desire to avoid conflict. And yet, when Jesus challenged the Pharisees, he knew he was entering into a potentially dangerous conflict. Many Presbyterians are in the habit of declaring that human affairs are "in God's hands," but this isn't what Jesus taught. As he warned in Matthew 7:21, 'Not everyone who says to me, 'Lord, Lord,' will enter the kingdom of heaven, but the one who does the will of my Father who is in heaven."

Many of the members perceived Sandra to be an incarnation of the devil or the wicked Queen Jezebel who used their church as part of her alibi when she murdered Betsy Bagwell, but they felt there was nothing any of them could do about it. Their ministers apparently lacked the will to suspend or excommunicate her. This resulted in an unfathomably strange situation that lies at the heart of this story. Highland Park society and institutions had no customs or procedures for dealing with a woman like Sandra.

For a while I was tempted to blame the society's women for failing to oppose the Jezebel in their midst. None of the ladies who were mortally afraid of Sandra warned Alan Rehrig about her—not even with an anonymous note sent to his office—even though they became mortally afraid for him. We often speak of "women's gossip" as an ignoble thing, but it is gossip, far more than law enforcement, that regulates society. Most of the time, people behave themselves to avoid reputational damage. When I visited Sandra in pretrial detention in 2007, she told me that her bad press in Dallas was "the gossip and slander of hypocrites." In her case, this gossip had no regulating or corrective effect, which rendered female society powerless to oppose her. Caroline Rose Hunt—the first female deacon in HPPC history, and one of the church's most influential members and benefactors—knew about Sandra's callous treatment of Bobby, and she knew about the suspicious circumstances of Betsy's death. And yet, she too seems to have concluded there was nothing to be done about Sandra.

To be fair, the women of Sandra's generation were raised to believe it wasn't their place to handle high conflict situations in the public forum, and they felt their primary duty was to protect their families. Directly confronting danger was, they believed, the job of their husbands, many of whom were lawyers. Thus, in the final analysis, Sandra remained unopposed and uncensured because Highland Park's male leadership simply couldn't handle her. Against the seductive and "frightening" woman, as Dr. Bagwell described her, men were powerless. And so, Sandra was confident that none of HPPC's ministers or deacons would speak out against her, neither to the police nor to the press, and nor would they say a word to Alan Rehrig. Indeed, Pastor Clayton Bell wed the unsuspecting young man to her at a ceremony at the Mansion on Turtle Creek.

CHAPTER 81
"YOU ASK FOR MIRACLES; I GIVE YOU THE FBI."

Just as Sandra perceived that no one in the HPPC would oppose her, she calculated that the Oklahoma County District Attorney's Office would be similarly weak-minded in dealing with her. According to detectives Ron Mitchell and Steve Pacheco, in the spring of 1986, Oklahoma County DA Bob Macy stated his eagerness to prosecute Sandra. Macy was famous for being a tough DA who, like Henry Wade in Dallas, was willing to bring circumstantial evidence cases before a jury. In the spring of 1986, he told Gloria he intended to impanel the grand jury to indict Sandra. This got her hopes up, but then months passed with no grand jury proceedings. In November, Gloria called Macy's office and was told that Alan's murder investigation had been turned over to the FBI.

In 2019 I had a long conversation with a retired FBI agent who'd worked in the Oklahoma City office in the nineties and ultimately had a major falling out with the Bureau because of its catastrophic mishandling of the Oklahoma City bombing. He wasn't familiar with Alan's case, but he found it intriguing, and he wondered why the culprit had gone to such trouble to transport Alan's body from Dallas to Oklahoma City.

"This suggests that the culprit believed there was a substantial advantage to the investigation being handled by the OKC police and DA's office. Did the suspect have a relationship with an influential man in OKC? I also think it's strange that the FBI took the case, because murder investigations are almost always handled by state law enforcement. You should submit a FOIA request for the FBI's case file."

This I did, and after months of waiting, I finally received notice from the FBI's Information Management Division that it had located approximately 1,242 pages and audio media files potentially responsive to my request. For fifty pages, I would have to wait approximately five months. For all 1,242 pages, I would have to wait approximately sixty-six months (five and a half years). I reduced the scope of my request to "the first fifty pages of the case file the FBI opened in 1986." About eight months later, I received an electronic copy of 21 of 50 pages. The other 29 pages were redacted altogether. The pages I did receive were riddled with white-out redactions.

Despite all the redactions, the document revealed that the FBI investigated Sandra for "ITAR-Murder, MF, and Conspiracy." The ITAR (International Traffic in Arms Regulations) charge struck me as puzzling. Was Sandra suspected of involvement in illegal, international (military grade) arms trafficking? The "MF" charge referred to Mail Fraud. "Murder" and "Conspiracy" referred to the murder of Alan Rehrig and the belief that the prime suspect had an **accomplice**.

An early passage of the file refers to the death of Betsy Bagwell as follows:

> Complete circumstances surrounding that case or unknown, however, it is believed that investigation conducted in that case would have been limited in that it was believed to have been a suicide.

The file then states that, about a month after Alan was murdered, Oklahoma City investigators received a tip that the subject of their investigation had an accomplice who helped her to transport Alan's body to Oklahoma City, and possibly flew her back to Dallas in a private plane.

[Subject's name redacted] **along with an associate** [name and description redacted] **have been determined through Oklahoma City investigations to be closely tied to the** [name and description redacted] **purchase cocaine from a known associate of** [name and description redacted] **that being** [name and description redacted] **gets his supply predominantly from the** [name and description redacted].

Oklahoma City police department homicide detectives assigned to the murder of Allen Rehrig strongly believe that [name redacted] **either assisted** [name redacted] **directly in transporting Alan Rehrig's body to Oklahoma City from Dallas or that** [name redacted] **back to Dallas after** [name redacted] **drove Allen's body to Oklahoma City.**

In other words, the OCPD strongly believed that Sandra's accomplice was a cocaine dealer. I was not surprised to read this, and it struck me as plausible. Cocaine came on strong in Dallas in the early eighties and was the drug of choice for its monied class. During Gloria Rehrig's trip to Dallas in the spring of 1986, Frank Monroe, Sr., told her that, according to Al Teel, Sandra had been spotted at the Mansion with well-known cocaine dealers. The mystery "package" that Sandra told Betsy she needed to pick up at Love Field made me wonder about smuggling. A few weeks before Betsy's death, one of her friends saw Sandra in the gate area at Love Field, waiting for a passenger to arrive. She was wearing sunglasses and a scarf, clearly not wanting to be recognized, and was conspicuously uncomfortable when the lady walked up to greet her. With Sandra's elegant, upper-class appearance, she could have picked up cocaine shipments at Love Field without arousing suspicion, and transported them to a dealer friend, perhaps one with a clientele who frequently dined at the Mansion.

There was also Sandra's habit of accusing her victims of what she herself was doing or scheming to do. She told her friend, Barbara Crooks, that she was shocked, *shocked,* to discover that Alan had made unauthorized clothing purchases on her (fictitious) Neiman Marcus card. She told Bill Dear that Alan had tried to kill her at the lake, when in fact (according to Emily) she had asked her son Britt to kill Alan at the lake. She told Oklahoma City police detectives and Bill Dear she feared that Alan was using cocaine and consorting with dealers. Thus, long before I read the FBI case file, I suspected it was Sandra who was using cocaine and consorting with dealers.

The rest of the redacted twenty-one-page report reveals little of how the FBI proceeded with its investigation, though it makes an intriguing reference to a terminally ill witness in California who should be "interviewed as thoroughly and expeditiously as possible." Dr. Bagwell also mentioned this witness in his 1986 interview with OCPD detectives. Sandra visited him shortly before Betsy's death, and then called him shortly afterward. The man told Dr. Bagwell's brother David that he believed Sandra to be a witch or an incarnation of the devil.

The latter pages mention the additional charges of "FBW" (Forfeiture by Wrongdoing) and "Civil Rights." As the *D Magazine* feature reported, FBI investigators in California, Oklahoma City, and Dallas were still investigating Sandra at the time of publication in April 1987. Though the Bureau ultimately produced another 1,200 pages in its case file, it never charged Sandra for any of her suspected violations.

CHAPTER 82

CONFUSION AND
CONTRADICTION

For a prosecutor to persuade a jury, it's important for him to present a compelling case theory that is supported by the known facts. The OCPD believed Alan had driven directly to the storage warehouse because he'd told Phil Askew that he was meeting Sandra there. The detectives perceived that after 5:00 p.m. on a Saturday, the warehouse was an isolated place with no one around to witness the murder. Sandra's suggestion that Alan had suddenly decided to drive to Oklahoma instead of to his appointment at the warehouse wasn't credible. Nevertheless, the theory that he was murdered at the warehouse had a major problem.

None of the press reports mentioned that the warehouse had an on-site manager and that his living quarters were attached to the office. Moreover, the facility was equipped with a mechanism for recording when a renter entered the storage area by typing his personal code on the entrance keypad. I only discovered these facts years after I began researching this story. According to the manager's records, no one entered Alan's code on the evening of December 7, 1985. Additionally, the warehouse manager stated the following in his January 11, 1986, interview with Bill Dear, P.I.:

On December 7 Saturday, at approximately 5:00 p.m. to 5:30 p.m., I was sitting in our living room watching television ... I remember getting up and looking out the window towards the parking area in front of the gate leading into the mini warehouses. I do not recall why I looked out at the time as I frequently do even without being attracted by a noise or activity. As I looked out the window towards the parking area where my van was parked, which is about sixty-five feet from my window to the general area, which is marked off with five parking spaces, I observed a small car parked in the third space with the front of the vehicle facing Northwest Highway. I could see a person seated in the driver's side of the vehicle. From where I was, I could not see if it was a man or woman. It was definitely occupied by one person. The window I was looking out of towards the parking area is tinted. You can look out, but no one can look in. I know the sun was setting, and with the tinted windows, I could not tell you just what color this small type of car was nor could I describe the person sitting in the drivers seat.

The phrasing of this statement seems a little contrived, suggesting that Dear may have done some leading of the witness. The 41-year-old man was married with two young children. His wife confirmed that, at 5:15 p.m., he was at home with his son while she was out shopping with their daughter. Like most men, he could have been vulnerable to seduction by Sandra, but probably not to the point of aiding and abetting the murder of Alan Rehrig. A friend in the storage business told me the owner, Watson & Taylor, hired solid couples to attend their facilities.

Sandra told the OCPD and Susan Albrecht that she arrived at the warehouse around 5:15 p.m. and waited for Alan. Though the warehouse manager did not identify the driver of the small car, his statement still lent credence to Sandra's story and had obvious utility for a defense attorney. I was unable to refer to the OCPD's case file because the agency steadfastly refused to let me see it. The best clues I could find were in a partial transcript of Sandra's deposition taken by Gloria's probate attorney on June 15, 1987.

It's a remarkable fact that on Thursday, December 5, 1985, the interior of Alan's Bronco was professionally cleaned by a detailing service. This, and the fact that he'd been separated from Sandra since November 1, meant that any objects, fibers, or fingerprints traceable to her was highly suspicious. The following timeline is assembled from Sandra's statements.

Friday, December 6, 1985

Early afternoon: Alan visits Sandra's house "in the early afternoon" to talk. She gets into his Bronco with one of her cats, which he pets while they are talking.

Later that afternoon: Sandra has a phone conversation with Alan at his office. As she recounted the conversation: "We talked about Christmas plans and what we were going to do for Christmas. He said he bought Emily a necklace and some earrings." Either during their earlier conversation at her house or during this phone conversation, they planned to do their errand to the warehouse on that (Friday afternoon).

Later that same afternoon: "Alan called again and said he was going to see his friend instead of us doing our errand at the warehouse. And I needed to go by and pick up the necklace. So, I went up and picked up the necklace ... at his office garage, which is where the Sherry Lane National Bank is. ... He had left it [the necklace] in his truck. And he told me to just get into the truck and get it out. So, I went and got it out of the back seat." This was the second time that afternoon that, according to Sandra, she got into his truck.

Saturday, December 7, 1985

9:00 or 10:00 a.m.: Sandra calls the Askew residence to speak with Alan "to find out what time he wanted to meet me that afternoon. He wanted to meet me after some big game was going on. He said he had to see this game. And because I had a full schedule that day, there was only a limited amount of time where I could meet him. ... We decided to meet at 5:00 ... At the warehouse storage center."

5:15 P.M.: Sandra arrives at storage warehouse and waits for Alan, then leaves the warehouse, then finds a payphone on Northwest Highway to call the Askews. "I then dropped by Neiman's to pick up little Christmas things and a bottle of nail polish. And I went on home. I think I got there about 6:15 or so."

All the above statements are dubious. Going down the list:

1). According to Alan's colleagues, Friday, December 6 was a busy day that did not afford Alan time to go Christmas shopping, visit Sandra, have two phone conversations with her, and plan to go to the warehouse that afternoon. Her neighbor told OCPD detectives that she went to a 12:30 p.m. movie with Sandra. Assuming the film was about two hours, it finished at 2:30 p.m., which put Sandra back home at 2:50 at the earliest. Sandra's claim that Alan visited that Friday afternoon contradicted her vehement assertion to Gloria Rehrig on December 10 that she hadn't seen him in a month.

2). If Alan visited Sandra's house at around 3:00 p.m. and she talked with him, why did she get into his car with her cat? According to Gloria, Alan loathed her cats, and would *not* have petted one in his freshly detailed car.

3). Why did she feel such an urgency to get Alan's Christmas present for Emily on December 6 that she made a trip to his office to retrieve it from the back seat of his car? Why didn't she tell him to bring it on their errand to the warehouse or drop by to present it to Emily? All these implausible stories struck me as an obvious attempt to explain any traces of her or her cat that could have been found in the Bronco.

When I read the warehouse manager's statement, I suspected the warehouse was a red herring. Sandra knew the detectives would regard this meeting place as gravely suspicious and focus their investigative effort on it. They would then become terribly frustrated to discover there was no record of Alan visiting the facility that evening. The coup de grace for their theory was the manager's claim that, between 5:00 and 5:30, he glanced out the window and saw a small car in the parking lot.

CHAPTER 83
SLEIGHT OF HAND
AND MISDIRECTION

Sandra's neighbor, Margaret, told the OCPD detectives that she had a conversation with Sandra during the first week of December, a few days before the weekend.

> She told me that Alan told her that he wanted to set up a meeting at the warehouse and go through the storage stuff and get his camping gear. Nothing about splitting stuff up. I advised Sandra, gee, don't go by yourself. Take someone with you. She was making an issue of him getting stuff that didn't belong to him.

In her deposition, Sandra stated that she and Alan had initially planned to go to the warehouse on Friday, but later he said he needed to see a friend, so they agreed to run the errand the next day (Saturday). She then stated that she called Alan on Saturday morning around 9:00 or 10:00 "to find out when he wanted to meet me that afternoon."

Her statements imply that she had to pursue Alan to nail down a meeting time at the warehouse, but this contradicts what she told Bill Dear on December 19, 1985. As Mr. Dear related in his memo of the conversation for her defense attorney, Vincent Perini:

> Mrs. Sandra Rehrig also stated that on December 7, 1985, she talked with Alan at the residence of Phillip Askew. She originally had an appointment to meet Alan at the storage shed on Northwest Highway, where they had some personal belongings stored, at 11:30 A.M.; however, she called him and postponed the appointment until 5:00 P.M. She said she proceeded to the storage shed on Northwest Highway as agreed, but Alan never arrived at the meeting place.

Alan apparently told her that he would like to fetch *his* camping gear from *his* storage unit, but he had to go through her to do it because she had put her combination lock on the unit because "she was making an issue of him getting stuff that didn't belong to him." He probably told her he would *like* to attend Jimmy Askew's birthday party and to watch the SMU-OU game that Saturday afternoon but could still run out to meet her at any time, or he could have met her the following day (Sunday).

In Sandra's June 1986 interview with Susan Albrecht, she stated that she and Alan had planned to meet on Sunday for a one-year anniversary brunch at the Mansion. Before or after this brunch would have been a far more suitable time to visit the warehouse. For that matter, Sandra could have told Alan the lock's combination. Indeed, if Alan had been a disagreeable man, he would have cut the lock from *his* storage unit with bolt cutters. Instead, he was trying to be agreeable to avoid additional confrontation with his soon to be ex-wife.

Everything about Sandra's story indicates the storage warehouse meeting, which she postponed till 5:00 p.m., was a setup for Alan to disappear on Saturday evening, just before she was scheduled to go out with Dr. Frank and his wife Barbara. Down to the smallest detail, his disappearance resembled Betsy Bagwell's disappearance on a Friday evening three years earlier.

1). Sandra and Betsy were estranged; Sandra and Alan were estranged.

2). Sandra and Betsy ran a special errand to Love Field; Sandra and Alan ran a special errand to the warehouse.

3). Betsy was last seen going out to meet Sandra around 4:30 p.m.; Alan was last seen going out to meet Sandra at 4:55 p.m.

4). Sandra called the Bagwell residence at 6:15 p.m.; Sandra called the Askew residence at 6:15 p.m.

5). After parting company from Betsy, Sandra went shopping at Preston Center; after Sandra's planned meeting with Alan, she went shopping at Neiman Marcus.

6). After Betsy's disappearance, Sandra went to dinner with Stanley and Barbara Crooks; after Alan's disappearance, Sandra went to dinner with Dr. Allen and Barbara Frank.

A puzzling feature of this story is why Phil Askew was so confident that when Alan left to meet Sandra, he was *certainly* headed straight to the storage warehouse, and nowhere else in between. In my successive interviews with Phil, he did not remember Alan emphasizing that he was driving straight to the warehouse. He only remembers that, for some reason, he believed this was the case.

It's an important detail because it's what Phil told the OKC detectives, which prompted them to focus their investigation on the warehouse. Phil's belief could have originated in Alan's Friday afternoon telephone call with Sandra. As she stated in her 1987 deposition, Alan was at his office when they spoke, and it was during this conversation that they agreed to meet the following day (Saturday) at the warehouse. It was a safe bet that Alan would mention this plan to Phil on Friday afternoon at the office or that evening at the Askew residence, where Alan was staying.

I suspect that when Sandra (by her own admission) called Alan at the Askew house at 11:30 a.m. on Saturday, she proposed *not* meeting at the warehouse, but at a different location. She apparently calculated that Alan wouldn't bother telling Phil and Judy about this change of plans, probably because he had no reason to tell them the particulars of their meeting. Nevertheless, it was still a gamble, which is why she called the Askew house at 6:15 p.m.—first to make sure Alan hadn't told them about the change of plans, and secondly to emphasize that Alan was supposed to meet her at the warehouse. Her call apparently solidified in Phil's mind that this was indeed the case.

In Sandra's 1987 deposition, she said that, after Alan didn't show up at the warehouse, she found a payphone on Northwest Highway to call the Askew residence.

> I called the house where he had been living, the Askews. And Phil answered the phone. And I asked him if Alan was late or what happened to Alan. And I told him that Alan hadn't come. And he said, "Well, maybe Alan went to your house." And I said, "No, I don't think he would have done that." And so, he told me he would let me know if he heard anything from him, that he would call me, or have Alan call me. And then I called my kids after that. I thought, well, maybe Phil was right, and he went by the house. And I can't remember which of my daughters I talked to. I think it was Kathryn. And she said that Phil had just called there and asked if Alan was there, which I thought was strange.

Phil and Judy Askew had never seen the deposition transcript, and when I showed it to them in the summer of 2021, they were both baffled by it. Neither had *any* recollection of Phil asking Sandra this question or calling the Bridewell residence and asking one of Sandra's girls if Alan was there. Both believed that, at the time of Alan's departure, he was headed directly to the warehouse. They were also astonished to see Sandra's statement that Alan had visited her at home on Friday, December 6. Both had a distinct recollection of Alan being nervous and excited on Saturday because he was about to see Sandra for the first time in over a month.

Regardless of whether Sandra's statements were true or false, she must have had her reasons for making them. Either Phil did, in fact, remark, "Maybe Alan went to your house" and forgot he'd said it, or Sandra fabricated his statement as a pretense for claiming that her daughters were at home around the time Alan was murdered. Whatever the case, it's clear OCPD should have regarded Sandra's garage as a possible crime scene and investigated it.

It's a plausible theory that Sandra told Alan to stop by her house (on the way to the warehouse) and to pull into her garage (on the back side of the house, facing the alley) to load the possessions he'd left there when they separated. As he pulled into the garage, she shut the garage door. While Alan was distracted looking to the left at her, standing in the garage entrance into her house, her accomplice approached the vehicle from the right, opened the door, and fired the first shot into the right side of Alan's chest. Her accomplice then got into the passenger side of the vehicle and maneuvered Alan's upper body between the gap between the front seats, pushed it onto the backseat floorboard, and fired the second shot into the back of his head.

Sandra immediately drove her son's car to the storage warehouse, where she arrived around 5:30 p.m. and parked in front of the manager's office so that she would be seen, apparently waiting for Alan. Her accomplice could have immediately driven Alan's Bronco to Oklahoma City and caught a Southwest fight back to Dallas, or she could have locked the vehicle in her garage while she went out with the Franks and made the trip to OKC during the early morning hours.

An alternative theory is that Alan was murdered in the covered parking garage at his office building at 5956 Sherry Lane. This could explain why he departed the Askew house at 4:55 p.m. instead of 4:35 p.m. It was only a 5-minute drive to his office instead of the 25-minute drive to the storage warehouse. Sandra had viewed his office parking garage the day before (when she visited it purportedly to fetch Emily's Christmas present) and ascertained that it wasn't equipped with video surveillance. Even now, 38 years later, the 5900 block of Sherry Lane is dead quiet on a Saturday evening after 5:00 p.m. The probability of anyone noticing Alan's Bronco entering the parking garage of the 5956-office building and thinking anything of it was slim to none.

Theoretically, when Sandra spoke to Alan at the Askew residence at 11:30 a.m. on Saturday, December 7, she presented him with a ruse for meeting at his office on Sherry Lane. Perhaps she requested to review some documents he kept in his office such as his car title. Maybe she proposed the office as a quiet and private place to talk. The covered parking garage resembled the garage at Love Field and the garage at the Preston Center Medical Building, just one block away, where Dr. Paul Radman had been accosted by a gunman seven years earlier.

In this scenario, Alan agreed to meet her at the office building at 5:00 p.m. Sandra or an accomplice arrived early to make sure no one else was around. Alan pulled into the garage and parked. Sandra approached his vehicle like she was going to get into the passenger seat to talk, and then shot him right as she opened the door. Alternatively, she got into the passenger seat, and while they were talking, her accomplice approached the vehicle from the passenger side. Sandra opened the passenger door and got out, thereby giving the gunman a clear path to shoot Alan.

From Preston Center, Sandra drove 20 minutes east on Northwest Highway to the storage warehouse, where she arrived around 5:30 p.m. and parked in front of the manager's office so that she could be seen, apparently waiting for Alan to arrive. From the parking garage, located next to the North Dallas Tollway, it was a straight shot to 635 East to I-35 North to Oklahoma City. The accomplice could have immediately driven the Bronco straight to Oklahoma City and caught a Southwest flight home to Dallas, or the Bronco could have remained in the parking garage while Sandra went out with her friends, and then driven to OKC in the early morning hours.

CHAPTER 84
THE TOTALITY OF CIRCUMSTANCES

Regardless of how precisely the murder of Norman Alan Rehrig was carried out, the totality of circumstances persuades me that Sandra was the culprit. Her lies about her age, then about being pregnant and miscarrying twin boys, revealed her psychopathic deception and manipulation of Alan at the inception of their marriage. As Detective Steve Pacheco stated in the 2007 *Dateline* episode, she had the obvious motive of claiming the $225,000 life insurance. No other criminal enterprise is consistent with the circumstances of Alan's car and body being found in Oklahoma City.

Then there were Sandra's expressions of foreknowledge that he would be found in Oklahoma, and the contradiction between her statement that she never saw Alan on the night of his disappearance and her answer in the affirmative when the Dallas police officer asked her if Alan had been wearing shorts and a navy sweater when she saw him last.

During her first and only interview with the OKC detectives, she made verifiably false assertions that Alan was into drugs, gambling, and random encounters with gay men. As Detective Kyle Eastridge said in the Kurtis

Productions documentary, "The whole basis of her interview was to impugn Alan's character to make it look like somebody else did it besides her." As Eastridge also remarked in the same documentary, Sandra's claim that Alan had tried to kill her the previous summer at the lake after she fell off the jet ski was another major lie, as was revealed by witnesses who were at the lake that day.

Although Eastridge didn't elaborate the significance of this lie, it is consistent with a defining trait of psychopaths—namely, their marked tendency to project their own designs onto their victims. Emily's testimony to the Oklahoma multi-county grand jury in 2007 should be viewed in this light. She claimed to have a clear memory of her brother Britt telling her in 2001 that Sandra had asked him to run over Alan with the jet ski. Though the grand jury apparently concluded that her testimony was hearsay because Britt refused to confirm it, the story is credible.

Then there was Sandra's tacit expression of guilt in her refusal to assist the OCPD and her mother-in-law in their efforts to find Alan's killer. Throughout her interview with Susan Albrecht, she expressed her desire for the police investigation of her husband's murder to end without success in catching the culprit. There are simply no other plausible suspects, and no other reasonable explanation for Alan's murder. As Detective Eastridge put it in the Kurtis Productions documentary, "Whenever you pursue another lead, it always comes back to her. She had the motive to kill him; she had the opportunity to kill him, and she was the last person that we know of to see him alive."

Given the strong conviction Eastridge expressed on national television, one wonders why he was initially so unresponsive to Detective Jayne Todd's multiple requests in 2007 that he renew his investigation of Sandra Bridewell for the murder of Alan Rehrig. Since 2008, the OCPD and DA's Office have been conspicuously tightlipped about Alan's murder. Neither Eastridge nor DA investigator Mike Burke responded to my requests for interviews, and Burke flatly told Gloria Rehrig that he wouldn't talk to me. Upon hearing this, my attorney who specializes in the Oklahoma Open Records Act told me he wondered if the police had made a mistake and were concealing it.

According to a witness who contacted Gloria Rehrig—a biologist who'd worked in the OCPD crime lab—there were multiple lapses in storing, handling, and evaluating evidence during this period. This raises the concern that evidence in Alan's case was lost, thereby prompting the DA to drop the matter instead of seeking an indictment. For example, a fast-food hamburger wrapper, bearing fingerprints, was apparently found in Alan's Bronco. Skip Hollandsworth mentioned it in his 1987 *D Magazine* story, as did Gloria's probate attorney, David Wise, in his prefatory notes to Sandra's deposition. According to Wise, the OCPD detectives stated unequivocally that this hamburger wrapper bore Sandra's fingerprints. If this was indeed the case, it raises the suspicion that the OCPD lost this critically important piece of physical evidence.

On the other hand, it strikes me as unlikely that Sandra made such a sloppy mistake, and this makes me wonder if the hamburger wrapper bore the prints of her accomplice. It could have also been yet another red herring, planted by Sandra or an accomplice, who could have (while wearing gloves) snatched it from the trash area of a fast-food restaurant. She likely knew that if the police ever obtained her fingerprints, these would not match the prints on the wrapper, which would provide her defense attorney with potent ammunition.

Another suspicious element of Sandra's 1987 deposition was her statement that Alan petted one of her cats in his car on Friday. This is a wildly implausible statement, and it raises the suspicion that she was—for some reason that is not evident in my partial copy of the deposition transcript—concerned that cat hair had been found on the seats or floor of Alan's freshly detailed Bronco. If this was indeed the case, a hypothetical explanation was that hair transferred from her clothing to the car seat or from a blanket (on which hair from her cats was adhering) used to cover Alan's body on the long ride from Dallas to Oklahoma City.

A promising possibility for serving justice was lost because the Oklahoma City and Dallas Police departments didn't work together on the case. Alan's murder in 1985 should *not* have been viewed in isolation, but as connected with the shooting death of Betsy Bagwell in 1982 and David Stegall in 1975. Dallas and Oklahoma City law enforcement should have performed a thorough joint investigation of all three deaths. The FBI should have assigned a profiler in its Behavioral Science Unit to perform a signature crime-scene analysis of all three. During the trial of the Austrian serial killer Jack Unterweger, about whom I wrote my first book, the FBI profiler Gregg McCrary testified that because the different crime scenes shared multiple striking similarities, a suspect who could be linked with just one murder should be regarded as suspect for all of them.

The David Stegall and Betsy Bagwell murders were both staged suicides in which a single shot was fired from a .22 caliber pistol into the victim's temple. In Betsy's case, the firm muzzle contact suggested the shot was the work of an experienced shooter who then moved her upper body between the front seats and into the back seat area, and then onto the front passenger seat. In Alan case, the assailant moved his upper body between the front seats and onto the back seat floorboard. Both crimes appear to be the work of an assailant who was very deft with a pistol.

Dr. Bagwell told OCPD detectives he believed that Sandra had used an accomplice to murder Betsy. As a matter of longstanding principle and habit, Sandra never did *anything* that she could get a man to do for her, so it's a plausible theory that she recruited a hitman to do such brutal and dirty work, perhaps the same one to murder Betsy and Alan. This is consistent with the fact that moving the dead bodies within the confines of the cars required considerable physical strength. The extremely bold and aggressive man who shot Dr. Paul Radman in Preston Center two years after David Stegall's death was an example of the kind of hired gun who worked in Dallas during this period.

CHAPTER 85
ROBERT SMITH

Robert Smith reminded me of David Stegall. He was, like Sandra's first husband, in his thirties and the father of three children when he died of a purportedly self-inflicted gunshot in his own home. Also, like David Stegall, he was a successful professional, but also struggling to keep up with the Joneses. Again, like David Stegall, because his death was quickly ruled a suicide, it received no press coverage. The one exception was a small notice in the *Park Cities News*, written by Susan Albrecht, who was researching Alan Rehrig's murder when Robert died. Like me, she found it extraordinary and frightening that Alan's first cousin was shot in his car, just as Alan had been shot in his car six months earlier. When I contacted Susan to ask about her research, she was friendly and cooperative, but she wasn't encouraging.

"If you pursue this, your own life may be in danger," she said.

"Did anyone threaten you when you were reporting it?" I asked.

"No. But look at what happened to Robert Smith?" she said.

Gloria's probate attorney, David Wise, shared Susan's fearful perception. For several mornings in a row, around the same time Robert Smith was shot, someone in a pickup truck aggressively tailed David on his daily drive to the Cooper Clinic for exercise. Because it was still dark at 5:00 a.m., and because of the glare from the truck's headlights, David never saw the license plate. However, it was clearly the same pick-up truck every morning and clearly an intimidation tactic. It worked, prompting David to send his wife and children to her parents' house in Virginia for several weeks.

One night when I was visiting Gloria Rehrig in Edmond, we went out to dinner with her older sister (and Robert's mother) Winie. Like Gloria, 91-year-old Winie showed no infirmities of age. The two ladies walked at a normal pace from the parking lot into the restaurant and to our table. Both had strong, clear voices and razor-sharp memories. Both had experienced the death of their two children. Gloria had lost Alan to murder and Philip to cancer. Winie had lost Robert to purported suicide and Cynthia to cancer. Winie and her husband Robert Smith, Sr. were actively participating in the investigation of Alan's death at the time Robert was shot.

"Robert was definitely afraid of Sandra," she said. However, as it became clear during our conversation, Robert was also having trouble with his wife, and he expressed this in his purported suicide note. Winie didn't wish to discuss the matter further than this. She dearly wanted to maintain good relations with her three grandchildren—the only family she had left apart from Gloria. Discussing Robert's suicide with me could anger Robert's widow Glady, which could alienate her grandkids from her.

Glady didn't wish to speak with me, but her daughter Heather agreed to meet me for lunch. The friendly and cheerful woman was a teacher at Highland Park High School. I found her engaging and I enjoyed our lunch together, but she didn't shed much light on her father's death. She remembered him as a fun, humorous, and loving father, and yes, Sandra had given him the creeps. On the other hand, after Robert was found, they discovered that several photos of him with Glady were missing from family photo albums. He had apparently gathered and destroyed them.

"My mom has no doubt that he committed suicide," she said.

I met Robert's son Matthew for happy hour drinks at Lucy's Lot restaurant in Grapevine, just west of DFW airport. In our initial phone conversation, the week before, he'd been friendly and seemed comfortable discussing his father's purported suicide with me. He confirmed that his dad had been afraid of Sandra, especially after he was nominated successor Administrator of Alan's estate. Yes, it seemed very strange that his father had locked himself in the garage, in the family car, and shot himself in the side of the torso with a hunting rifle he'd recently gifted to his only son. If the bullet had missed his heart, it would have been an extremely painful death. Why didn't he just start the car and go to sleep from carbon monoxide poisoning? And if he was determined to shoot himself, a frontal shot to his heart with the .44 Magnum he carried in his briefcase promised a surer and quicker death than a shot to the side of his torso with the rifle. Robert was a deer hunter, and as anyone who has ever hunted deer knows, unless the shot directly strikes a vital organ, the wounded animal may live in agony for some time.

One of the police officers had remarked that Robert's hand position—both folded in his lap—seemed inconsistent with his extending his right arm to depress the trigger. As it turned out, the high-velocity shot lacerated his heart's left and right ventricles, which probably resulted in instant death. Thus, after he depressed the trigger with his extended right arm, it seemed unlikely he could have pulled his right arm back to his body and placed his right hand in his lap.

On the other hand, on the day of his death, his father had been eager to get all the kids out of the house. For years Matthew asked himself the question: *Did dad tell me to return the bicycle to my sister's friend so that he could be alone to kill himself, or was he expecting a visitor, possibly a dangerous one?* Finally, there was a note his father had left for him in his dresser drawer.

"Did you save it?" I asked him.

"No, but I remember what it said—something like 'You're now the man of the house, so be sure to look after your mother and sisters.'"

"Anything else?"

"Yeah, something that seemed really weird. He wrote, 'And always remember to be safe with guns.'"

I didn't say it to Matthew, but I thought that this note, allegedly penned by his father, was not weird, but *preposterous*. People in a suicidal frame of mind do strange things, but it seemed to me that it would take an exceptionally bizarre man to write such a note to his fourteen-year-old son just before shooting himself with the hunting rifle he'd just gifted his son. I was reminded of the letter that Sandra claimed to have found behind a picture frame, purportedly authored by Bobby Bridewell's alleged mistress and mother of his illegitimate child.

Matthew's demeanor was different when I met him in person. In the interim between our phone conversation and our appointment, he had spoken with his sister and didn't like what she'd reported about our lunch conversation. He beat me to Lucy's Lot and was already nursing a drink when I arrived. As I approached the table, he looked up at me with a cold expression. He had the same striking blue eyes as his father, whom I'd just seen in a photograph.

"Man do you have your father's eyes," I blurted out.

"I've often heard that when I've visited my dad's parents in Oklahoma, which is why I don't visit much anymore," he said. "I spoke to my sister," he continued. "She said my grandmother told you my dad's marriage with my mom made him unhappy. Well, that's just total bullshit. It was my dad's parents who made him unhappy, not my mother."

I wasn't expecting this, especially coming right as I sat down, and I didn't know how to react. He seemed unaware of the content of the purported suicide note, in which his father had expressed profound unhappiness with his mother. Matthew mentioned examples of his grandparents distressing his father. He was still angry at them, and apparently angry at me for opening this old wound. I started to ask if he'd witnessed his grandparents' abusive behavior, or if he'd only heard about it from his mother, but then thought better of it.

"It seems your father's death triggered a family debate about why he was unhappy and who was to blame," I remarked. "But what if he didn't commit suicide? What if he was murdered?"

"I wondered about that for a long time," he replied, "and it fucked me up until I was thirty. But then I told myself I just didn't want to think about it anymore, so I decided to put it behind me."

"I'm very sorry about your father's death," I said. "But I must say, I don't believe that his death and others in Sandra's circle were properly investigated. I'm now working with a retired North Carolina detective and with Gloria to investigate these suspicious deaths on my own time and resources. One of the biggest obstacles is the reluctance of family members to talk. I believe this is one of the main reasons why Sandra has gotten away with so much over the years. It's as though she can sense that her crime will intersect with a family conflict that will become the focus instead of focusing on her."

"Isn't it always that way?" he said.

"Not with other suspicious deaths I've researched before this story. The Oklahoma City cops also won't share their investigative reports, even though I'm willing to keep pursuing this in Dallas and all over the country."

"I'm sure they just don't want you to see how lazy and careless they were," he said. "You ought to know by now that Oklahoma is a total shithole."

He abruptly stood to leave.

"You seem unhappy about what I'm trying to do," I said. "I'm sorry I've upset you."

"You haven't upset me," he said, softening, his beautiful blue eyes suddenly more friendly. "But maybe Sandra just isn't worth it. I mean, at her age, surely she's not preying on anyone anymore." I didn't answer, but just smiled and shrugged.

CHAPTER 86

A CAN OF WORMS

After I spoke with Matthew, I tracked down Alan's old friend Karl McKinney, who'd borne the terrible responsibility of identifying Alan's body. He still had a vivid memory of his old friend's murder and the subsequent investigation. When I asked him if he knew anything about the death of Robert Smith, he fell silent for a moment.

"Now that's a can of worms I don't want to open," he said.

"Why not?" I asked.

"Because I sensed there was something going on with Robert and that it's probably best not to speculate about it."

"Do you believe it had something to do with Sandra?"

"All I can say is that, after Alan was murdered, it seemed like Robert was under pressure. And then one day I got a call from an Oklahoma City detective who was investigating Alan's murder. He said he believed that someone among Alan's family and friends was leaking information about the investigation to Sandra."

"You think it may have been Robert or his wife Glady?" I asked.

"I don't know," Karl replied. "The cops interviewed several of Alan's friends and family members, and there was a lot of talk about the investigation."

Nina and Bill Raef had been the closest friends of Robert and Glady at the time of Robert's death. I found their address on the Incident Report. Thirty-four years later, Nina still lived in the same house, and she graciously agreed to speak with me. She too had perceived that Robert was under pressure after Alan's death—like something apart from grief was weighing on him.

"Before Alan's murder, he was always such a humorous guy, and I remember how much he loved to tell jokes. Afterwards, he became preoccupied and irritable."

This reminded me of something that Gloria had told me during our first meeting—namely, that in the early days of Alan's relationship with Sandra, when everyone had perceived her to be a lady of property, Robert had asked her for a personal loan.

"Are you sure about that?" I had asked Gloria.

"Yes, because Alan was very unhappy about it."

Though Sandra didn't have any money to loan Robert, it's likely she didn't tell him that. She may have told him she'd think about it, and asked to see a statement of his assets that could secure the loan if, *God forbid*, something happened to him that impeded him from repaying it. Notable among his assets was his life insurance policy with a $500,000 death benefit for his wife. Finally, if Robert indeed provided her with a financial statement, the document may have borne his signature. A hypothetical scenario is that Sandra herself did not loan Robert any money but introduced him to a man who *seemed* respectable but who in fact was a loan shark—one who could, following Robert's death, pressure his widow to pay off the loan with the life insurance death benefit. This is speculative, but it could explain the perception that Robert was under pressure after Alan's death.

As a matter of fact, neither Robert's garage nor his house had been secure. According to Nina Raef, on the night of Robert's death, Glady couldn't enter the garage's back door because it was locked. Glady didn't carry a key to the door because it was seldom locked. Thus, a hit man could have easily snuck up the alley, jumped the fence into the backyard, and let himself into the garage. Likewise, according to Nina, the Smith children were "latchkey kids" who often let themselves in the front door using a hide-a-key. Often when she dropped off the Smith girls, she watched them from her car to make sure they found the key and were able to enter the house. Anyone observing the house could have seen this.

There was also a single sentence in the DPD Incident Report that contained two conspicuous details:

THE COMPLAINANT HAD THE SETBELT STRAPPED ON HIM ... AND A RIFLE, CALIBER .243 RUGER, SERIAL #77042400, WAS LYING ACROSS THE SEAT, THE END OF THE BARREL WAS AGAINST HIS RIGHT SIDE.

1). Why would Robert buckle his seat belt in a car parked in a locked garage before shooting himself? The buckled seatbelt suggested he'd either just pulled into the garage or was about to pull out when he was shot.

2). By a remarkable coincidence, I have the same Ruger Model M77 .243, and am familiar with its powerful recoil. Even if the butt had been braced against the passenger side door when Robert depressed the trigger, the rifle would have kicked violently, and it struck me as very unlikely the end of the barrel would have come to rest against his right side. This raised this suspicion that the gun position was staged to enhance (to a naïve viewer) the perception that Robert had fired it himself.

As was the case with Betsy Bagwell and David Stegall, I was able to obtain the crime scene photos of Robert's death (**Appendix IV** presents my analysis). They indicate that he was probably shot by someone else, who then staged the scene to look like a suicide.

CHAPTER 87
THE "SUICIDE NOTE"

An especially complex feature of the crime scene was the note that investigating officers found on the right side of the windshield, handwritten on a single piece of paper from a yellow legal pad.

7-14-86

Glady—

Stress and Pressure too Much!

I'm Not *good enough and don't measure up to your standards.*

I hope you can find someone to put up with your constant bitching (MR Perfect)

Good Luck

  Robert

P.S.
I hope the $500,000 will last.

It's notable that the first line is written in neat print, which was Robert's usual style. The first two words—"I'm Not"—of the second line are also in print, but the remainder of the letter (reproduced here in italics) is in cursive, which his mother found surprising, as she'd never known him to write in cursive. Also remarkable is that, apart from the P.S. referring to the life insurance death benefit, the letter makes no reference to Robert's impending death. In all other respects, the content could be that of a bitter "Dear John" letter.

To draw any firm conclusions about the note, it would be necessary to perform a rigorous analysis to determine if it's authentic. For optimal impartiality, this would involve a comparison of the suicide note with other known samples of Robert's handwriting supplied by someone other than his life insurance beneficiary. The mere fact that Sandra knew Robert's wife—and the fact that she knew Dr. Paul Radman's wife (the beneficiary of his large insurance policy)—should have been examined by police investigators.

Additional consideration should be given to the possibility the note was only partly written by Robert, or written by Robert under duress— i.e., at gunpoint, trying to buy time. Multiple witnesses shared the perception that he seemed to be under pressure that began in the wake of Alan's murder. These witness accounts should have served as the basis for an inquiry into what was going on in his life. The possibility that Robert had asked Sandra for a loan in the early days of her relationship with Alan should have been investigated. Did he show his financials to her, thereby making her aware of his life insurance policy with the $500,000 death benefit? If so, did she introduce him to a loan shark who put pressure on Robert and Glady, thereby making Glady mad at her husband for exposing her and her children to a dangerous criminal? Alternatively, was Sandra exerting pressure on Robert through some other means—perhaps some form of blackmail?

As was the case with David Stegall and Betsy Bagwell, the Dallas Police Department kept the case open for only a few days and then closed it upon receiving notice that the Medical Examiner had ruled the manner of death a suicide. Between the initial Incident Report dated July 14, 1986, and the concluding Supplement Report, dated July 20, 1986, no investigative action apart from the initial death scene examination is documented. The Incident Report notes that REPORTING PERSON [GLADY] SMITH STATED THAT APPROXIMATELY 6 MONTHS AGO, A COUSIN OF THE COMPLAINANT HAD BEEN MURDERED, AND AT THIS TIME IT IS UNKNOWN IF THERE IS ANY RELATION. To have determined if there was a relation would have required a thorough investigation of what was happening in Robert's life, and with whom he'd been interacting in the run-up to his death. However, judging by the available DPD records of this case, none was performed.

The fastened seat belt and position of Robert's hands are highly suspicious and should have prompted a full police and forensic medical investigation. How exactly the central nervous system is affected by a high velocity rifle shot that lacerates the left and right ventricles is, I suppose, a difficult thing to research. In film footage of firing squads shooting rifle bullets through the hearts of the condemned, the victims seem to collapse instantly. However, because their hands are typically tied behind their backs, it is impossible to observe their arm and hand reflexes. After reaching hard to his right to depress the trigger and fire the bullet through his heart, did Robert have sufficient central nervous system function to draw his right arm back to his body and rest his right hand on his lap, in perfect symmetry with his left hand? Readers who have studied death by gunshot to the heart are invited to contact me on my author's website (authorjohnleake.com).

CHAPTER 88
SUBURBAN NOIR

Cause for Alarm!, a 1951 film starring Loretta Young, has been described as a notable example of "Suburban Noir." Ms. Young plays a housewife named Ellen who spends most of her time nursing her invalid husband, George, who is dying of heart disease. George suspects she is having an affair with his friend and doctor, Ranney Grahame, and that they have been slowly killing him with overdoses of his heart medicine. George writes a letter to the District Attorney, accusing Ellen and Ranney of murdering him. He claims their motive is to be together and collect his large life insurance death benefit. He asks Ellen to give a sealed letter to the postman, which she does. He then tells her the letter's contents and draws a pistol and threatens to kill her. In the excitement of this confrontation, he has a heart attack and dies.

Up until this moment, the audience believes George is being irrationally jealous, bitter, and paranoid. Ellen's marriage to him seems emblematic of the oppressive role that society expects women to play— that of dutiful wives who ask little for themselves. It's a stultifying arrangement in which husbands seem naturally inclined to becoming possessive, ill-mannered, and undesirable. Married life, in which the familiarity of cohabitation may easily breed contempt and resentment, is the natural launchpad for a film noir story.

Ellen's panicked effort to intercept the letter before it's delivered to the DA's office causes the audience to wonder about her innocence. Dr. Grahame shows up and repositions George's body in the bed to make his death look like a simple heart attack. Just as Ellen's hysteria about the letter reaches a fever pitch, the postman rings and returns it to sender for insufficient postage. The film concludes with Dr. Grahame burning the incriminating document. By all appearances, Ellen was a perfectly innocent suburban housewife, but looks can be deceiving.

When Sandra was in her twenties and thirties, some remarked to her that she resembled Loretta Young. Once, when Al Tatum surprised her by dropping in around cocktail hour, she looked especially ravishing, and confessed to him that she was about to go out on a date.

"I thought you were him when the bell rang, so I did my best Loretta Young imitation when I opened the door."

I suspect that Sandra had watched *Cause for Alarm!* and probably every other film noir hit of the forties and fifties—a panoply of people plotting and executing murders while creating alibis and red herrings. Noir often features a femme fatale—usually a married one—who seduces a man and persuades him to knock off her husband for the life insurance. The husband is usually portrayed (or represented by the femme fatale) as boorish and tyrannical, which evokes the white knight instincts of the paramour, who, at some point, realizes that maybe the husband wasn't so terrible after all. A brilliant twist of this convention was presented in *To Die For* (1995) in which a femme fatale (marvelously played by Nicole Kidman) seduces a couple of dopey high school kids and coaxes them into murdering her husband, whom she portrays as a monster. When they go to his house and hold him at gunpoint as though they are robbers, he is disarmingly affable, and beseeches them not to take his wedding band because "My wife will kill me if she sees me not wearing it."

My favorite noir film is *Double Indemnity* (1944) in which the insurance salesman, Walter Neff (played by Fred MacMurray) is seduced by the housewife, Phyllis Dietrichson (played by Barbara Stanwyck). While Phyllis drives her husband to the Burbank station to catch a night train to Palo Alto, Walter lies on the backseat floorboard. On a dark street near the station, he springs up and strangles her husband, whom he then impersonates and boards the train. As it heads north, he steps out onto the rear observation platform to smoke a cigarette and "accidentally" falls off. Phyllis drives her husband's body to the designated place by the railroad, and they put it on the tracks at the spot where investigators will deduce that he fell off the train.

Later Walter discovers that Phyllis has killed before and that she has another boyfriend who is probably planning to kill him. Her apparent desire and love for Walter was just an act. In fact, she isn't capable of feeling love or even empathy. *Double Indemnity* was the inspiration of *Body Heat* (1981) starring Kathleen Turner and William Hurt. Whenever Walter approaches Phyllis's house, he smells honeysuckle in the air, which he associates with his intense longing for her. In *Body Heat* it's the wind chimes hanging around the girl's house, gentling swaying in the sultry, south Florida breeze, that seem to goad the young man to his fate.

The message is clear. Because men are so compelled by sexual desire, there is no hope for them as they are drawn to the femme fatale. They are doomed. Sandra understood this, and she used it with extraordinary effectiveness to seduce and blackmail married men—not only to extort money from them, but also to ensure their silence if they were ever called to serve as witnesses of her crimes. Like all femme fatales, she played the sexual seductress and damsel in distress with equal skill. Her ice-cold cunning, manipulation, constant lying, and zero empathy are all on display in the women of film noir.

In trying to understand what makes such people tick, many have turned to Otto Kernberg's theory of malignant narcissism, Simon Baron-Cohen's zero negative empathy disorder, or Robert Hare's psychopathy checklist. These researchers have provided a useful interpretative framework for recognizing psychopaths, but their concepts can't quite explain the mystery of a femme fatale. A man who enters a relationship with her is doomed not only because of her inability to love, but also because his own flaws will be laid horribly bare as the relationship unfolds. Every man has weaknesses, and the femme fatale will exploit them with devastating effectiveness. Especially vulnerable are conscientious men who are aware of their imperfections, as their susceptibility to feeling guilt will seem to validate her accusations. Such men are the female psychopath's favorite prey.

Under the steady barrage of her emasculating psychological warfare and gaslighting, only an aggressive male psychopath could turn the tables. Normal, law-abiding men don't stand a chance. As the idealizing, honeymoon phase ends as she becomes bored and resentful, the dehumanizing begins. The extreme stress of the relationship brings out the worst in a man, thereby making it all the easier for her to justify ruining or even murdering him. If he asks her why she wants to destroy him, she may answer with real conviction that it's all his fault.

CHAPTER 89

THE REGULATORS

Just before Christmas, 2022, I called each member of a group that I (in my private thoughts) call the Regulators. All are women, and they are the only people in this story spanning forty years who made a persistent effort to stop Sandra's depredations. First, I called Gloria Rehrig, who, at ninety-two, was still as alert as ever. Every year the holiday season seemed to kick off around December 7—a day that continued to live in infamy for her—and it always made her sad. She always answered the phone on the second ring and was always keen to answer my questions and help me in any way she could. While love between men and women is often fickle, hers for her child hadn't faded a shade since 1985. She told me she'd recently fallen and injured her hand, but her spirits were characteristically high, and she thanked me profusely for my ongoing efforts to research and write this story.

Then I called Jayne Todd—the retired Brunswick County, North Carolina Sheriff's Deputy who had the distinction of being the only law officer who'd ever succeed in persuading a DA's office to prosecute Sandra for a crime. She achieved this outcome through extraordinary effort. As she pointed out to the Brunswick County DA, who was considering dropping the case due to the relatively small sum that Sandra had fraudulently charged on Sue Moseley's credit cards, "She probably would have done far worse to Miss Sue if we hadn't intervened when we did. She must be stopped now, or it could be far worse for her next victim." Jayne's brother had recently died of cancer, and she spent much of her time looking after her invalid father, but she too was characteristically cheerful and wished me the best of luck in finishing my book.

After I spoke with Jayne, I called the private investigator, Carrie Huskinson, who was struggling with heart problems but hanging in there. Carrie was the only person I knew of who'd succeeded in intimidating Sandra, who had seduced her client's husband. One evening, Sandra called her client's house and boldly asked to speak with her husband—just as she'd often called the Bagwell house and asked to speak to Dr. Bagwell. Carrie happened to be visiting when the call came in, and she got on the phone.

"Listen Sandra, you don't know who I am, but I know who you are, and I know what you are trying to do. If anything happens to my client, I will kill your children, starting with your youngest, because I know she's your favorite." Sandra hung up and never called the house again. To be sure, Carrie would never hurt anyone, but she understood that the only way to deal with Sandra was by aggressively pushing back. By all appearances, not a single man had ever been firm with her, much less put her in her place.

After I spoke with Carrie, I invited Glenna Whitley to join me for dinner at our favorite restaurant in her neighborhood. Over the years, Glenna had maintained a public record of Sandra's past, her movements around the country, and her various scams. The electronic editions of Glenna's reports had alerted countless people to Sandra's identity and the potential danger they were in by bringing her into their lives and homes. While most of the ladies in Highland Park were terrified of making any statements about her that could make it into print, Glenna boldly wrote about her again and again. Much of the language she used to describe Sandra was extremely cutting.

"Were you ever afraid she would retaliate?" I asked her over dinner.

"Sometimes I thought about it, and Peter [her husband] worried about it. I guess I always figured that Sandra was motivated by material gain, and not revenge against someone like me."

I then asked her if she, as a woman, understood why Sandra didn't apply her intelligence and talent to a gainful occupation.

"Why was she so focused on seducing and exploiting men?" I asked.

"I don't know," Glenna replied. "I can only make the unoriginal guess that it began somewhere in her childhood, in her relationship with her father and stepmother. As much as I always wanted to bring her to justice, I must acknowledge that her early years were marred with trauma. First, she was adopted, then she lost her mother in a car accident, then she grew up with a stepmother who may not have been kind to her, and then she lost Bobby Bridewell to cancer. I suppose it's possible she suffered other abuse as well. The mystery to me is why she apparently found it impossible to get on a straight and narrow path. I think of all those years between 1989 and 2012, when I'd periodically get a call from the latest frightened person whom she was conning. Seems like it would have been a lot easier just to lead a normal life."

Gloria, Jayne, Carrie, and Glenna all understood that the persistent failure of society and law enforcement to stop Sandra made her ever more dangerous and destructive. All four of these ladies did their absolute best for law, order, and justice. They are the moral backbone of this terrible story.

When DPD officers arrived at the Stegall residence on the morning of February 22, 1975, they had no obvious reason to suspect the pretty housewife and mother who'd never been under suspicion for committing a crime. The pitiable spectacle of the emotional woman apparently conditioned their perceptions of the crime scene—a scene that was consistent with a man who'd been shot in the head while he lay sleeping. The pistol lying on the bed under the victim's outstretched left hand, and the razor blade cartridge in his right hand, looked staged, but these apparently did not strike the investigators as suspicious enough to warrant questioning the widow's claim that her husband had committed suicide.

Seven years later, when DPD officers were confronted with the shooting death of Betsy Bagwell, the circumstances were extremely suspicious. At that point, the earlier shooting death of Sandra's first husband should have raised a red flag. The failure of Betsy's friends to alert law enforcement, and law enforcement's lack of diligence, enabled Sandra to remain free to prey on her next victim. Getting away with murdering Betsy emboldened Sandra to murder Alan Rehrig.

There is no statute of limitations for the prosecution of murder. The murder of Alan Rehrig should have resulted in a thorough reevaluation of Betsy's case. Yet another occasion for reevaluating Betsy's case came in 2007, when Sandra was arrested for identity theft. This prompted Carrie Huskinson to renew her investigation of the Dallas murders. She obtained copies of the Betsy Bagwell death scene photos and contracted Steven Wilkins—Forensic Investigations Manager at the Pierce County Sheriff's Department in Tacoma, Washington—to perform an analysis of the images. Mr. Wilkins concluded that Betsy had *not* committed suicide. Carrie gave copies of his report to Detective John Coughlin and the private investigator Al Teel. She also called the Dallas County Medical Examiner and Dr. Bagwell, but neither expressed interest in seeing Wilkins's report.

No matter how many times I look at the dreadful images of Betsy—dead in her car or dead at the medical examiner's office—I still get upset. She was only forty years old—thirteen years younger than I am now. I think about all the good times I've had since I was forty. The sight of these images and the murder they document are a perfect outrage. It seems to me that every man and woman who could have helped to serve justice for Betsy let her down—her husband, her friends, her church pastor, the police, the medical examiner, *everyone*. Even after Alan Rehrig was murdered three years later—a crime that warranted a vigorous reexamination of Sandra Bridewell in the matter of Mary Elisabeth Bagwell—these same people let Betsy down again.

Most of those intimately involved in this painful story were opposed to me "dredging it up," and many are angry at me for doing so. And yet, as they are aware, terrible stories like Betsy's don't go away just because we cease talking about them. Concealing a dreadful truth to avoid conflict is like allowing a predator to roam free in the community or complying with the directives of an incipient tyrant. Such failures to take difficult but necessary action are like ignoring early signs of cancer. In all cases, turning a blind eye to the problem doesn't eliminate it. On the contrary, failing to confront these malignancies in their early stage only makes the inevitable reckoning with them far more terrible. Likewise, it seems to me that we never expunge the guilt of failing to do our duty to someone who loved and trusted us. In my experience, we are haunted by it even more as we grow older and more vulnerable, and it can only be expiated by telling the truth and making amends.

CHAPTER 90
EPILOGUE

After I finished writing this book, I contemplated trying a second time to persuade Sandra to grant me an interview. The only media interview she ever gave was with Susan Albrecht at *Park Cities People* in the spring of 1986. Since then, she has turned down every request, and she refused to tell me her side of the story when I visited her in jail in 2007. To be fair, she was, at that time, facing a trial—a matter of far greater importance than telling her side of the story to a book author. Sixteen years later, it occurred to me that I should take another crack at having a conversation with her.

I was reluctant to send a letter to her P.O. Box. I estimated the chance of her replying was slim to none, but it would give her notice of my intention to publish this book, which she could conceivably use to her advantage. Because my years of research have persuaded me that she is an officially undetected serial killer, I no longer feel an obligation to seek her side of the story. The only account she has ever offered—that David Stegall and Betsy Bagwell were suicides, and Alan Rehrig was consorting with dangerous drug dealers and gambling bookies—is demonstrably false.

I wanted to tell her why I believe she murdered David Stegall, Betsy Bagwell, and Alan Rehrig, and to propose that she confess and ask Gloria

Rehrig (a true Christian) for forgiveness. As Sandra has long professed to be a Christian, she is familiar with the religious concepts of confession and penance, and how these could save her soul from eternal damnation. My plan was to approach her in person and invite her to tell her side of the story over dinner at the best restaurant in town. A journalist friend in Graz, Austria named Hans Breitegger pulled this off with the Austrian serial killer Jack Unterweger in 1992, before the warrant was issued for his arrest. Jack didn't reveal anything incriminating, but he did engage Hans in a fascinating conversation.

Sandra has long maintained multiple PO Boxes, but she hasn't generated a public record of a physical address since she left North Carolina in 2012. I asked a top private investigator to find her. About a week later he told me it was the second time in his forty-year career he'd been unable to run down a single record of a subject's location (as distinct from a PO Box). Shortly after he informed me of this, I had a conversation with a wise lady who admonished me that I was indulging in the worst kind of intellectual pride.

"You're not going to persuade Sandra to confess, and don't think for one second that you can outsmart her. You're pretty good at ascertaining reality, but she is an expert at manipulating it. Only a man of overwhelming spiritual strength and humility could even begin to get a confession out of her, and you're not him." I thought about this, and it occurred to me that my friend was describing the sort of character one finds in the pages of Dostoevsky, such as Father Zosima, the Elder in *The Brothers Karamazov*. Dostoevsky readily came to mind because for years I'd marveled at the strange irony that Sandra produced and attended a stage adaptation of *Crime and Punishment* shortly before Alan was murdered.

At the time she produced the play, it was, for her, a perverse vanity project. However, now that she is seventy-nine years old, maybe it's now possible for her to look back on her life and recognize what Dostoevsky was trying to tell us. **No one ever gets away with anything**. Every lie and deception, every betrayal, act of selfishness and exploitation deforms us. When we commit transgressions, we must conceal them to avoid penalties and we often live in fear of exposure. These hinder us from being free and experiencing carefree joy. We're often tempted to believe that, by means of deception, we can warp reality so that it will give us money, pleasure, and status. And yet, for reasons that we struggle to understand, those who yield to this temptation always end up in a miserable place with no real friends, peace, or satisfaction.

CRIME SCENE PHOTO ANALYSIS: BETSY BAGWELL

A. General Body Position

Though Betsy's feet are still on the driver's side floorboard, her midsection is lying across the center console, her torso is lying on the passenger seat, and the top of her head is lying on the far-right edge of the passenger seat. Her hips and thighs are on the right side of the large steering wheel, and her right thigh is on the far-right side of the seat. Both of her arms are stretched back towards the console, and her right, upturned palm, cradling a .22 caliber revolver, is braced between her right thigh and the driver's side of the gear shifter. This body position is wildly inconsistent with the proposition that she shot herself in the head and then slumped to her right. I performed experiments with a 1980 Mercedes 300 TD station wagon and a woman the same height and weight as Betsy. The bucket seats are designed to hold the driver and passenger in a comfortable, upright posture, with lateral supports to prevent sliding while turning. The seat configuration prevents more than minor slumping in either direction. A person sitting in the seat who relaxes will simply sink down into the seat and be held in place by the lateral supports. Betsy's upper body could not move across the center console without her left thigh hanging on the bottom of the steering wheel. Coordinated effort is required to slide both legs to the right of the steering wheel and to move one's upper body across the center and onto the passenger seat.

The muzzle pressed to Betsy's right temple not only fired a bullet into her brain, but also the muzzle blast (the explosive shockwave produced by the highly pressurized gas of the propellant combustion). This blast would have greatly amplified her lethal brain injury. In the unlikely event that she remained alive and mobile for some time after the shot was fired, the position of her body and arms was inconsistent with the proposition that *she* shifted her torso onto the passenger seat. This would have required repositioning and bracing her arms and elbows. The photographs reveal that someone else moved her torso to the passenger seat, and then staged her arms to try to make it appear that she simply slumped to the right after she fired the shot into her brain.

B. Blood on Betsy's Right Thigh and Right Hand

Drops of blood have fallen from the gunshot wound on Betsy's right temple or from blood running from her nose onto her right thigh and then run a short distance down the skin before drying. The direction of the flow is clearly visible. It shows that her thigh was rolled in the opposite direction when the blood dropped onto it, ran down the skin, and dried. After the blood dried in this position, someone moved her body all the way to the right, which caused her right thigh to roll to the right (opposite) direction from its position when the blood was deposited on it.

Betsy's right hand is lying next to her right thigh. There is a clear transfer stain on the palmar side of her right thumb and light smudges on the palmar side of her hand above her thumb. Blood stains on her pinkie, ring finger, and middle finger resemble the pattern on her thigh, but are smudged. The smudge pattern on her middle finger mirrors the smudge pattern on the adjacent region of her thigh. Also conspicuous is the lack of any blood visible on the gun in her hand. All the above is wildly inconsistent with the proposition that she fired the shot with her right hand and slumped to her right while still clutching the revolver. The smudged bloodstains on her fingers and the transfer stain on her thumb appear to have been deposited when her right hand was rotated to the right to turn her palm up and place the gun in it. The action of moving and rotating her hand caused the palmar side of her fingers to touch the blood deposits on her thigh, which caused the blood smudges on her finger pads and blood deposits under her pinkie and ring-fingernails.

C. Transfer Stains on Left Thigh, Right Sleeve, and Gear Shifter

Three blood transfer stains on Betsy's left thigh are inconsistent with the proposition that she shot herself with a pistol in her right hand and then slumped to the right while still grasping the revolver. Three of her left fingers are clearly visible in the photos, and they don't have a spec of blood on them. There is also a transfer stain on her right sleeve and a transfer stain on the right side of the gear shifter knob. The photos show the victim as she was found—before the paramedics could have inspected the wound on the right side of her head (lying flat against the passenger seat)—which excludes the proposition that the paramedics caused these transfer stains.

D. Blood on the Right-Side Panel of the Driver's Seat

Blood drops on the right-side panel of the driver's seat indicate that the wound on the right side of Betsy's head was in proximity with the right-side panel when the blood was deposited. These blood stains contrast with the blood drops on Betsy's right thigh. The latter stains could have *only* been deposited when her head was positioned forward, over her right thigh. Her upper body and head moved a considerable distance between depositing blood in these two different locations.

E. Blood Smear on the Passenger Seat

A large blood smear on the passenger seat extends around the seat's left (facing forward) lateral support, indicating that the side panel is smeared as well. This indicates that her head went back, between the front seats, towards the back seat, and then returned forward with the bleeding right side brushing against the side panel and then across the back of the front passenger seat.

F. Blood Spatter in Back Seat.

Medical Examiner Field Agent Gray noted in his Investigation Report: "blood spatters in back seat." This indicates that Betsy's bleeding head was presented to the back seat before it came to rest on the front passenger seat.

G. Gun and Parking Ticket Position

Betsy's right, upturned palm, cradling a .22 caliber revolver, is wedged between her right thigh and the driver's side of the gearshift—a position that secured the weapon in her hand. Likewise, the revolver is wedged between her thigh and the gearshift. The bottom of the grip is pressing into her thigh. The gun's barrel is pressed against the parking lot ticket, bearing the 6:05 time stamp, thereby holding it against the ashtray cover. The ticket is not leaning against the semi-vertical, laminated wood cover—it is pinned in place with the ticket's bottom edge above the console's base. Were it not for the muzzle pressed against it, the ticket would have probably slid down to the top of the gearshift. This indicates that someone slid the parking ticket between the gun muzzle and ashtray cover. The right hand, gun, and parking ticket position display clear signs of staging.

H. Luggage Tag on Passenger Floorboard

A plastic laminated airline luggage tag with a zip tie is lying on the passenger side floorboard. As the reporting officer noted in the Incident Report, the tag is inscribed with the name BAGWELL and Betsy's home address and phone. As witnesses have attested, Betsy was an exceptionally organized and fastidious person. There is no reason to believe that she just happened to have a luggage tag lying on the passenger side floorboard while giving Sandra a ride to Love Field to rent a car. Her purse and wallet, containing her DL and checkbook, were found in her car, so there is no reason to believe that she left the luggage tag on the floorboard to identify her after her death. I believe it is highly probably that the culprit left this object on the front passenger floorboard of her car.

THEORY OF THE MURDER
OF BETSY BAGWELL

As stated in the main narrative, Sandra does not have an officially documented alibi because she was never the subject of a homicide investigation. Nevertheless, it is likely she took steps to create one in case the police questioned her about her whereabouts at the time of the murder. According to the 1987 *D Magazine* report, she told the police that after she left Betsy at the church at 5:00 p.m., she went shopping in Preston Center. Sandra understood the police would regard the Love Field parking ticket as establishing that Betsy's death had happened after 6:05 p.m. The conspicuous placement of the ticket, between the pistol muzzle and the ashtray cover, has a staged quality, indicating the culprit wanted to make sure the police saw it. Sandra planned the crime so that she could—with minimal risk of being contradicted by a witness—claim she parted company from Betsy at 5:00 p.m. and then went shopping in Preston Center (it's about a seven-minute drive from the church to the mall).

While Betsy's upper body was found lying on the front passenger seat, it was also, at some point, presented to the back seat area. This is evident from the medical examiner field agent's report, which noted "blood spatters in back seat." Why did the culprit temporarily move her upper body between the front seats, towards the back seat area before depositing

it on the front passenger seat? Two hypothetical scenarios come to mind:
1). Betsy's upper body inadvertently fell between the two front seats while
the culprit was moving her body from the driver's seat to the passenger
seat, thereby presenting her bleeding headwound and nose to the back
seat area.

2). Betsy's upper body was deliberately pulled between the front seats and
into the back seat area.

Another tantalizing feature of the documentation of Betsy's murder is
found in the Incident Report. The DPD officer who wrote the report
noted the parking ticket with the 6:05 p.m. stamp. However, he also noted
the statement of a witness named Terry Kline, a white female from
Bridgeport, Texas.

WIT KLINE STATED THAT SHE HAD BEEN AT THE
AIPORT PARKING LT NEAR THE COMP M
BAGWELL'S CAR SINCE 16:30 P.M. AND DID NOT
HEAR ANY GUNSHOTS.

This appears to be a straightforward statement. Did the reporting officer
interpret this to mean that the witness had been *in the location* since 16:30
without actually seeing Betsy's car till after 18:05? The wording does not
express this qualification, though, to be sure, the statement only says the
witness "did not hear any gunshots" and mentions nothing about *seeing* the
car. Only thoroughly questioning the witness could yield clarity about this.

After much time and effort (and the assistance of an exceptionally
skilled investigator) I tracked down "witness Kline," whose surname was
misspelled by the DPD officer who wrote the Incident Report. The
proper spelling of her surname is Klein. She considered it possible that
she visited Love Field in the summer of 1982 and waited a long time for
a visitor's flight to arrive—apparently one that was badly delayed.
However, she had no memory of a woman found dead in her car in the
short-term parking lot. She surmised that the officer must have told her
little about the incident, otherwise she would have remembered it.

If Klein's testimony was correct and Betsy's car was already in its place in the lot around 4:30 p.m., it meant the culprit or accomplice entered the lot a second time in a separate vehicle at 6:05 p.m. to acquire the ticket that was found in Betsy's car. In 1982, there was no video surveillance in the parking garage and no mechanism for registering a particular car entering the lot with a particular ticket. Someone could have surveyed Betsy's car from a distance to make sure the body had not yet been found, and then, at an opportune moment, passed by, opened one of the front doors, and inserted the 6:05 parking ticket in less than five seconds. Even if he was seen opening the car door and reaching into the vehicle, he would appear to be the owner of the car fetching something from the console.

An alternative theory is that Betsy was murdered in her car in a different location, with fewer people around, than the Love Field parking garage. After she was shot in another location, her upper body was maneuvered between the front seats and into the back seat area, and then transported to the airport. After entering the lot at 6:05 and finding a favorable spot, the culprit moved her upper body from the back seat to the front seat, performed the final elements of staging, and then walked away. Three and a half years later, Alan Rehrig was murdered while sitting in the driver's seat of his vehicle. His upper body was then maneuvered between the front seats and placed on the back seat floorboard with his legs lying between the fronts seats while the culprit drove his vehicle to Oklahoma City. It's a plausible theory that Sandra or her accomplice followed the same procedure for murdering Alan because it had proved effective in murdering Betsy.

What follows is a **theory** of how Sandra could have carried out the murder of Betsy Bagwell and constructed a seemingly authentic alibi. In considering any theory of a complex crime, it's important to bear in mind that even the most meticulously planning culprit may have to alter her plan in real time in response to unforeseen conditions and events. A plausible and coherent theory of the murder of Betsy Bagwell is that Sandra initially planned to commit it on the morning of July 16, 1982, during her first trip to Love Field with Betsy. According to this plan, Betsy would be found in her car in the airport parking lot with her suitcase in her car. When Dr. Bagwell called Sandra, she would tell him (and the police) that Betsy had come over that morning for "girl talk." She had been depressed about her marriage and feared her husband was sleeping with his nurse and possibly other women. She was therefore planning to leave her husband and retreat to their house in Santa Fe. Upon hearing Sandra's story, the police would think Betsy had been in a suicidal frame of mind while also contemplating running away. By all appearances, she had driven to Love Field but shot herself in the parking lot instead of going into the terminal and buying a ticket.

Unbeknownst to Betsy, her morning trip with Sandra to Love Field to pick up a package was, in fact, to meet Sandra's accomplice, who was (in theory) carrying Betsy's suitcase that Sandra had recently stolen from her Santa Fe house. The original plan was to murder Betsy in her car at Love Field. However, during their morning trip, Sandra or her accomplice didn't like the situation in the parking lot. Perhaps it was an unexpectedly busy day, with too many people coming and going. And so, they aborted their initial plan. Sandra told Betsy the package was scheduled for a later flight. While Betsy met her friends for lunch, Sandra and her accomplice went back to the drawing board. In theory, they chose the covered parking garage of the Preston Center Medical Building where David Stegall (and his colleague Paul Radman) had officed. On a summer Friday after 5:00 p.m. the floor furthest from the entrance would likely be completely devoid of people.

At 4:30 p.m., Betsy and Sandra drove back to Love Field to pick up the package and to rent a car for Sandra. They parked in the lot near the rental agency, and Betsy waited to make sure Sandra succeeded in getting a vehicle. Sandra returned to the car a few minutes later and said she'd left her driver's license in her car. This time, (she claimed) her car had stalled in the parking garage of the Preston Center Medical Building, where she'd gone for a check-up around midday. They drove to the building and parked in the garage next to Sandra's allegedly stalled car. While Sandra got into her car to retrieve her driver's license, her accomplice (hiding in the parking lot) approached Betsy's car from behind, got into the backseat with this pistol already drawn, reached between the front seats, and shot her in the right side of the head. The shot and muzzle blast probably knocked her unconscious, and she remained seated in the driver's seat, with blood running from her headwound down the right side of the seat to the seatbelt buckle, on which blood is visible in one of the photos.

At this point, just after 5:00 p.m., Sandra drove her car from the garage to a shop in Preston Center a block away, parked on the street, and went inside to make a purchase. Back in Betsy's car, the gunman waited for Betsy to stop breathing, and then maneuvered her body to get her hips and thighs clear to the right of the large steering wheel. As he pushed her upper body forward to move it around the seat's lateral supports, drops of blood fell from her headwound or her nose onto her right thigh. Following this action, the gunman pulled her upper body between the front seats and into the backseat area. Blood from her headwound or nose deposited the blood spatters later observed by Medical Examiner Field Agent Gray. Blood was also transferred to the gunman's right hand.

Betsy's body remained in this intermediate position while the gunman got out of the backseat and into the front seat. While maneuvering Betsy's thighs to the far-right edge of the driver's seat, he transferred the finger-shaped bloodstains to her left thigh. At around 5:45 p.m., he left the parking garage and drove Betsy's car Love Field by way of Northwest Highway and Lemmon Avenue to reduce the chance of anyone in the Park Cities recognizing Betsy's car. He entered the airport's covered parking garage at 6:05, found a spot and parked. At an opportune moment when no one was around, he pulled her upper body forward between the front seats and placed it on the front passenger seat. He then braced the revolver in Betsy's right hand against the gear shifter and stuck the parking ticket between the muzzle and ash tray cover. For some reason he decided against leaving Betsy's suitcase in the car, only its luggage tag on the floorboard. He then got out of the car and walked into the terminal and called Sandra's house from a payphone around 6:15 p.m. to tell her he'd just completed the job at Love Field. She hung up with him, called the Bagwell house, and asked to speak with Betsy. The point of this call was to establish that she (Sandra) was already at home at the time that Betsy's car entered the lot.

The original plan to murder Betsy at Love Field that morning was logical because it would create the appearance that Betsy had simply driven to the airport by herself and committed suicide in the parking lot. However, the logic of the plan's Love Field element was lost that afternoon because Betsy's daughter Wendy saw her mom set out with Sandra. Maybe Betsy told Wendy that they were "running an errand" without mentioning Love Field, which emboldened Sandra to go through with her original plan. It seems that Sandra didn't think this through. Her plan was to tell the police that she and Betsy had simply met for "girl talk," and to say nothing about going to Love Field that afternoon to rent a car. She apparently realized she'd made this potentially catastrophic mistake when she spoke with Dr. Bagwell on the phone at La Tosca and he revealed that Betsy had called him at work and told him about "the letter" and their earlier trip to Love Field. Sandra reflexively denied the letter's existence but conceded that they'd gone to Love Field to rent a car (but had been unable to because she'd forgotten her driver's license).

CRIME SCENE PHOTO ANALYSIS: DAVID STEGALL

A. General Body Position

David Stegall is wearing pajamas and lying on his right side in a typical sleeping position. The right side of his head is resting on a pillow and his arms are resting on the bed in a comfortable sleeping position.

B. Position of Head

Blood has pooled on the pillow underneath the right side of David's head and face. This pool of blood has partly run off the edge of the pillow through a few contours in the fabric. Otherwise, the large pillow is entirely free of bloodstains, indicating that his head did *not* move after the shot was fired.

C. Bed Covers Position

Generally, he is under the covers as though he were sleeping. In the first three photos in the sequence, his left hand and most of the pistol are concealed by covers. The fourth photo was taken after an investigator drew the covers down to expose the left hand lying on top of the pistol. It was physically impossible for David to have pulled the covers over his left hand, resting on the pistol, *after* he fired the shot through his head with his left hand. Who did? It's hard to imagine the investigators didn't notice this and ask Sandra about it. She could have claimed that she or one of the doctors whom she called after she discovered David that morning had drawn the covers over his left hand, though there was no reason why anyone would do this.

D. Left Arm, Left Hand, and Gun Position.

I was not able to establish with certainty if David was left-handed, right-handed, or ambidextrous. The medical examiner field agent noted that he was left-handed/ambidextrous. David's left arm and left hand are lying in a natural-looking sleeping position. His left hand, with fingers outstretched, is lying on top of the bolt and frame of the pistol. This is incongruous with the proposition that he fired the shot with his left hand. I experimented with lying in this exact position and aiming the muzzle of my Ruger Standard .22 at my head as David must have aimed it if he had fired the shot. To hold the pistol in this position, it is necessary to cock the shoulder back and exert a fair amount of muscular effort. *After* David pulled the trigger and the bullet went through his brain, creating a shock wave in his skull, it is doubtful he had the nerve and muscle coordination to continue gripping the heavy (2.19 pound) target pistol as he extended his left arm back to a comfortable sleeping position, then lay the pistol on the bed, then released his hand from the grip and retracted his index finger from the trigger guard, then lifted and extended his hand and fingers to rest them on the gun. To be sure, both Lynne Herold and the renowned forensic pathologist, Jan Garavaglia, cautioned me against drawing a firm conclusion based on the gun position. Both scientists regarded the gun position as suspicious, but they also told me they are familiar with cases of gunshot victims moving a lot after being shot in the head. However, a notable feature of David's case is that no other part of his body moved after the shot was fired.

E. Close-up Wound of Entrance

According to the medical examiner's report, the gunshot entrance wound to David's left temple was *not* a contact wound, but a "close-up wound of entrance." This means that David did *not* rest the muzzle on his left temple but held the muzzle at a slight distance from it. This makes no sense. If you lie on your right side and raise the gun with your left hand to fire it into your left temple, the entire weight of your arm and the pistol are bearing down. Trying to hold the pistol in this position without resting the muzzle on the temple is awkward and difficult and makes it much harder to be sure of one's aim. This is one reason why almost all self-inflicted gunshot wounds to the head are *contact* wounds. In a 1992 review of 199 suicidal gunshot wounds to the head in the database of the Dallas County Medical Examiner's Office, none were noncontact wounds. In a subsequent study of 1,704 suicidal gunshot wounds performed by Vincent Di Maio and his colleagues, only 2.1 percent were noncontact wounds. Dr. Jan Garavaglia found the **non**-contact wound to be the most suspicious feature of David Stegall's death—a circumstance *far* more consistent with homicide than suicide.

F. Position of Incised Wounds on Right Forearm

All three incised wounds on the inside of David's right forearm are well above the point on the wrist where the radial artery runs near the surface. Two incisions run across the arm (along the short axis); one runs diagonally. None of the incisions came close to lacerating the artery. As a medical man, David certainly understood that making these incisions would have no lethal outcome, though they would certainly cause pain and distress.

G. Timing of Incisions

All three of the incised wounds bled, indicating the incisions were made while he was still alive, and his heart was pumping. However, droplets of blood around David's nostrils indicate that blood entered his nasal passage after the shot to his head was fired, then mixed with air, and were then ejected from his nose in the form of exhaled droplets. This indicates that David continued breathing for some period after the shot was fired through his brain.

H. Position of Right Arm

The blood from the incised wounds has pooled—along with a large volume of blood from the head wound—along the side of his right forearm lying on the bed, which forms a depression in the sheet. Because the bloodstains are limited to the area around his right forearm and head, it is clear that his right forearm never moved after the incisions were made. This indicates that he did *not* initially make the incisions to his forearm, and then get out of bed to grab the pistol after he realized he wasn't going to bleed out. Thus, if David himself fired the shot, he had to have brought the loaded and cocked pistol with him to bed before he made the incisions. This again raises the question: why would he make the three pointless (though painful and distressing) incisions to his forearm when he was ready, able, and willing to shoot himself in the head?

I. A Statistically Anomalous Complex Suicide?

Since David's death in 1975, several studies have been published about the phenomenon of "complex suicide"—that is, suicide in which more than one suicide method is applied. Complex suicides are categorized as "planned" when two methods are used simultaneously to make sure that death occurs. In "unplanned" complex suicides, other methods of suicide are employed after the first one fails or proves too painful. Numerous planned suicides have been documented in which persons ingest drugs and use firearms. Numerous unplanned complex suicides have been documented of persons cutting their wrists and then inflicting stab wounds, hanging, or jumping from a height. However, in reviewing the literature on complex suicide, I couldn't find a single case of a person incising his forearm and then shooting himself. No toxicology analysis was performed in David's case, making it impossible to ascertain whether his consciousness was impaired by alcohol and or other substances.

J. No Blood Visible on Razor Blade and Left Fingers

His right palm is turned up, and lying in it is a cartridge of Gillette TRAC II razor blades. Lying on the bed near his right forearm is a razor blade. No blood is visible on the blade, nor is any blood visible on the sheet next to the blade's cutting edge. To be sure, only one side of the blade is visible, and the image quality of the blade is not sufficient to draw a definite conclusion. However, the fact remains that blood will readily adhere to and display bright red on a steel blade, and there appears to be none whatsoever on the blade lying on the bed. This suggests that this blade was either *not* the instrument that made the three incisions (each over two inches long) or it was cleaned afterwards, possibly to remove fingerprints. David's left fingertips are sharply in focus in the photos, and there is clearly no blood on them. If he made the three incisions to his right forearm with the razor blade, he had to have grasped the blade with his left thumb and at least one of his left fingers, most likely his index. Because the blade is so narrow (8 millimeters), the fingertips will necessarily be very close to the cutting edge. Again, to qualify: the entirety of David's left thumb and fingers is not visible in the photos, but most of the thumb tip and all the fingertips are, and not a spec of blood is visible on them. At one end of the diagonal incision there is a transfer bloodstain on the skin adjacent to the incision. This stain is about the size and shape of a fingerprint. That there is no blood visible on David's left fingertips suggests that someone else's finger transferred the blood.

Summation: As a dentist he had access to powerful medications on which he could have overdosed and died after falling unconscious instead of inflicting pain and violence to himself in his family home. He did not leave a suicide note. The proposition that he stole the pistol from his friend Bill Hardy instead of buying an inexpensive pistol at a pawn or sporting good shop is implausible. Sandra frequently visited her friend Linda Sue Hardy at her house and could have easily stuck the pistol in her purse. Sandra's claim to investigators that she didn't hear—i.e., wasn't awakened—by the shot fired in the small, one-story cottage is extremely unlikely.

The death scene photos display several features that are not consistent with suicide, as well as elements of staging. David's outstretched left hand, resting on the pistol, is markedly inconsistent with the proposition that he fired the pistol into his left temple—an action that would have, with high probability, resulted in his left arm going limp and falling straight down instead of extending back out into a comfortable sleeping position. That the gunshot wound to his left temple was not a contact wound is an extreme statistical anomaly for a suicide and inconsistent with David lying on his right side and raising the heavy pistol above the left side of his head. In this position, resting the muzzle on his left temple for comfort and surety of aim was the obvious action for a suicide. Likewise, the purportedly complex suicide involving incisions to his right forearm (completely missing the radial artery) and a gunshot to his head is an extreme statistical anomaly and perfectly inconsistent with David's understanding of anatomy.

How exactly Sandra performed the murder is a matter of speculation. A large pillow pushed against the headboard suggests she was seated upright in bed, right next to him, perhaps pretending to read by the light of the bedside lamp on her side while he slept with his back turned to her. In one of the crime-scene photographs a book is visible on the nightstand. So as not to wake him, Sandra didn't touch his left temple with the pistol's muzzle but held it at close range. She then shot him in the head and planted the pistol under his outstretched left hand. To enhance the appearance that David committed suicide, she slashed his forearm three times and placed the razor cartridge in his right palm. Realizing that her fingerprints were on the razor blade, she wiped it clean and then placed it on the bed next to David's right arm.

Chief Medical Examiner Di Maio should have ordered a toxicology analysis in David's case, which could have revealed alcohol and sedatives in his blood and yielded a clue about his cognitive state at the time he was shot. Hypothetically, Sandra spiked an after-dinner drink with a sedative to reduce the risk of him waking up. In this scenario, Sandra (or an accomplice) could have snuck into the bedroom after David fell asleep, positioned herself next to the bed, and then turned on a flashlight at the last second to aim the pistol at his temple and fire the shot.

CRIME SCENE PHOTO ANALYSIS: ROBERT SMITH

A. General Body Position

Robert is sitting behind the wheel on the station wagon's bench seat. His legs extend straight down to the floorboard, but his upper body is slumped to the left so that his left shoulder and head are leaning on the driver's side door. The lap seat belt is fastened firmly around his waist.

B. Arm and hand position

His arms are in a normal sitting position with his wrists resting on the tops of his thighs and his hands in his lap. It is notable that the final resting location and position of the arms, wrists, hands, and fingers, including the flexion, is the same for both the right and left side. This suggests that, just before the shot was fired, both hands were in the same position, doing the same thing, such as gripping the steering wheel at 9:00 and 3:00 o'clock. Moreover, that the high velocity rifle shot lacerated the right and left ventricles of his heart suggests that he would have been instantly and totally incapacitated. Thus, the position of the right hand—resting in the right side of his lap, mirroring the left-hand position—is not consistent with the proposition that he extended his right arm far to the right to depress the